Heroines of the Qing

Heroines of the Qing

EXEMPLARY WOMEN TELL THEIR STORIES

Binbin Yang

UNIVERSITY OF WASHINGTON PRESS *Seattle and London*

THIS BOOK IS MADE POSSIBLE BY A COLLABORATIVE GRANT
FROM THE ANDREW W. MELLON FOUNDATION.

Publication of this book also was supported by a
Faculty of Arts Research Award from the University
of Hong Kong.

© 2016 by the University of Washington Press

20 19 18 17 16   5 4 3 2 1

University of Washington Press
www.washington.edu/uwpress

Library of Congress Cataloging-in-Publication Data

Names: Yang, Binbin.
Title: Heroines of the Qing : exemplary women tell
    their stories / Binbin Yang.
Description: Seattle : University of Washington Press,
    2016. | Includes bibliographical references and
    index.
Identifiers: LCCN 2015042764 | ISBN 9780295995496
    (hardcover : alkaline paper)
Subjects: LCSH: Women—China—History—18th
    century. | Women—China—History—19th
    century. | Women authors, Chinese—History.
    | Women—China—Intellectual life. |
    Femininity—Social aspects—China—History.
    | Sex role—China—History. | Power (Social
    sciences)—China—History. | Virtue—Social
    aspects—China—History. | Confucianism—
    Social aspects—China—History. | China—
    History—Qing dynasty, 1644–1912.
Classification: LCC HQ1767 .Y354 2016 | DDC
    305.4095—dc23
LC record available at http://lccn.loc.gov/2015042764

To Fang Liu 方劉

CONTENTS

ACKNOWLEDGMENTS

The completion of this book would be unimaginable without the very generous help I have been fortunate to receive over the years. The book is the result of a three-year research project, but my research interest in "exemplary women" and their writings started over ten years ago.

Professor Beata Grant has been my inspiration. She opened my eyes to the extremely rich reservoir of women's writings in late imperial China and led me into this exciting research field by guiding me in the key issues and questions raised by scholars and the useful angles from which to approach these writings. During my long journey of exploring this material, she was always generous with her time and support and went out of her way to help me overcome many difficulties. Her insightful mentorship and her powerful intellect are simply *exemplary*.

I am tremendously indebted to Professor Robert E. Hegel for his continuing support. He kindly offered to read my book proposal and sample chapters several times, providing timely and astute responses. His encouragement is one of the main reasons this book is now in print.

Professors Miriam L. Bailin, Letty L. Chen, Pauline C. Lee, and Steven B. Miles were the readers of some of my earlier works, from which I have drawn a few examples in writing this book. Professor Bailin stimulated me to think about women's situations in broader cultural contexts. Professor Chen offered incisive suggestions about the framework and organization of book projects in general. Professor Lee was full of support despite the shortcomings of my earlier works. Professor Miles pointed out the significance of the historical sources concerning an exemplary woman from the Qing period, which laid the first brick for this book project.

My sincere gratitude goes to Professor Grace S. Fong for accepting the invitation to a mentorship workshop for my book at the School of Chinese, the University of Hong Kong in April 2015. Long before the workshop, she read and commented on my manuscript and provided crucial help when I reshaped some of my key concepts and framing devices. I would like to take this opportunity to pay tribute to her scholarship. Besides benefiting from her insight on women's writings in late imperial China as various forms of life history/writing—a major contribution she has made to the field—this book draws a great number of primary sources from the digital database of Ming Qing women's writings that she is building and most graciously making available to researchers. I also am deeply grateful to Professor Shu-mei Shih for organizing the mentorship workshop and for being an amazing support for the junior faculty at the School of Chinese. She has made great efforts to find opportunities for us to have our work known by a wider academic community.

The many insightful suggestions of Professors Dorothy Ko and Xiaorong Li have also been crucial to the reformulation of this book's overall conceptual frame and main arguments, in addition to saving me from the embarrassment of mistakes. It was owing to their very generous help that I was finally able to complete this book. The remaining mistakes are mine.

The publication of this book was possible because of the executive editor, Lorri Hagman. She helped me incorporate suggestions for revision and prompted me to think beyond my original framework. My writing became much clearer owing to her meticulous editing. I also appreciate the kind assistance provided by Beth Fuget, Kathleen P. Jones, Tim Roberts, and Tim Zimmermann. My friend Manling Luo's marvelous new book, *Literati Storytelling in Late Medieval China* (University of Washington Press, 2015), has been my guide during completion of revisions as well as style changes.

In drafting a grant application for this book in the fall of 2010, I benefited from the numerous useful comments and suggestions of Professors Louise Edwards, Cuncun Wu, Clara W. Ho, and Aihe Wang. Special thanks go to Professor Edwards for offering me help throughout this project, ranging from suggestions on writing to publication tips and support at critical stages. Professor Kam Louie, the former dean of the Arts Faculty at the University of Hong Kong, was extremely supportive of junior faculty, and I am so happy to be able to finally tell him that I have completed the project he had warmly encouraged me to pursue. During the course of conducting research and presenting my research results in conferences, I became especially indebted to Professors Allan Barr, Ronald Egan, Nanxiu Qian, and Maureen Robertson for their valuable input.

My colleagues and friends at the University of Hong Kong have been a constant source of inspiration and comfort, and they deserve special credit. J. Charles Schencking was a perspicacious reader of my book proposal and sample chapters. He offered perspectives of a historian working on a different cultural context and very useful advice regarding publication. He and Janet Borland were always brimming with support and compliments. Isaac Yue, Siu-fu Tang, Lucas Klein, Peiyin Lin, Pui Ling Tang, and I formed a support group by going to each other's book presentations and workshops. I have learned immensely from their projects. I would also like to thank Roslyn Hammers, an art historian and my colleague, for her valuable input, especially concerning chapter 2.

This book is the result of a research project funded by the General Research Fund of Hong Kong during 2011–15. I am grateful for the very generous financial support that greatly facilitated my research: it funded my many research trips to the major libraries and museums in mainland China, my purchase of the newly available research materials, the trips I made to present papers at international conferences, and, toward the later stages of my project, the teaching relief that allowed time for me to put down my research results in writing. I would also like to express my great gratitude to the members of the Arts Faculty Research Committee of the University of Hong Kong for conferring on me the 2015 Arts Faculty Research Award for Junior Pre-Tenure Professoriate Staff (under the category of cumulative research activities over a three-year period) and for kindly allowing me to use the award to cover part of the expenses for the publication of my book. Mr. Edward Shen, the Arts Faculty Secretary, was immensely generous in offering assistance when I applied for the GRF grant and the Faculty Research Award.

Shorter versions of chapters 1, 3, and 4 have been previously published as journal articles in *NanNü: Men, Women, and Gender in China*; *Frontiers in Literary Studies in China*; and *Modern China*, respectively. I would like to thank the journal editors Harriet Zurndorfer, Chun Zhang, and Kathryn Bernhardt for their kind help and insightful suggestions for revisions. I greatly appreciate the permission of Brill and SAGE to incorporate and adapt parts of those articles. My great thanks go to the National Library of China, the Palace Museum of Beijing, and the University of Hong Kong Library for granting me permission to use reproduced images from their collections.

My parents, Huang Xiuhua and Yang Xusheng, have been there for me throughout my work on this project. Their love for me and the early education they provided me—which inculcated in me a passion for literature—are among the main reasons I have made it this far in my academic career.

This book is dedicated most affectionately to my husband Fang Liu. I promised him a book years ago, and now I can finally acknowledge his unbounded support, which sustained me through the most stressful times of academic life.

Unless otherwise noted, translations of official titles in this book follow Charles O. Hucker's *A Dictionary of Official Titles in Imperial China*. I am grateful to one of the anonymous readers for recommending this useful reference. All translations not otherwise specified are mine.

For the sake of consistency and clarity, I refer to historical figures by their family and given names. I mention their style names, sobriquets, or honorific titles only when it is absolutely necessary for my discussion.

Heroines of the Qing

Introduction

Produced within a robust biographical tradition and a vigorously implemented court reward (*jingbiao*) system, life stories of "exemplary women" (*lienü*) continued to shape and reshape the constructions of ideal womanhood throughout Chinese history.[1] By the Qing period (1644–1911) this dominant discourse of female exemplarity had helped formulate a set of normative values that were integral to the consolidation of a kinship system based largely on patriarchal authority and patrilineal succession.[2] By promoting women's fulfillment of their kinship-based duties as key to the prosperity of their (husbands') families or lineages and the moral good of society at large, it placed women at the fulcrum of the Chinese kinship system.

This book carves out a new terrain of research in the discourse of female exemplarity through a major shift in focus, namely, from a predominantly male-authored biographical tradition to women's autobiographical practices uncovered from the newly available corpus of their writings. This approach does not presume that writings by the women themselves are necessarily more transparent than biographical texts or involve any ultimate truth about these women's lives. Rather it focuses on rhetorical strategies of *self-representation*, highlighting in particular how the normative values of female exemplarity were appropriated by these women for self-empowering purposes. It thus allows rectification of what some recent studies have identified as the "silences in and limitations of formal biographical texts [about women]."[3] Most important, this approach brings to the fore the discursive productions as dynamic processes in which women actively intervened as writing subjects, particularly by articulating their exemplarity in their own terms. It thus opens a window into women's self-authored exemplary life stories, which suggested to them a path to fame and social honor. A study like this is possible only because of recent developments in the field of women's writing culture in late imperial China.

HISTORICIZING THE DISCOURSE OF FEMALE EXEMPLARITY

Historical records in China abound in accounts of exemplary women of various types. Mothers were admired for raising their sons to be men of virtue, despite all the vicissitudes of life. Wives were recognized for their deference to their husbands and for, whenever needed, also stepping forth to admonish those who were led astray. Daughters were lauded for filially serving their parents and in-laws, as well as for sacrificing their own bodies in extreme situations (e.g., slicing flesh from one's own body to use as medicine for a sick or dying parent or parent-in-law). We need, moreover, take only a cursory look at local gazetteers to learn of the enormous number of heroic martyrs, chaste widows, and faithful maidens who were glorified for their fidelity to their deceased husbands or fiancés, particularly during the late imperial period.

The earliest models of exemplary women are found in the hagiographical canon of the Han scholar and bibliographer Liu Xiang (ca. 77–ca. 6 BCE), *Biographies of Exemplary Women* (Lienü Zhuan).[4] Originally incorporating both good and bad examples of female conduct—to admonish the Han emperor Cheng (51–7 BCE) regarding his selection of imperial consorts and, in turn, to have "royal teachings" proceed from the domestic sphere to the public realm[5]—Liu Xiang's work nonetheless spawned a long biographical tradition that focused exclusively on female virtue. Major dynastic histories following the Han routinely included sections for exemplary women. Local gazetteers followed the fashion from at least the Song (960–1278) onward. And a plethora of biographical subgenres for women flourished outside official history beginning in the Tang period (618–907). Some provided material for official biographies of exemplary women. Others, such as the numerous epitaphs written for women (around 1,500 extant pieces from the Tang), created an "overwhelmingly dominant discourse on gender roles" in addition to serving the emotional and memorializing needs of the women's families.[6] Liu Xiang's canonical work itself enjoyed lasting popularity and was incorporated into a massive moral literature targeting a female audience. Together with other widely circulating moral guides for women—such as *Classic of Filial Piety for Women* (Nü xiaojing) by Lady Zheng (ca. 8th century), *Analects for Women* (Nü lunyu) by Song Ruoxin (d. 820), and *Female Exemplars* (Guifan) by Lü Kun (1536–1618)—the elaborately illustrated and amended editions of Liu Xiang's work became a prevalent presence in gentry families during the late imperial period.[7] With momentum added by a booming print industry, life stories of exemplary women inculcated moral principles in female readers and also appealed to a broader readership through their enhanced dramatic effects.[8] The concept of female virtue shifted during this long process, from a wide range of admirable qualities emphasizing the portrayal of women as "intellectual and moral agents"—including wise counsel, rhetorical skill, and political acumen, for example—to predominantly widows' fidelity to their deceased husbands, resulting in what is now generally referred to as "the cult of female chastity."[9]

Concurrent was the development of a bureaucratic system of conferring court rewards on moral exemplars. The Han government introduced the system by placing insignia at the residences of "filial sons, obedient grandsons, chaste women, and righteous wives [xiaozi shunsun zhennü yifu]."[10] While the categories of moral exemplars underwent modifications through time, governments of subsequent dynasties strengthened the system by exempting households of the awardees from corvée labor and by developing a set of statutes specifying the criteria and the nomination and review procedures. Numbers of chaste widows who received court rewards rose dramatically during the late imperial period even as the other groups of moral exemplars continued to be recognized.[11]

In the broadest terms this dominant discourse of female exemplarity underwent metamorphosis across time as the result of the dynamic state-society interactions and negotiations, and by the Qing period it had penetrated into all levels of society. The state had a big stake in promoting female exemplarity as a means of inspiring moral transformation in its subjects. The elite, ranging from the most successful official title holders to the lower gentry, produced a voluminous literature glorifying their virtuous women as part of their larger strategies of achieving success in intense social competitions and perpetuating their elite status. Although women who already held official titles due

to their husbands' status were excluded from the reward system beginning with the Yuan (1260–1368), the elite managed to get around the
system when the regulations were loosened and pooled all kinds of
social and cultural resources to promote their virtuous women. The
massive social stratum of commoners, on the other hand, became the
primary object of imperial benevolence during what can be described
as the "democratization" of the reward system (i.e., only commoners
were entitled to nomination for court reward)—which simultaneously
justified unprecedented state intervention into their daily lives.[12]

Much has been revealed about the complexities surrounding the
intensifying impact of this discursive tradition beyond its implications
as state ideology, especially through the lens of newly explored historical sources. Legal case records shine a light on the production of
gender norms as an ongoing process imbricated in everyday encounters between the changing paradigms of imperial agendas and ordinary people's lives.[13] Elite discourses such as mourning literature and
family biographies also yield intriguing details of how the emotional
needs of their male authors shaped the exemplary lives of women,
besides leaving clues to the affective bonds and psychological tensions
within the families.[14] Moreover, unconventional biographical sources
by and about women are being uncovered, enabling a fresh feminist
analysis in which these exemplary lives are not merely mouthpieces
for male sentiments and ideological agendas or, worse, part of an old
"truth" about China, which conveys little more than the long shadows that a monolithic Confucian patriarchy cast over women's lives.[15]

FEMALE EXEMPLARITY AND WRITING AS A PATH TO FAME

Recent publications have delineated the socioeconomic and cultural
changes that brought about a flourishing writing culture among elite
women during the late imperial period.[16] There were two high tides
of women's literary activities: from the late Ming to the early Qing,
and from the High Qing to the late Qing period.[17] The first emerged
with the fashion for collecting and publishing women's writings in
the sixteenth century, which can be attributed to a variety of factors but perhaps most significantly to commercial expansion and the
printing boom in the lower Yangzi region. This first high tide was
characterized by the prominence of literary courtesans who associated with the leading male literati of the time, as well as women from
illustrious families who took the initiative in establishing women's

literary circles.[18] During the second high tide, by contrast, courtesans lost their cultural glamour and elite women came to dominate the stage of women's literary activities.[19] This period, roughly from the second half of the eighteenth century through the nineteenth century, also witnessed the greatest number of published women writers. Hu Wenkai's seminal study, *Research on Works by Women from All Dynasties* (Lidai funü zhuzuo kao), records more than 3,600 women writers from this time, exceeding the total number of those from all previous ages.[20]

Their sweeping cultural impact notwithstanding, these high tides of women's literary creativity were fraught with contention, which culminated in the Chinese equivalent of the *querelles des femmes* in the late eighteenth century.[21] Central to the debates was the perceived antithesis between female talent (*cai*) and female virtue (*de*): a woman in unrelenting service to her family would not immerse herself in frivolous literary diversions or expose herself to the public eye in literary gatherings and by putting her poetry in print—not the least because doing so risked fishing for fame. The problem with a woman's pursuit of literary fame lay primarily in the fact that the concept of writing (*wen*), as the domain of Chinese high culture and as a gateway to the governing body of the imperium, suggested male privilege. A woman assuming the role of a writing subject must necessarily have transgressed the basic gender norms governing the inner (*nei*) sphere of kinship-based duties and the outer (*wai*) sphere of officialdom and public service. Her literary works hence smacked of the frivolous or even the licentious.[22]

Ironically, a way out of the dilemma lay in a vehement attack that the scholar Zhang Xuecheng (1738–1801) launched on Yuan Mei (1716–97), the greatest connoisseur of women's poetry during the eighteenth century. Condemning Yuan's unbounded idealization of female talent, Zhang valorized women's learning as first and foremost a moral force derived from classical learning and contributing to the intergenerational transmission of the Way (*Dao*). By providing the moral guidance essential to the success of husbands and sons, women's writings suggested a source of moral inspiration transforming the inner/outer dichotomy into "a seamless, unitary social order centered on the home and bounded by the outer reaches of the imperium."[23] Women's literary endeavors, in other words, founded their legitimacy on their moral strength. Thus did the greatest achievements of High Qing women's poetry anthologized by the woman poet Yun

Zhu (1771–1833) become the hallmark of the imperium's cultural and moral triumphs.[24]

One may go further to argue that, in the context of elite families' social competition, a woman's assertion of moral authority often turned into a strategy of self-promotion and social capital for her family, and in turn suggested a path to fame and social honor. An example from the nineteenth century offers a glimpse into these dynamics. Wang Ying (1781–1842), a widow in a salt merchant's family of Yangzhou, was not nominated for a court reward (buhuo qingjing) on the basis that, widowed at the age of thirty-five, she did not meet the age requirement for rewards to chaste widows. (Rewards were generally bestowed on women fifty and older who were widowed at thirty or younger.)[25] Someone urged her son Cheng Bao (1805–60), then a student, to "reduce her age and submit it to the higher administrations [jiannian shangwen]." Cheng firmly declined and said, "My mother has an innately honest nature, and has always taught me not to be deceitful. How would I dare to tarnish her reputation?"[26]

Instead, as soon as he earned the provincial graduate or juren degree (1828), Cheng Bao commissioned a painting glorifying Wang Ying as a virtuous widowed mother teaching her son by an autumnal lamp (Qiudeng kezi tu), and he started to solicit inscriptions from the elites. After he earned the metropolitan graduate or jinshi degree (1833) and was assigned to a post on the Board of Works, he circulated the painting among his colleagues and senior officials. Inscriptions for the painting grew steadily over the years into a rich corpus of essays and poetry by 120 authors, including those by such eminent figures as Bao Shichen (1775–1855) and Ruan Yuan (1764–1849). By the time Wang Ying celebrated her sixtieth birthday (1840), she had earned a reputation among the elites as an exemplary mother and the transmitter of her family learning (jiaxue).[27]

Wang Ying, however, was not an ordinary chaste widow who relied solely on her family connections to make the case for her. Her image as the transmitter of family learning can indeed be attributed to the fact that she hailed from a family of both scholarly and mercantile backgrounds and brought her fine heritage of learning to the salt merchant's family that she married into. She was selected into the Qing dynastic history's section for exemplary women specifically because of the moral strength of her writings.[28] As one of her biographers stated, through her writings she "established proper words [liyan deti]" for women to model, and it was from these writings that the biographer "selected what were particularly vital and wrote them down, so as to prepare for the historians' selection [of her into official history]."[29] Circulating as manuscripts among Cheng Bao's connections around the same time as the painting, these writings served as a family project through which Wang Ying's moral voice reached the upper echelon of the elite. They were a testimonial to her ascent to authority in a range of family and lineage affairs, particularly her coordination of fewer family means (following her husband's death) toward the success of her son Cheng Bao and the metamorphosis of her family's social status.[30] Although no record shows that Wang Ying did eventually obtain a court reward, the moral strength of her writings ensured her place in the official dynastic history as an exemplary woman.

Cheng Bao's reaction to the suggestion of age fabrication—though intended to illustrate the moral integrity of his mother—inadvertently divulged the dark truth of social competition. The reward system faced challenges from fraudulent nominations and corruption as early as the Song. The Qing government had to constantly adjust its policies on the criteria and procedures of the court reward as a means of coping with such challenges.[31] Precisely because of the intensity of competition, the reward was not easily obtained. A case in which a woman died during the protracted review procedures—which often took years—was terminated because rewards were not usually bestowed posthumously. Some women simply did not live long enough to win the reward.[32] While the woman was alive, she needed support from her family or lineage, neighborhood elders, and local luminaries to make the case for her because nomination and review depended on these social relations.[33] As the cases examined in this study will show, a woman's access to social and cultural resources and, more important, the initiative she took to maintain and put to effective use her social relations were often crucial to her success in obtaining social honor.

Wang Ying's success suggests the important role that a woman's writings played in her (and her family's) pursuit of social honor. She is only one example among the many women writers from the late imperial period who realized the ambition of literary and moral immortality (buxiu) through establishing their words (liyan)—an ambition that was exclusive to men by the very definition of writing. Recent studies have shown that this notion of literary immortality was by no means lost on women and have offered new insights into the "agency" women exercised in their writings by "momentarily or figuratively acting in non-kinship defined roles," such as poets, critics, artists, connoisseurs, and travelers.[34] The purpose of the present study, however, is not so much to probe women's literary identities outside the kinship system as to explore how they used their writings to *promote themselves as exemplars of female virtue* defined precisely by their kinship roles.

Results of these women's self-promoting efforts varied: some did succeed in obtaining court rewards or entering official histories; others established their moral reputation among elite audiences without obtaining official recognition; still others—in rare instances—encountered silence from elite society due to the potentially subversive nature of their writings.[35] But it was their writings that produced records of their self-promoting strategies and their assertion of moral authority. Outside the long and uncertain journey toward state recognition, in other words, writing suggested to these female authors a more certain path to immortality—that is, to undying moral as well as literary repute.[36] By examining these writings as the female authors' path to fame and social honor, this study simultaneously illuminates the broader social trends underlying the publication and circulation of their writings and the wide range of practical and emotional needs their writings served. An increasingly accessible corpus of women's writings in the form of personal collections (*bieji*), produced in the second high tide of women's literary creativity, will lead us to the world of the female authors.

CONCEPTUAL FRAME, SOURCES, AND GENRES

Women's writings during the late imperial period appeared in various forms, including joint publications (*heke*) and anthologies (*zongji*), but predominantly as personal collections. In brief, these were individual collections of works by a single author rather than the anthologies or joint publications of multiple authors. Over nine hundred women's personal collections from the Qing period have been identified.[37] A large number of these writings, which were formerly difficult to retrieve from various rare-book collections in China's major libraries, are now becoming easily accessible because of large-scale reprinting projects in China and digital archives in North America.[38]

Personal collections traditionally comprised primarily poetry or essays and hence were alternatively titled collections of poetry (*shiji*)

or collections of essays (*wenji*).[39] They often included biographical
material about the author such as prefaces and epilogues penned by
contemporaries or the author himself or herself, as well as the correspondence between the author and his or her social connections. As
the entire corpus of an author's works, such collections sometimes
also contained a rich variety of literary genres in addition to poetry
and essays. Biographical studies on a certain author can benefit from
retrieving detailed information about his or her life and works from
his or her personal collection.

Personal collections, which contain *biographical* material, became
increasingly *autobiographical* in the late imperial period. In fact, as
an individual's poetic works, personal collections developed their
autobiographical tendency from the canonical idea that "poetry was
the expression of one's intent [*shi yan zhi*]," as stated in the Great
Preface to the *Book of Odes* (Shijing). Stephen Owen has argued that
from the ninth century on, such collections were increasingly organized by chronological order and edited by the poet himself. The
result was a form of "interior history" that unfolded as the poet made
editorial choices and arrangements.[40] During the late imperial period
women started to engage actively in the editing and publishing of
their own works, particularly poetry.[41] Although women's literary
activities during this time depended to a great extent upon male support, and in many instances men no doubt participated in publishing
women's works, there is ample evidence for women's involvement.[42]
Specifically women's extensive engagement with personal collections
appeared concurrently with and can be attributed to another trend
of the late imperial period, namely, the gathering by both male and
female authors of their poetic works into personal collections, which
was comparable, as Grace S. Fong argues, to "keeping a diary or personal journal."[43]

Fong further perceives an author's poetry collection as a form of
"life history/writing" produced through the interplay between the
"texts" (i.e., the poetic works) and the "paratexts" (i.e., the framing devices that guide the reader's interpretation of the texts, written
either by the author himself or herself, or by a person other than the
author). She uncovers a range of paratexts that are particularly significant in the construction of life histories, including prefaces, biographies, accounts of conduct (*xingzhuang*), epitaphs (*muzhiming*),
postscripts, records or notes (*ji* or *zhi*), inscriptional verses (*tici*), and
critical comments (*pingyu*) and portraits. These paratexts fill in the

gaps and silences left in the poetic works, supply the logical flow and narrative continuity expected of life histories, and sometimes engage in lively dialogues with the poetic works.[44] The paratexts in women's poetry collections, according to Fong, were written mostly by those other than the authors themselves. These paratexts hence offered a kind of "threshold" into the "inner quarters" of the women's poetry collections, taking up the task of presenting and praising the work. Examining a woman's poetry as framed by numerous paratexts can offer insights into the forces shaping the interpretations of her self-representation and the kinship and social networks underlying the production of her life writing.[45]

The idea of poetry as "interior history" and the use of personal collections of poetry as "life history/writing" provide the overall conceptual frame for the present study. The women's personal collections examined in the following chapters were, by their very nature, various forms of life history/writing in dynamic interplay with the numerous texts (or paratexts) shaping their interpretation and reception by the audiences—sometimes generating a textual or semiotic continuum wherein the author and her audience engaged in extended conversations (see chapter 2), sometimes creating tension between the perspective of the author and her audience or revealing the gaps at one place yet filled in at others (see chapter 3). On the other hand, the newly available corpus of women's personal collections contains a wealth of materials written by women *aside from poetry*, including biographies (*zhuan*); records or notes (*ji*); eulogies (*zan*); elegies (e.g., *jiwen* or *lei*); tables of historical figures (e.g., *houfei biao*, literally "tables of empresses and imperial consorts"); autobiographical accounts (e.g., *zishu*); genealogies (e.g., *jiapu* or family history; *zongpu/zupu* or lineage history); protocols on ancestral rites (e.g., *cisi zongyue*); letters (including a very peculiar form of letter addressed to the deceased, or *mingshu*); travel accounts; instructions and lecture notes for children; moral guides for women; inscriptions or commentaries on poetry; paintings or writings about paintings; commentaries on the classics; historical studies; studies of astronomy and mathematics; political essays; and medical treatises. Read in the light of the textual continuums or tensions outlined earlier, this reservoir of materials offers unprecedented insight into these women's lives and their writing careers.

The cases explored in this study represent a small but illustrative sample of writings that reveal the female authors' manipulation of the textual spaces of their personal collections. In selecting the cases I was first drawn by a few particularly outspoken voices, which redress the "cavernous silences" often shrouding women's exemplary life stories in traditional biographical writing.[46] These female authors showed no qualms about expressing a range of "negative" emotions, such as anger, frustration, anxiety, and bitterness. Family discord and secrets—taboo aspects of these women's lives[47]—are represented as well, as the women sought attention and claimed recognition for their sacrifices and contributions. My analysis, however, neither focuses exclusively on such expressions of emotions nor uses modern perspectives to fit them neatly into a scheme of women's subversion of the Confucian patriarchy in terms of a radical rejection of both this kinship system and its normative values. Even the boldest forms of women's self-expression explored here were built on an emphasis on moral values and on the dynamic give-and-take between these values and the female authors' expressive needs. What was subversive and powerful in these writings was their authors' active negotiation with and appropriation of the dominant discourse of female exemplarity, which had the effect of "resignifying the power discourse with subversive citations *from within*" (my emphasis), as a recent volume on Chinese women's biography proposes.[48]

These writings draw the reader's attention also because they tell remarkable stories: these are personal histories of surviving ordeals or accomplishing daunting feats and of mustering all available social and cultural resources to achieve fame and social honor. It is crucial, therefore, to examine these stories along the entire life course of their authors and in the broader scope of the social relations and competitions in which they were embedded. Moving from a few outspoken voices to this broader canvas entails a twofold approach, which emphasizes women's self-empowerment in writing and their construction or writing of their personal histories as their social and cultural projects.

A study of women's self-empowerment also raises the question of the *self* of Chinese women, which needs to be conceptualized in terms of the historical contingency of Chinese womanhood. As Tani Barlow argues in her seminal study, the terms *funü* and *nüxing*, representing the concept "women," are "historical artifacts" born of Chinese modernity in the early twentieth century. There was no universal or transcendent category of "women" defined outside the kinship roles of the Confucian family system.[49] However, to dismiss kinship-defined womanhood as being either devoid of the self or fragmented (i.e., divided by kinship roles) is to assume the modern myth of the self as an autonomous and unitary individual. Just as the Confucian gentleman achieved self-cultivation through a matrix of social roles and relationships, the female authors in this study derived their sense of self from their kinship-defined roles and empowered themselves with the moral authority inherent in these roles. Both men and women as gendered subjects in premodern Chinese society must be understood through this prism of the *relational, role-based self* rather than by the standards of the *autonomous, egoistic self* in the Western philosophical traditions.[50] Moreover, since all relationships in premodern Chinese society were at once familial and social—the family being bound into a unitary social order[51]— the self defined by kinship relations was also very much a social being embedded in the family-society-state continuum. It will become clear by the end of this study that the female authors' *self*-empowerment in this sense had significant implications for resignifying the power discourse and redefining women's roles as active agents of nation-building around the turn of the twentieth century.

Given the significance of poetry as the primary form of self-expression for women (as it was for men) during the late imperial period, this particular genre has received by far the most attention in studies of women's literary productions from this time.[52] In addition to poetry, however, this book highlights a variety of literary and artistic genres that have been little explored but that open new trajectories of inquiry into women's writing careers during this period. My purpose is not simply to suggest that women did not write poetry alone or to showcase the rich variety of literary genres found in the newly available personal collections.[53] Genres carry varying degrees of emotional weight, as a recent study of the early Qing mourning literature proposes. Tributes in prose, for example, tended to avoid contentious issues, while poetry often unveiled complexities behind the more orderly commemorative accounts. Authors writing in multiple genres sometimes created "a complex interplay" between these genres.[54]

While all literary and artistic genres offer insight into the little known aspects of these female authors' lives, they serve different expressive functions. Poetry offers an effective vehicle for the expression of poignant emotions, hence inserting a few particularly disruptive voices into the normative values of female exemplarity (see chapter 1). Portraiture emerged as a widely used artistic genre for self-representation among artists and elites starting in the sixteenth century, allowing the subjects of these portraits to generate publicity for themselves in elite society and to convey a broad array of social and cultural messages.[55] Surviving samples of women's portraits and self-portraits, together with a profusion of textual material such as colophons and inscriptions, demonstrate that women actively engaged with this artistic genre for autobiographical purposes and asserted moral authority through the visual representations of their exemplary stories. A look at the careers of the professional women painters reveals at the same time how a woman's economic contributions changed her perception of her importance to her family (see chapter 2). Family genealogy may not be explicitly autobiographical, yet it situates a woman's life within the context of her (husband's) family history and, in rare instances, magnifies the family tensions and taboo issues that poetry, for example, provides only a glimpse of. The ritual authority inherent in this genre also allowed a woman to fill the power vacuum of the patriarchal family in times of transition and to resolve family disputes according to her own wishes (see chapter 3). Family letters provide intimate details of daily life, including women's domestic duty of guarding family health. This understudied aspect of women's medical knowledge readily lent itself to addressing the new exigencies of the late Qing era. In political essays and medical treatises by women we witness earlier models of female domestic caregiving being incorporated into a scheme of national strengthening and expanding from the domestic sphere to the political and the national (see chapter 4).

Inquiry into women's use of these literary and artistic genres challenges the stereotypical definition of women's "proper sphere" and reveals that women crossed the boundaries of domains that were traditionally—and are too often still—assumed to be closed to them.[56] Women who were considered exemplary by normative kinship values crossed boundaries that defined knowledge, economic roles, political engagement, and ritual and cultural authority. Ultimately, then, this book also offers new insights gained from examining the hitherto little studied genres of women's writings.

CHAPTER I

Breaking the Silence

Cases of Outspoken Exemplary Women

Implicit in the concept of "poetry as the expression of one's intent" was the Chinese poetics that privileged spontaneity and unmediated self-expression of the poet, which in turn generated the basic assumption in premodern Chinese literary criticism of an integral relationship between the poet's inner life and his or her poetic works. Recent scholarship, however, has pointed out that Tao Qian (365–427; also known as Tao Yuanming), for example, consciously manipulated his reader's reaction and constructed a self he desired his reader to see. The very fact that the poet took care to emphasize spontaneity at every stage of his composition reveals his awareness of and self-conscious defense against readers' suspicion of his double self.[1] Tao Qian's obsessive attention to spontaneity may be seen as an example of the tension between reality and fiction in autobiographical writing.[2]

The result of growing tendencies from the ninth century on for a poet's works to be organized in chronological order and edited by the poet himself was a form of "interior history" constructed by editorial choices and arrangements.[3] This concern with individual interior history spawned the genre of chronological biography (*nianpu*)—the chronological ordering of notes for an individual's life that could help his or her contemporaries write biographies beyond the usual eulogizing narratives in official historical writing.[4] For the purpose of this study, it is the nature of a poet's personal collection as interior history—carefully organized and edited for the reader to see—that also makes a woman's collection of poetry a useful source of her autobiographical writings. The woman poet and critic Shen Shanbao

(1808–62), for example, used her poetry collection to construct a life story and took control of the reading process through the strategy of "self-censorship," which helped to create a consistent textual subject as a filial daughter and a dedicated young poet.[5] Gan Lirou (1743–1819) organized her poetry collection by explicitly tracing her progression through the life phases of womanhood and, by this means, wrote herself into family and social histories.[6] Women poets like Shen and Gan could assume literary identities in their writing that transcended their kinship roles, such as travelers, critics, and artists.[7]

The purpose of this chapter is to explore how women established themselves as exemplars of female virtue defined precisely by their kinship roles while articulating in the most poignant terms their uneasy relationship with these normative roles. The cases I discuss reveal stunning outspokenness, manifest either in the authors' efforts to foreground their dilemmas and sacrifices or, oftentimes, in their expression of such "negative" emotions as anger, frustration, anxiety, bitterness, and despair. Of note are rhetorical strategies with which they mediated their expression of emotions and told their extraordinary life stories as the exemplary mother, wife, and daughter-in-law.

LIU YIN (1806–1832): THE FIRST WIFE ADOPTING THE VOICE OF THE SECOND WIFE

Liu Yin was known as Filial Woman Liu (or, more precisely, Filial Daughter-in-Law Liu) from the county of Wujin, Jiangsu. She was lauded primarily for her devoted care of her severely ill mother-in-law, which led to her own exhaustion, illness, and finally death at the age of twenty-seven.[8] Around fourteen years after her death, her husband Miao Zhengjia (?–1846), also a poet, gathered the poetry drafts she left and obtained funds to have them printed in 1846 as her personal collection, *Remaining Drafts from the Dreaming-of-the-Moon Tower* (Mengchanlou yigao).[9]

Like many personal collections of works by exemplary women, the main body of Liu Yin's collection is accompanied by a large number of eulogizing texts: three prefaces, two biographies, inscriptions (thirty-seven poems by twenty-six persons, including nineteen local literati, six gentry women, and a nun), two epilogues, and an introduction, all bent on creating a hagiographic profile.[10] These texts show that Liu Yin demonstrated a wide range of exemplary behaviors in addition to that of filial piety. When she was young she was said to have admired the character of her grandfather Liu Shuchu (fl. eighteenth century), who was recorded in the local gazetteer for his filial behavior.[11] When dissidence arose in her family regarding her engagement to Miao Zhengjia (whom her grandfather chose to be her fiancé, though another relative tried to persuade her to marry into an affluent household), she composed a verse to express her disdain of wealth and her insistence on fulfilling her engagement despite the destitution of the Miao family, modeling herself upon the celebrated Han dynasty exemplary wife Meng Guang.[12] After her marriage to Miao, she took on all the household duties and served her mother-in-law and grandmother-in-law respectfully, calmly, and happily despite hardships. In order to help the Miao family through financial straits, she wove late into the night and pawned her dowry to pay for the debts of her father-in-law, who stayed in Guangxi for a long time to avoid creditors, in the hope that he could come home.[13] When her parents tried to persuade her to stay in her natal home after the funeral of her grandfather (so she could have more comforts), she firmly declined. She capably took care of the household while Miao traveled to attend civil service exams and to take teaching jobs in gentry families, and never troubled him with difficulties at home.[14] She urged him to glorify his family name, comforted him when he was in distress, and admonished him when he could not restrain his temper. Miao was unable to establish a career; his friend Gu Huaisan (fl. nineteenth century), a historian, glossed over his frustration by comparing him to Qu Yuan (ca. 339–278 BCE).[15] Liu also dedicated herself to the care of her children. When her first son died, she herself nearly died of grief and disease. After her second son survived malaria, she was emaciated. Throughout this quite standard language extolling Liu's exemplarity, the enormous load of work put on her—and her alone—by this destitute family is evident. Her service to her ill mother-in-law was only the last on this long list of household duties that were sapping all her energy. In the words of Miao, she was "like a tree that was long withering from inside and therefore collapsed at the first gust of wind."[16]

What these texts share is their emphasis on Liu's unfailing efforts to control her emotions—namely, her perseverance through ordeals without complaining. Liu was not "emotionless," yet when she expressed emotions, this only enhanced her exemplary profile. As an affectionate wife, she was said to "find harmonious delight" in the time she spent with Miao even when they had little to live on; as a loving mother, she was heartbroken at the death of her first son, shedding tears and blood in turn; as a filial daughter-in-law, she worried that her second son's malaria would grieve her mother-in-law, so she held him in her arms day and night to care for him.[17] On the other hand, Liu was also represented as knowing exactly when to check her emotions. She held back tears when Miao once again failed the civil service exam, and comforted him with just the proper words.[18] When she herself was dangerously ill, she was able to "make all efforts to act as if she had been completely well" so she could care for her ill mother-in-law. Even days before her death, she urged Miao to return to his job, smiling and speaking normally as she saw him off.[19] In short, Liu's exemplarity lies in her perfect management of the balance between the expression and the suppression of her emotions according to appropriate rites.[20] Thus did Zhang Wenhu (1808–85), the author of one of the prefaces to Liu's collection, characterize Liu's poetry: "It carries a forlorn tune, yet its character can be compared to that of the pine that stands prominently on the height of ten thousand feet and that undergoes frost and snow without withering."[21]

One is tempted nonetheless to wonder whether Liu herself might tell the story differently. Would the writings of this woman crushed by her household duties tell of moments when she lost the perfect balance, either between the expression and the suppression of her emotions or between the sorrow and the "character" of her poetry? Would she never reveal anxieties, frustrations, or pain that did not have the positive effect of highlighting her exemplary profile?

Liu was not a prolific poet. Yet, given her overwhelming workload, the fact that she found time to write poetry at all surprised some of the authors of the eulogies,[22] and may suggest the importance of poetry for her as a vehicle of self-expression. In fact, even a cursory look at the thin volume that Liu left (sixty-eight poems in total, only around half of which were composed after she was married) reminds us how useful it is to approach the lives of exemplary women the other way around, that is, by examining how they represented themselves rather than how they were represented.[23] Liu's poems about extreme cold, illnesses in her family, and the hardships of life in general are in shocking contrast to what Miao refers to as the total absence of hunger, cold, illness, and pain in her letters to him.[24] What she was said to endure calmly and "would rather die than mention" did find expression in her poetry and did affect the balance of which she was said to be in perfect control.[25]

Take the example of a few of Liu's mourning poems. It may not be surprising that, as a loving mother, she should write grief-laden poems for her deceased son. Although the *Book of Rites* conveyed that infant deaths were not worth mourning, a mourning literature for children emerged during the ninth century and reached its apex during the late imperial period.[26] The woman poet Xi Peilan (1762–1820?), for instance, wrote sixteen "Songs of a Broken Heart" for the deaths of two of her sons, in which she directly confronts the *Rites* to justify her grief.[27] What is most remarkable about Liu's mourning poems, however, is not so much her expression of grief as her effort to express her frustration about the conflicting demands on her:

空說懷中玉燕投，	In vain it was said that he was the jade swallow who flew into my bosom,
一期才過便回頭。	After one short year he died.
重闈白首腸都斷，	In the inner quarters, my white-haired mother-in-law is heartbroken,
我縱傷心淚敢流？	How dare I weep for my own grief?
寒宵績紡暑繅絲，	On chilly nights I wove, on hot days I reeled silk,
那有工夫更弄兒。	How could I have a moment for my son?
今日思量慚鞠育，	Thinking of this today, I am mortified by my neglect of him,
任伊啼笑沒人知。	He was left there to cry and to laugh—nobody knew![28]

Liu's effort to control the expression of her own grief foregrounds her concern for her mother-in-law in the first poem, turning the occasion for mourning into that of illustrating the virtue of filial piety. At the same time, however, this very effort also heightens the effect of what it is meant to repress. The phrase "How dare I" bespeaks the conflict of emotions—between those of a grieving mother and those of a filial daughter-in-law. In highlighting her awareness of the need to prioritize her filial concerns over her motherly feelings, she lays bare the pain that being a filial daughter-in-law could entail.

In the second poem the sense of conflict comes out in even clearer terms. Liu frankly admits her neglect of her motherly duties yet attributes it to other household duties that competed for her attention—in particular, weaving almost unceasingly so that the household could survive. Though a symbol for female industriousness throughout Chinese history, weaving is here used not to foreground Liu's virtue but rather to relieve an excruciating sense of guilt: these duties had conflicting claims on her, and she could not but sacrifice her motherly duties for the sake of her household duties. Therefore, far from being the woman who capably handled all difficulties so her husband would not need to worry, as the eulogizing texts try to convince us, Liu reveals—with an undertone of resentment?—that she could barely manage the distribution of her time.

Liu's emotional uncertainty finds its most peculiar expression when she speaks as a wife. In poems addressed to her husband, she distributes her moral advice constantly, using her own example (how she happily takes all the familial duties onto herself so that Miao can pursue his career) to urge him to glorify his family name.[29] While these poems reassure us of her role as the moral guardian of her husband, as represented by the eulogizing texts, there is also something disturbing in them—not only when there is a clear sense of superiority in Liu's tone but also when this admonishing voice loses its confidence. In a long poem Liu wrote in imitation of the famous Music Bureau (Yuefu) verse "Chanted for a Companion Who Would Grow Old with Me" (Baitou yin), which Zhuo Wenjun (second century BCE) addressed to her husband, Sima Xiangru (179?–117? BCE) when he was about to take a concubine, we witness, to our shock, Liu imagining herself dead and adopting the voice of the second wife to admonish her husband. This most remarkable piece exposes the uncertainty and anxiety underlying Liu's confident tone.

As the poem opens, Liu's poetic voice compares her situation to that of "a new flower blossoming on the old twig," while informing us that the "old flower withered a long time ago." She then identifies herself explicitly as the second wife of Miao: "I am your second wife." Elaborating on the affections between this second wife, "I," and Miao, the poetic voice draws our attention to the luxuries that Miao bought her in order to please her. (At this point we cannot but recall the destitution of the Miao family and wonder what has changed its fortune.) Instead of taking pleasure in these luxuries, she suddenly kneels before him and, begging for a detailed story, inquires about Miao's deceased first wife. The following is apparently what she learns; note that the poetic voice switches abruptly from a humble tone to one of reproach:

前妻來歸日，	When your former wife married you,
值郎貧賤時。	You were poor and humble.
無薪炊屐屨，	Out of firewood, you had to burn your door latch;
無粟朝忍饑。	Out of grain, you endured hunger since dawn.
畜妾今日富，	Now you are rich, and take me into your house,
忘郎昔日貧。	Having forgotten the meager means you had in the past.
豈惟忘昔貧，	It is not only poverty that you've forgotten,
並忘舊時人。	But the one who was with you in days of old.

舊人為郎死，	She died for you,
死後幸有子。	Luckily there was a son she left.
勸郎續弦膠，	She urged you to take a second wife,
家事須料理。	As there were household matters to manage.
瀕危持郎手，	On her deathbed she held your hands,
惜此呱呱兒。	Telling you about her worries for her baby:
棄置從後人，	"I have to leave him to your next wife,
生死從爾為。	It is up to you whether he lives or dies.
妾身付泉壤，	Although I am departing to the land of the dead,
妾魂守家門。	My soul will guard this household.
孤兒眼中血，	The blood from the eyes of this orphan,
新人掌中痕。	Will explain the bruise in the palm of your new wife."
郎言聽未終，	I had not heard the end of your words,
新婦聲暗吞。	Before I, your new wife, started to weep.
結髮尚寡恩，	If you have little affection for your first wife,
新婚何足論。	What is there in you for your new marriage?
願移愛妾意，	Please take what you have indulged on me,
先慰泉下魂。	To appease the soul in the underworld![30]

In this peculiar lecture the second wife admonishes the husband, urging him to give his affections to his deceased former wife. Liu appropriates the voice of the second wife to vent her own anxiety about her marriage.

Anxiety underlies the confident voice of reproach: What would happen if Miao succeeded in establishing a career—which Liu always pushed him to do? Would he remember her sacrifices for him if she died of overwork and if he took a second wife? And how would her successor treat her son? Would that woman be an evil stepmother? Would Liu's claim that her soul would always be there, watching the household, be a useful warning? Would Miao be put to shame by the second wife's condemnation?

At some points in this poem Liu herself appears to be accusing Miao of lack of gratitude for the sacrifices she has made. Her voice breaks in when the voice of her successor quotes her. After all, we might wonder, how would the successor know vivid details of the first wife's deathbed scene? Liu may have us believe that these are from the words of Miao ("I had not heard the end of *your words*; / Before I, your new wife, started to weep"), yet she cannot explain why Miao would present them in such a way as to be used against himself. This problematic relationship among the voices shows that the poem is a thinly disguised piece of ventriloquism wherein the puppet character of the second wife speaks all the concerns of the first wife and exposes the tension in the marriage that the latter not only voluntarily walks into despite all warnings but literarily invests all her life in.

Was there anything in her relationship with Miao that warranted Liu's anxiety? Or was the poem an effort to call attention to her own sacrifices? Was she questioning the worthiness of her sacrifices? Was there any sense of regret in the bleak picture that she painted for her future—that she would die of overwork yet would soon be forgotten by her husband? Due to the dearth of relevant sources, we may never find precise answers. The entry on Miao in the "Writers' Garden" (Wenyuan) section of the Jiangyin gazetteer reveals nothing more than that he had an unrestrained character and excelled in poetry yet failed to establish a career.[31] The eulogizing texts in Liu's collection make standard references to the deep affection the couple had for each other, while at the same time making passing comments on Liu's need to admonish her wild (*kuang*) husband. Nonetheless we do know that there is a subtext between the lines with which Liu fashions her own profile. To quote Lu Yitong (1805–63), the author of one of the epilogues to Liu's collection, who astutely senses the tension in the piece:

> As I read *Remaining Drafts from the Dreaming-of-the-Moon Tower*, particularly the poem "Chanted for a Companion Who Would Grow Old with Me" . . . I wondered why it carries such a sorrowful tune. At the very time the poem was composed, the couple were deeply attached to each other. Even though they had to put up with poverty, diseases, ill fortunes, and separations, these ordeals did not weaken the bond of affections between them—how would one expect that she would go to such an extent [with her sorrow]? . . . It was as if she had predicted what would happen in the future. Could it be that she was treating others well just so that she would not be treated poorly by them?[32]

XIE XIANGTANG (1800?–1870): WHEN A MOTHER DISPENSED HER MORAL ADVICE

Xie Xiangtang was from Pingyang in Zhejiang. The entry on her in the local gazetteer identifies her as a gentry woman (*guixiu*, literally "talents from the inner quarters") who excelled in poetry and was known particularly for her poem "Precepts for My Son" (Shi'er) as well as for a poem mourning the death of her younger brother, a poet, Xie Qingyang (fl. nineteenth century). The entry also celebrates her as a chaste widow, mentioning briefly that her husband, Jin Luoxian, frequented the entertainment quarters and died before the age of thirty. To continue the family line Xie adopted a son from the Jin lineage.[33] It was to her adopted son therefore that Xie addressed her "Precepts."

Unlike that of Liu Yin, Xie's personal collection, *Drafts of Poetry and Song Lyrics Written after Womanly Work* (Gongyu shici gao), appeared in print as an appendix to the personal collection of her brother Xie Qingyang. As such it did not receive much attention. No eulogizing texts are found in it, and neither are prefaces or epilogues of an introductory or commentary nature except a preface penned by Xie herself.[34] But for the terse entry from the Pingyang gazetteer there is not much of a story about Xie's life. Yet she is attention-worthy precisely because this lack of detail about her life contrasts so strongly with her will to communicate and to gain recognition through her own writings. Were it not for these writings she would be just another chaste widow listed in a local gazetteer, and we would never know of the critical role that she played in restoring her family's fortune.

At the beginning of her collection Xie does not reveal an intent to claim recognition. Like many gentry women poets preceding her, she is too busy defending the act of writing itself. Her preface focuses on the inevitable paradox of a woman writing about herself: If she "feels ashamed of boasting [about] herself beyond limit, and submits to the admonition that having no talent [is a virtue],"[35] then why does she spend so much time writing? What purpose do these writings serve if not self-promotion? Xie's awareness of the need to justify herself (and the fact that she followed the custom among many earlier women poets of categorizing her collection as "drafts written after womanly work") reminds us that the tension surrounding women's literary pursuits during the previous centuries endured.[36] Xie's own reasons for writing, however, are far from clear. At one point she seems to be wavering between the claims that women write to illustrate virtue and that one's feelings cannot but be expressed through poetry. In the end it is these feelings that Xie draws our attention to.

Xie characterizes her poetic works as "sorrowful songs" (*beiyin*), without which the "agonies" (*kuzhong*) in her cannot be vented. In fact, the last line of her preface indicates a wish not only to vent the pain but to have it known by others: "*Who would know of* a tiny fraction of the agonies in me?" (my emphasis). Xie is referring to her widowhood, which she qualifies thus: "a person is titled 'not-yet-dead,' and a grass is named 'living alone.'"[37] And what needs to be known, it turns out, is not the pain itself but rather the concrete life situations that come with the pain.

One of these situations that pressed on Xie's mind was that her husband's family was left with no heir. The phrase "to continue the family line" (*chengtiao*) appears at several places in her collection. In one of her mourning poems she specifies that this is the reason she does not commit suicide upon the death of her husband.[38] In a poem that she dedicates to a deity, she expresses her wish that the latter bless the family with an heir so that the family line could continue.[39] Read in this context, what Xie characterizes as her "heart-broken words [duanchang yin]" may not spring specifically from deep affection for her deceased husband but rather from a quite different concern.[40] Echoing the title of the celebrated collection of song lyrics by Zhu Shuzhen (1135?–80?), a Southern Song woman poet who suffered from an unhappy marriage, Xie's "heart-broken words" carry a disturbing undertone.

Particularly disturbing is the assertion that Xie makes in some of her mourning poems, in which she is shedding "tears yearning for a son [sizi lei]."[41] She describes the last days of her husband, Jin Luoxian, cryptically:

瘦骨不盈把，	He was less than a handful of bones,
全非當日形。	All his former looks had gone.
傷心何至此，	It grieved me to wonder how it had come to this,
惡餌誤芳齡。	It was what he fed on that ruined his prospering life.[42]

Xie never specifies what caused the death of Jin apparently in the prime of life. The poem does make a vague reference to "bad food" or "evil bait." If, based on his shocking state, it is hard to believe that he was suffering from simple food poisoning, then the alternative interpretation that he had taken "evil bait" may suggest a different sort of illness, as well as a different relationship with Xie. Did Jin's illness have anything to do with his habit of visiting the entertainment quarters?

Moreover, even as Xie grieves over the illness and death of Jin, nowhere in this poem—or in the seven other mourning poems under the same title—can we spot a single word that suggests any bond of affection between the couple. In fact, Xie is utterly silent about her marital relationship, which goes quite against the custom of writing mourning poems for a deceased spouse, which often contain memories of the intimacies between husband and wife or the hardships they went through together to highlight the loss and grief.[43] A case that contrasts most distinctly with Xie is the late Ming poet Bo Shaojun (d.

1626), who turned her one hundred mourning poems into a hagiography for her deceased husband in addition to using them to express her enduring grief. (She died of grief soon after.)[44] It seems that Xie's marriage left her with neither memory nor heir.

Only after many years did Xie disclose the key to her curious silence about her marriage.[45] Having gone through much hardship to raise her adopted son to the age of twelve, the age to embark on a virtuous path toward glorifying the family name, she now had important moral advice to dispense in "Precepts for My Son." It was when Xie spoke in the admonishing voice of a mother rather than the "heart-broken" voice of a widow that concealed parts of her life began to unfold.

Xie's sixty-six-line poem opens in an explicitly autobiographical tone and with a clear sense of pride: "I originate from a household of Confucian scholars, which exudes the fragrance of brushes and ink." In the ensuing elaboration on her illustrious natal family background and the fine education she received, however, anger at her deceased husband erupts, along with emphasis on her own contribution to restoring his household from financial ruin to prosperity:

自從適汝父，	Ever since I married your father,
筆硯多拋荒。	I have abandoned my brushes and inkstone.
汝父喜揮霍，	Your father was a profligate,
家事慵屏當。	Who was too lazy to deal with household matters.
輕肥事裘馬，	He indulged in sensual pleasures of all kinds,
錢刀等秕糠。	And squandered our wealth as if it were worthless.
千金不為惜，	A thousand taels of gold meant nothing to him,
日夜窮歡場。	He would spend days and nights in brothels.
漸至誇台築，	Gradually debts piled up,
遂以腴產償。	To pay for which we sold off our fine properties.
我苦進規勸，	I made all efforts to give him my counsel,
故輒思更張。	And led him to abandon his former path.
喜心竊自謂，	Delighted in my heart I said to myself:
捕牢鑒亡羊。	"Good that he can learn from his previous lessons!"
詎謂丁厄運，	How could I know that ill fortune was soon to befall,
一疾入膏肓。	And that, once he was ill, there was no cure for him.
行年未三十，	Hardly had he reached the age of thirty,
下招來巫陽。	Before spirits came down to gather his soul.
籲嗟我命薄，	I bemoaned the bitterness of my fate:
綠鬢稱未亡。	In the prime of my youth I was titled "not-yet-dead"!
爾時未有汝，	At that time I did not have you [as my son],
寂寂守空房。	All by myself I lived in these empty chambers.
我非身惜死，	It was not that I was unwilling to give up my life,
所計在久長。	I was thinking for the long-term well-being of this household.
孀居十餘載，	During over ten years of my widowhood,

朝夕淚盈裳。	My tears soaked my robe from dawn till dusk.
嗣任得元晏，	Luckily the heir I found for this household was so fine,
稍覺寬衷腸。	Which gave comfort to my grieving heart.
井臼躬操作，	I personally performed all housework,
米鹽策周詳。	And meticulously calculated all expenditure.
一日復一日，	As days went by,
漸漸充倉箱。	I filled trunks and warehouses.
為築新棟宇，	I had a new mansion built,[46]
為復舊田莊。	And former family land and properties recovered.
雖幸收桑榆，	Although I had the fortune of retrieving what has been lost,
辛苦已備嘗。	There is no hardship that I haven't tasted![47]

In this extensive moral dissertation that Xie addresses to her adopted son, we unexpectedly run into her confession of her unhappy marriage: her husband not only frequented the entertainment quarters, as the entry from the Pingyang gazetteer reveals, but in fact brought his household to bankruptcy with his extravagant habits. The open criticism with which Xie describes his life of debauchery and his squandering of their family wealth bespeaks a clear sense of anger—even after all these years. Was this profligate even worthy of her grief and, more important, of the sacrifices she had to make in remaining a chaste widow for him?[48] Here we get the sense that Xie's earlier silence about her marriage is a way of critiquing it and of venting her anger. After all, one is not supposed to display anger at the deceased in mourning poems, yet one can leave the mourning blank, as it is with Xie's mourning. She is too absorbed in mourning the fact that she is left with no son to mourn the death of her husband. Moreover, even though the direct cause of Jin's death remains a mystery, the words Xie uses in her earlier poem to explain it here invites an interpretation other than "bad food." Were Jin's debaucheries the "evil bait" that eventually cost his life— even after he decided to "abandon his former path"?

A mourning poem by her brother Xie Qingyang specifically blames Jin's death on his addiction:

莫信名香能續命，	You should not have believed that the "famed fragrance" could cure you,
可憐毒餌竟傷生。	How sad it was that the poisonous bait took your life!
君所嗜非宜，頗涉自戕。	[Note:] You were addicted to what was harmful to you.
	It was very much like you had killed yourself.[49]

As Xie Qingyang puts it bluntly, Jin was responsible for his own death. It was his addiction (to opium? prostitutes?) that killed him and that incurred Xie Xiangtang's anger. The point, however, is not so much how Xie Xiangtang expresses her anger as how she bends her anger toward the end of polishing her own virtuous profile.

We may never find out how exactly Xie survived financially, as many aspects of women's participation in the economic activities of this time are still unknown. Did she make good investments with her dowry (considering that her wealthy natal family may have dowered her generously)?[50] In any case, dowry investment would serve as a much more convincing explanation than frugality alone, especially in this commercially vibrant area of Wenzhou.[51] Xie highlights her industriousness and frugality ("I personally performed all housework, and meticulously calculated all expenditure"), mentioning only activities within the boundary of recognized (and so "safe") female virtues.

Only after she finishes her self-valorizing dissertation (to contrast with her alleged disdain of self-promotion in her preface) does Xie finally turn to the moral education of her son. The remaining third of the poem establishes her as one of those high-minded mothers recorded by history who spurred their sons to make the best of what they had and to pursue a virtuous path to success. Central to her concern is the danger that her son might squander the "prime time" of his youth. Nothing but clichés here, perhaps, yet when read against what she has just revealed to her son, her message is clear: "Do not repeat the path of your libertine late father."

Xie would adopt this admonishing voice again, and not to her son alone.[52] She was blessed with a prosperous old age, living to the age of seventy, seeing her son married, having grandchildren, and making good use of the wealth she earned by her own efforts. And it is thanks to her own words that we get to know of the remarkable facts about this otherwise obscure yet no less exemplary facet of her life.

DONG BAOHONG (1820—1884?): WORDS OF "BLOOD AND TEARS" AS SELF-PROMOTION

Dong Baohong was a chaste widow from Zhenzhou, Jiangsu, who caught the attention of a number of local literati. Her personal collection, *Poetry Collection from the Drinking-Fragrance Pavilion* (Yinxiangge shichao), ironically features as its last poem one titled "Expressing My Feelings upon the Fact That I Have No Means to Have My Poetry Printed" (Yin shi wuli fuzi yougan), in which she writes,

"How blessed are those who'll be known for thousands of years to come! / Several times, I burst into tears as I thought of *Spring and Autumn*" and "The blood from my heart, alas, / Will forever be gone, as if swept away by currents."[53] "Blood from one's heart" (*xinxue*) is a stock expression of how much one invests in one's works. Dong clearly relies on such effort to win a place in history and hardly veils her jealousy of those recorded by the *Spring and Autumn Annals*, which was said to be compiled by Confucius himself. Dong thus draws our attention to how much publication of her work means to her.

A closer look at Dong's collection along with the eulogizing texts in it reveals that, having been widowed since the age of thirty, Dong both consciously sought attention for her fidelity to her deceased husband and used such attention to help herself survive. The collection starts with a preface and a "record" (*jilu*) penned by Liu Shu, director of a local shelter for chaste widows. Dong's native county, Zhenzhou, was part of the Yangzhou area, where the idea of a widows' shelter was first conceived by local literati in 1773. Before the mid-nineteenth century at least fifty-six such shelters were established, and more than 70 percent of them were located in Jiangsu and Zhejiang. During the remaining half of the nineteenth century another 132 shelters were established in an increasing number of provinces. As charity works run by local luminaries, these shelters provided financial aid in the form of food, monthly stipends, and/or accommodation for widows who lost the means to survive at the death of their husbands, especially during the Taiping Rebellion (1850–64) and afterward, when population loss amounted to over 50 percent in the lower Yangzi region. By this means these shelters motivated the women to remain chaste widows and protected them from their unscrupulous kin, who, out of financial consideration, often pressured them to remarry.[54] Liu Shu's preface for Dong's personal collection indicates therefore an important connection Dong made as a chaste widow.

Following Liu Shu's preface are twenty-one poems composed by eleven local literati in honor of Dong. Together these texts provide significant details about Dong's life. For example, Liu records that Dong came to the shelter during the sixth year of the Xianfeng reign (1856) and announced that she would commit suicide. Shocked and terrified, Liu asked why. Dong's answer reads very much like a written autobiography:

> I was born in a household of Confucian scholars, and learned the
> *Odes* and the *Rites* when I was young. During the twenty-second year

of the Daoguang reign [1842] I was married to Zheng Yue. After nine
years [1851], my husband died. On his deathbed he told me to remain
a widow in the household because my father-in-law was then traveling outside, and if the latter returned home, I could serve him as if I
were his son [fudai zizhi]. I respectfully marked the words of my late
husband and dared not forget. When it came to the third year of the
Xianfeng reign [1853], rebels from Guangdong took the city of Jinling
[Nanjing], and my father-in-law was trapped there. I had given birth to
a daughter, but she died some years ago. I was therefore all by myself
and had no one to turn to. I had long been thinking of following my
husband to the land of the dead! It was only because of the thought of
how much he had counted on me to serve his father [that I did not do
so]. Whenever I met someone who returned from the rebel-taken city,
I would inquire about my father-in-law, and someone told me that he
was still there. Therefore, although I wished to end my life, I could not
allow myself to do so immediately. After the rebels took the city of Yi
[Yizheng], I fled to the Liu Family Village. During the following year,
the rebels took the Liu Family Village, and I had nowhere else to go
but to return to the city of Yi. While my husband was alive, he held a
minor government post and we had little savings. Having experienced
plunder time and again by the rebels, what I had left was all gone. Plus,
the famine caused the price of rice to soar, and stores were all shut
down. The reason, indeed, that I would rather endure hunger than
end my life was that my father-in-law might still someday come home.
However, in the end he did not, and my situation turned even worse.
There was an elderly kinsman from my husband's lineage who constantly insulted me with filthy words. I knew that I could not remain a
widow in this household any longer and tried to hang myself, yet did
not succeed. Since then, I have been even more determined to commit suicide. The fact that I would choose to do it now rather than on
the day when my husband died may give rise to mistaken conjectures.
Therefore I list here my reasons so as to inform the Hall for Chaste
Widows. If, someday, my father-in-law does come back and I am not
here to serve him, I know that I have no excuse for my unfilial behavior, yet perhaps people will understand and forgive me.[55]

Liu informs us that this speech was indeed based on a written autobiographical account, matching the oral speech verbatim, which Dong
submitted to Liu before she left and after reciting the speech. Dong's
act, then, was carefully planned. Three days later she went to Liu
again, this time submitting to him a poem, in which she reiterated her
determination to commit suicide.[56]

Dong thus waited another three days not to execute her wish but to
reiterate it. The single most important theme in her narrative is her filial
concern for her father-in-law. Given that female suicide was celebrated
as a moral ideal since the Han dynasty, what would serve as a proper,

virtuous excuse for a woman to live on after her husband's death?[57] In many cases, if it was not to continue the family line it was to serve the in-laws,[58] yet Dong was left with neither children nor in-laws to take care of. Her only daughter had died, and, here at least, she does not mention her adoption of a son.[59] Her mother-in-law had died.[60] Her father-in-law had not returned from the rebel-taken city and may have died there. Consequently Dong's justification of her existence hung on the thin line of what she heard from the "someone" who fled back from Nanjing, namely, that her father-in-law was seen there and therefore might still be alive and come back "someday." Her entire speech thus reveals not so much her determination to die as her will to live.

That Dong sought the attention of the shelter at this particular moment can be attributed to the extreme poverty and hostility that confronted her and that she could no longer survive. The "rebels from Guangdong" she refers to can be no other than the Taiping rebels, who brought massive disruptions to the lower Yangzi region. Originating from this area, Dong bore her personal testimony to the rebels' occupation of Nanjing in 1853 and their ravages of areas in Yangzhou and Taizhou. Fleeing back and forth between counties of her native area, Dong lost all her belongings and thus faced the threat of death not because of any real pressure on her to follow her husband "to the land of the dead" but because she could barely survive the political and economic tumults of her time.[61] The insults from the elderly relative could have involved pressure to remarry, since economic reasons often underlay widow remarriages during this time.[62] Dong's alleged attempt to hang herself can be read as a strategy for resisting such pressure.[63] But if her real goal was to survive, then appealing to the shelter for chaste widows could be a practical means of gaining both moral and financial support. Such shelters were places where women sought protection rather than a venue for suicide, and according to Liu Shu, this particular shelter in Yangzhou had provided protection for more than a thousand local women.[64]

This act of seeking protection was remarkable in its rhetorical strategy. Dong drew with ease from a standard language of female virtue to characterize her dilemma, foregrounding her options: committing suicide, following her husband's deathbed wish and remaining a chaste widow, and serving her father-in-law in the place of his son. Interspersed among her petitions for attention to her moral rectitude were those for sympathy with her desperate situation. Liu was so impressed with Dong's "persistence in virtue" despite all the ordeals she went through that he soon arranged for her to be provided a monthly stipend and that her elderly relative no longer harass her so that she could "have the freedom to pursue her path of martyrdom."[65]

Dong's petition, then, succeeded in securing material support. Beyond this, however, it seems that she was also determined to write herself into history through the publication of her poetry and to claim for herself a place among those exemplary women lauded by local and dynastic histories. Around one fourth of Dong's poems were written before her marriage. The rest of her personal collection presents her life as a sequence of struggles with ill fortune and can be read in this sense as an expanded version of the speech that she gave at the shelter. Its contents may be classified as follows:

1. Three poems describing her devoted care of her husband while he was severely ill and expressing her concern for her father-in-law, who was traveling.

2. Eleven mourning poems that both express her deep affection for her deceased husband and foreground the dilemma she was put in, accompanied by a letter to him.

3. Twenty-four poems evolving from the theme of "expressing one's feelings" (*yougan*) that give poignant utterance to the loneliness and insecurity of her life as a widow.

4. Ten poems describing the tumults of her time and relating how she fled from the Taiping rebels, four of which detail specifically how she snatched a moment between her flights to pay tribute to her husband's tomb (no doubt intended as an illustration of her fidelity to him).

5. Eleven poems written in exchange with or in honor of local luminaries, showing her establishment of connections as well as her local reputation as a chaste widow.

6. An autobiographical essay, "An Account of My Lifetime Experiences" (Pingsheng jiyu fu), which summarizes her afflictions and precedes the last poem, "Expressing My Feelings upon the Fact That I Have No Means to Have My Poetry Printed."

All provide vivid details about how Dong dealt with her life travails on a day-to-day basis. The letter she wrote shortly after the death of her husband is especially revealing of the undercurrents of emotions surging beneath her promise of fidelity to him.

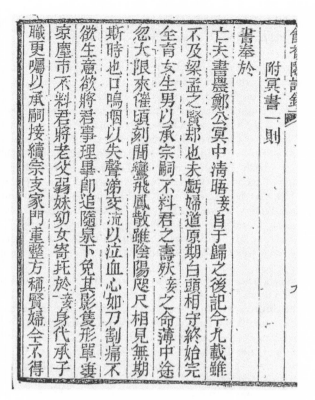

Figure 1.01. The first page of Dong Baohong's letter to her deceased husband. From Dong Baohong, *Yinxiangge shichao*, original page 9b. Reprinted by permission from the National Library of China.

In her opening greetings Dong explicitly addresses Zheng: "Written respectfully to my late husband, Zheng Shunong [courtesy name of Zheng], for him to read in the underworld." She then proceeds to elaborate on her affection for him, echoing her previous mourning poems regarding her "passionate love [*qingchi*]" for him. She describes how they treated each other like the exemplary Han dynasty couple Liang Hong and Meng Guang, how she expected that they would stick to each other till their hair grew white, how devastated she was by Zheng's death, and how determined she was to follow him to his grave—but for his deathbed wish that she should take care of his father, his younger sister, and their daughter;[66] continue the family line; and restore the household to prosperity. It is at this point that

Dong gains full justification for the purpose of her life. Yet her affection, or "passionate love," also slowly turns bitter:

> As I think of your last moments, I recall that you fixed your gaze on me intently as if you had a thousand things to say, yet were unable to say a word. You were, I suspect, worried that I was still young and that the household had but meager means: If I remarried, people would sneer. But I have always known by heart the rites of the inner quarters, and also known of the principles of chastity and righteousness. I swore that I would willingly stick to a quiet life of widowhood to fulfill your wish. However, what can I do with the facts that your father is in old age, that we barely have any savings, that the household has fallen to destitution—what should I use to feed the mouths of this household while we live for years without any income? Whom should I ask for food when our young daughter cries in hunger? Whenever I think of these things, I lose my mind. Although you asked me to live on, it was no different from putting me in the situation of death!
>
> As a consequence of the distress pent up in me, I fell ill, and constantly spat blood. My illness has grown more severe day by day. During the three years while you were ill, I did my utmost to take care of you, yet still you passed away. Now my illness has received no medical care at all—together with all my distress, I suspect that I will soon die. Quite unexpectedly, however, heaven and earth show their compassion. Moved by my woeful situation, a good gentleman Cheng from the Sericulture Office . . . graciously sends me a monthly stipend so I can maintain my chastity.[67] How should I ever repay such kindness? I hereby burn my letter to have this matter reach you in the underworld, so that you would feel grateful in your heart.
>
> . . . The few words of this letter are nonetheless made of an enormous amount of my blood and tears. If you indeed have a spirit, you may give out a sigh [for my situation]. Alas! This is all I have to say, and with deep respect I am burning my letter for it to reach you.[68]

The fact that Dong burned her letter in the hope of having it reach her deceased husband can be attributed to the popular practice of burning sacrificial essays (*jiwen*, otherwise translated as "essays written to mourn or console the deceased") in front of the grave. As early as the Han dynasty, funerary rituals included reading such essays aloud in order to speak directly to the deceased and burning the essays for them to reach the deceased, both indicating ritual as a means of communicating with the underworld.[69] Although by far I have found no other instances of letters to the deceased by women of Dong's time, copies of sacrificial essays were customarily preserved in an author's personal collection.[70] So was a copy of Dong's letter. Appended to her mourning poems, the letter was part of the funerary and mourning rituals preserved in printed texts.

The frustration, bitterness, and despair that surge forth from Dong's words of "blood and tears" were apparent to the authors of her eulogies, who used them to illustrate her adherence to chastity despite all ordeals (*kujie*)—the logic of which lay in that, the more desperate Dong's situation was and the more she suffered, the more determination and courage she demonstrated in sticking to the death-bed wish of her husband and consequently the higher recognition she deserved.[71]

It is with this language of suffering that Dong appeals to her reader. Her "blood and tears" paint a poignant picture of the phys-ical and mental suffering she endured. The "blood" in particular changes meaning from the metaphorical (i.e., a trope for one's grief) to the literal in that Dong did spit blood in her distress and illness. What she refers to as the blood from her heart therefore also takes on this association with concrete suffering rather than merely serv-ing as a stock expression of one's investment in one's writing.[72] At the same time, this language of suffering also serves to highlight Dong's moral principles, so that its subversive element of anger or bitterness is safely contained within a larger picture of her adherence to chas-tity despite all ordeals. Taking the chance of addressing Zheng's wor-ries, for example, Dong foregrounds her adherence to the "rites of the inner quarters" and to the "principles of chastity and righteousness" and asserts her determination to remain a chaste widow. And so she does, despite the impossibility of doing so and without considering any other option except perhaps that of death. In the larger context of her collection, suffering bears testimony to a "will of steel," as shown in a poem that follows shortly after: "Loneliness molds my intent of ice and frost; / Suffering forges my will of steel and stone."[73]

This language of suffering was what most appealed to the local literati who inscribed Dong's collection and what induced them to urge that a court reward be conferred on her and to propose that her life be recorded in *Biographies of Martyred Women* (Lienü zhuan).[74] The early Qing state in general conferred rewards on widows who had remained chaste since before the age of thirty to the age of fifty. By the Daoguang reign the criteria had been significantly loos-ened, to the effect that an unprecedented number of chaste wid-ows (93,668; 3,122 per year) were officially rewarded. The review process had also been simplified since the Yongzheng reign for the purpose of preventing corruption. Instead of relying on local administrations for nominations, the court required county magistrates to make public announcements and seek nominations from neighbors of the widows and lineage heads. Nominations went directly to the provincial level once they were approved by county magistrates instead of going through multiple levels of review among the local administrations.[75]

These changes made it necessary for Dong to launch a campaign for herself: by earning approval from local charity leaders and luminaries through her words of "blood and tears" she enhanced her chance of being nominated for the court reward through these connections. (She had no kinship ties to back her up, it appears; the only time she mentions such ties concerns the insults that were driving her to suicide.) Moreover, since court rewards were *not* conferred posthumously,[76] Dong could not leave it to someone else to make the case for her after she died. The publication of her poetry collection was thus her best chance of making her case and, by extension, of obtaining official recognition when she met the time requirement and leaving a name "for thousands of years to come."

The last poem of Dong's collection seems to have served as another petition for aid. In 1857, the year following her speech at the shelter for chaste widows, Dong took her collection to Liu Shu and asked for his preface. This time she was not asking directly for financial aid, yet her seeking a preface from her patron would have expressed her wish to have her collection printed. Liu gladly agreed to her request, bearing in mind the potential readers of the collection, and he urged them to look up to Dong's moral strength instead of simply admiring her poetic talent.[77] In the same year this collection came out in print.[78] It was very probably Liu who again arranged that funds be assigned for Dong's needs.

A copy of Dong's poetry collection held by the National Library of China indicates that she managed to have her collection printed again sometime after 1884, when she was in her sixties. A preface attached to this later copy reveals what she experienced after 1857. She lived as a widow for some thirty years before her only adopted son died. Having hardly anything to support herself, she moved into a Buddhist nunnery. In 1884 she took her volume of poetry to visit a Zhixuan, a local luminary or charity leader like Liu Shu. After reading her poetry, Zhixuan felt deeply for the hardships she went through and admired her unswerving adherence to moral values, and so organized a donation for her (see Figure 1.02).[79]

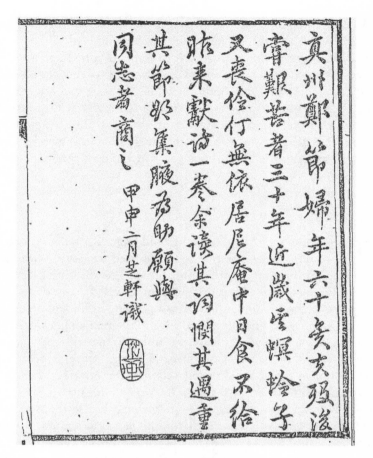

Figure 1.02 Preface by Zhixuan to Dong Baohong's *Poetry Collection from the Drinking-Fragrance Pavilion* (ca. 1884). Reprinted by permission from the National Library of China.

Despite her self-promotion, Dong's name does not appear among the chaste widows of Yangzhou who received court rewards. The majority of women listed in the "Chaste Widows and Filial Women" section of the Yangzhou local gazetteer published in 1874 were those who killed themselves or were killed by the rebels during the Taiping occupation, not chaste widows like Dong.[80] State policies had unfortunately shifted again by the time Dong met the time requirement for court reward, in part due to the phenomenal increase of female martyrs during the war, who needed to be honored.[81] But words, as

Dong had hoped, did save her from oblivion. If her words of "blood and tears" did not realize her ambition of being officially remembered, like those in the *Spring and Autumn Annals*, they nevertheless documented the efforts she made toward this end and allowed her to be read and known both during her lifetime and for years to come. These words also twice provided her with an effective survival strategy when she was threatened by starvation. Unlike the countless women who died in this area during the Taiping occupation, Dong survived not only the tumultuous years of the civil war but several decades after.

CONCLUSION

The cases of Liu Yin, Xie Xiangtang, and Dong Baohong show how the ideal of female exemplarity could be used to assert a woman's importance in history and to break the silence shrouding her life. Their accounts bring to light tension in otherwise idealized affection for their husbands, competing claims on their fulfillment of duties, the impossibility of surviving hardships while realizing a husband's deathbed wish, and, in one case, an unhappy marriage and bankruptcy brought by a profligate husband. Their writings delineated their dilemmas and allowed them to claim recognition for their critical contribution to their husbands' families and lineages.

Such writing was a strategy for establishing themselves as the real pillars of the family system, including its economic realm. Implicit in the self-promotion of these three women was the claim that only through their efforts were their families able to survive, continue the heir line, and recover former prosperity. To the extent that their self-promotion problematized the authority of their husbands, these women called into question the patriarchal values of the family system that were integral to their very existence as moral exemplars.

CHAPTER 2

Visualizing Exemplarity

*Women's Portraits and Paintings
for Self-Representation*

Portraiture is generally understood as a form of painting that captures
the visual likeness of an identifiable person in both Chinese and Western artistic traditions.[1] Early portraits from the Han period stood
in close relation to the literary genre of biography that took hold at
around the same time. Both can be characterized as the recording
of exemplary lives deeply embedded within state ideologies.[2] Despite
their tendency toward idealized types, however, famous examples of
the Han portraits set crucial precedents to the more individualized
portraits of the later ages. They are especially pertinent to a discussion of women's visual representations in two aspects.

First, archetypical images of exemplary women are found on a
set of painted screens that Liu Xiang, the author of *Biographies of
Exemplary Women*, commissioned in order to portray the women in
his hagiographies.[3] Reproduced or re-created portraits of these exemplary women circulated widely as moral guides for women during
the late imperial period, especially with the impetus provided by a
booming print industry. The commodification of these images further
led to their assimilation into traditions of entertainment and connois-
seurship.[4] Because of their popular appeal, these images inspired a
significant number of women's portraits that based their visual representations on the glorification of female virtue. Elite families commissioned and circulated portraits of their virtuous women, and the
attention obtained through the circulation of the portraits helped
elevate these families' social standing. The Qing woman painter
Chen Shu's (1660–1736) portrait, *Picture [of Chen Shu] Spinning at*

Night and Teaching the Classics [to Her Son] (Yefang shoujing tu),
is a widely cited example. The portrait was commissioned by Chen
Shu's son, Qian Chenqun (1686–1774), and was given by Qian as a
gift to the Qianlong emperor (r. 1735–95). The imperial attention it
obtained greatly enhanced the Qian family's reputation. Also because
of such imperial attention, Chen's paintings outnumbered those by
other women painters in the imperial collection of art.[5] Moreover, as
reading material for women, the popular images of exemplary women
fed the imagination of a female audience.[6] It will become clear in the
following discussion that these images provided the basis for women's
glorification of *themselves* as moral exemplars.

   This leads to the second aspect of the Han portraits as precedents
for later ages, namely, the use of portraits to gain publicity for exemplary lives. Examples include portraits of the founding generals and
ministers of the Han dynasty, which covered the walls of palaces and
memorial halls for these glorious lives to be commemorated and emulated.[7] While this practice of honoring meritorious generals and officials continued into the Qing period,[8] the actual means used to gain
publicity varied, and individuals from the broader strata of elite society resorted to the circulation of their portraits to get social exposure.
The elites commissioned large quantities of portraits of themselves
and their family members and elicited inscriptions from elite society.
Through this means a multitude of the subjects' admirable qualities
as defined either by moral values or the cultural sentiments of the
time reached an elite audience. By the Qing period it had become
commonplace for a male scholar or literatus to commission his portraits and encode his visual representations with cultural and social
messages.[9] Such popular use of commissioned portraits for publicity
further inspired women to address an elite audience through the circulation of their images.

PORTRAITS, SELF-PORTRAITS, AND AUTOBIOGRAPHICAL PAINTINGS

Strictly speaking, the self-portrait is a form of artistic *self-representation*, and the portrait is a broader form of artistic *representation*.[10]
This distinction nonetheless collapses in cases where commissioned
portraits shared with self-portraits the elements of *self-representation*
in the sense that the subjects dictated the terms by which they would
like to be portrayed and thus encoded their images with cultural or

social meanings they wished to convey. The making of these portraits involved dynamic negotiations between the subject and the painter and called into play, from the outset, the expectations and responses of an intended audience.[11] Together with the self-portraits of artists, these portraits belonged to an informal system, differentiated from the formal systems of ancestral, imperial, and religious portraits. They formed new trends of artistic self-representation during the three centuries starting in the late Ming period, indicating a heightened sense of the self among the artists and the literati, as well as a new cultural individualism at large.[12]

Autobiographical paintings are paintings that may not be labeled as portraits or self-portraits in the strict sense—given that they lack the visual likeness defining portraiture—and yet they demonstrate autobiographical tendencies and should be examined as artistic self-representation.[13] The Qing painter Zhang Bao (1763–ca.1833), for example, executed a hundred paintings to depict his lifetime travels and had these paintings printed as a series of collections titled *Drawings of Myself Floating in a Raft* (Fancha tu). Inspired by Zhang, the Qing official Wanyan Linqing (1792–1846) commissioned 240 paintings and used them as illustrations for his chronological autobiography, *Drawings of Fleeting Traces and Karma* (Hongxue yinyuan tuji). Human figures appear only in minimal sizes in the great majority of these paintings. It is the life experiences of the subjects—often represented by the places they visited or by family and social relations—that fill the spaces of the paintings. Many of these paintings hence have the visual effect of landscapes or, at the most, group portraits rather than portraits of an individual. (See Figs. 2.01 and 2.02 for the differences between autobiographical paintings and portraits.) To avoid confusion I use the term *portrait* or *self-portrait* when the painting demonstrates the visual likeness of an individual and the term *autobiographical painting* to refer to paintings such as those included in Zhang's and Linqing's collections.

I use this distinction with caution, however, because it does not capture the complexities of a range of related terms used in Chinese art—particularly the erosion of the boundaries between what was referred to as a "picture" or "painting" (*tu*) and what was specifically termed a "portrait" (*xiang*). A great majority of the portraits commissioned by the male literati were given the title of *tu* instead of *xiang*, which was used for more formal occasions.[14] Moreover, a portrait could alternatively assume the titles *xiaoxiang* (small portrait), *ying/*

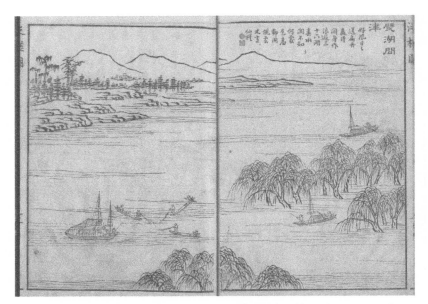

Figure 2.01a *Asking for Directions in Lake Pi*, by the male painter Zhang Bao. Source: Zhang, *Fancha tu*, painting no. 8, 11b–12a.

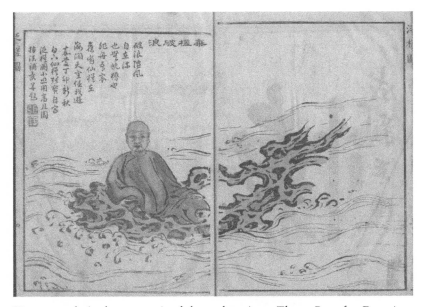

Figure 2.01b Author portrait of the male painter Zhang Bao, for *Drawings of Myself Floating in a Raft*. Source: Zhang, *Fancha tu*, 3b–4a. Reprinted by permission from the National Library of China.

Figure 2.02a *Composing a Poem in Honor of My Grand-mother*, by the male official Wanyan Linqing. Source: Wan-yan, *Hongxue yinyuan tuji*, vol. 1, painting no. 2.

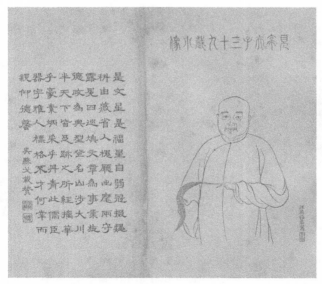

Figure 2.02b Author portrait of the male official Wanyan Linqing, for *Drawings of Fleeting Memories and Karma*. Source: Wanyan, *Hongxue yinyuan tuji*, vol. 1. Reprinted by permission from the National Library of China.

xiaoying (shadow or small shadow), *zhao/xiaozhao* (image or small image), *xieying* (painted shadow), *xiezhao* (painted image), *xiezhen* (painted image of the real person), or *huazhao* (painted image). Like *tu*, these terms were used for less formal occasions. A self-portrait, by extension, sometimes included in its title "painted by oneself" (*zixie* or *zihui*, e.g., *zixie xiaoying*, a portrait painted by oneself). This was nonetheless not always the case, since a self-portrait could also be designated a *tu*; it is often in the texts attached to the painting that we can learn the precise nature of the painted image.

WOMEN'S PORTRAITS AND PAINTINGS FOR SELF-REPRESENTATION

While formal ancestral and imperial portraits of both genders continued to be produced throughout the ages, portraits or self-portraits as a visual means of self-representation during the late imperial period were largely dominated by men. Women's informal portraits were no more than sparsely documented artistic endeavors.[15] The large quantities of "pictures/paintings of having leisurely enjoyment" (*xingle tu*) were typical of the (male) literati culture.[16] Studies of the print culture during the late imperial period rarely posit that women experimented with autobiographical paintings such as those included in Zhang's and Wanyan's collections.[17] Furthermore, despite a number of recent scholarly attempts to restore the active presence of women painters to the artistic world of late imperial China, few have taken note of women's portraits or paintings used for autobiographical purposes.[18]

A recent study by Mao Wenfang redresses this gender asymmetry by calling attention to the rich literary and painting traditions surrounding women's visual images during the Ming and Qing periods. The major cases of the study—the portraits of Liu Rushi (1618–64), Zhang Yiniang (ca. late seventeenth century), and Gu Taiqing (1799–1877)—highlight women's visual images as cultural imaginaries across great expanses of time and the various social purposes they served in elite societies.[19] Mao's exploration of valuable visual and textual sources notwithstanding, her study fails to search across the rich reservoir of women's writings from the late imperial period to map out broader trends of women's engagement with the portraiture genre. Lumping together figure paintings (or imagined "portraits") of romantic heroines and portraits of "real" women, moreover, she says much more about the social and cultural uses of women's visual representations than the autobiographical sensibilities imbricated in these visual images.

By contrast, women artists in the West—including those active during the timeframe of this book (i.e., eighteenth to nineteenth century)—exploited portraiture to expand their horizons as artists. Their self-portraits have been examined for their autobiographical sensibilities, their negotiations with their male-dominated profession, and their struggles to reconcile cultural ideals of femininity with what it meant to be a woman artist in their time.[20] This approach has received little attention in studies of women in premodern China.

Surviving samples of women's portraits from late imperial China provide a sense of the massive corpus of textual sources on women's artistic self-representation. Figure 2.03 is a portrait of the woman painter Cao Zhenxiu (1762–?), the daughter of the painter Cao Rui (ca. eighteenth century) and wife of the calligrapher Wang Qisun (1755–1817). Cao Zhenxiu was known to excel in paintings of plum blossoms as well as in calligraphy. The portrait bears a preface by Wang Qisun, which relates the episode of its production. Cao Zhenxiu wanted to have a portrait done for herself. Several times she tried unsuccessfully to commission it from Zhou Li (ca. eighteenth century), a renowned male portrait painter. Finally one day Wang Qisun invited Zhou Li to come to their house for a drink, and Cao Zhenxiu found the chance during the banquet to again make her request, to which Zhou gladly complied this time. He completed her visual image in less than half a day, and his ability to capture her precise appearance and character won her approval. Later Cao added the setting for the portrait: the architecture, the zither, the rocks, the bamboo, the crane, and the attendant who picks herbs by the rock. The portrait was therefore a work of collaboration between the subject and the painter. Clearly Cao had a precise idea of how she wished to be seen, and she overcame the odds in finding precisely the painter whom she regarded as capable of conveying her desired self-image.

Cao places herself in the center of the pictorial space and faces the viewer almost frontally. The way she holds a sprig in her right hand reminds us of the familiar portrayal of the Bodhisattva Guanyin in paintings of this time. The attendant hovering on the lower left corner (balanced by a crane on the right) enhances this effect in that both her position and her small size suggest a Buddhist supplicant. The bamboo further echoes paintings of the Bodhisattva Guanyin sitting in the bamboo forest.[21] Aside from this striking aspect of Cao's

Figure 2.03. *Portrait of Cao Zhenxiu*, by Zhou
Li and Cao Zhenxiu. Reprinted by permission
from the Palace Museum of Beijing.

self-representation, her additions to the setting are loaded with cultural meanings, which indicate her refined tastes and her membership
in an elite culture. The zither, the herbs, and the crane—among other
things—are standard allusions to the literatus hermit. The herbs may
also hint at Daoism or suggest Cao's medical knowledge.

While the precise messages encoded in Cao's portrait require a
more detailed analysis, my interest lies in how this sample can be
viewed in the context of her life as a woman painter and her interest
in the portraiture genre rather than as a random sample from a small

number of women's portraits that happened to survive. In fact, even a cursory look at the textual records about her life that Cao left makes it possible to situate her portrait in a whole range of women's artistic activities and social events related to the creation of their visual images. Cao's personal collection, *Drafts from the Pavilion of Composing Rhymed Verses* (Xieyunxuan xiaogao), keeps track of her painting career and socializing activities in the form of the numerous inscriptions she authored for paintings. Among these inscriptions thirteen were dedicated to women's portraits or autobiographical paintings (including eight poetic inscriptions, two prose inscriptions, and three eulogies) and seven to men's. These records alone indicate a livelier picture of women's engagement with the portraiture genre than the few extant samples might suggest. A Lady Shi, for example, executed a self-portrait to record her excursion to a mountain of plum trees. Two years after the completion of Shi's self-portrait, her husband came by and asked for Cao's inscriptions.[22] Two other examples (one poem and one short essay by Cao) record a self-portrait by the famous Ming woman painter Wen Shu (1595–1634). The portrait was still circulating during the Qing period and was reproduced by the painter Pan Gongshou (1741–94). In time this reproduction came into the possession of an official named Zhu, who then asked Cao for inscriptions. Cao's inscriptions in this case serve to delineate the trajectories by which an earlier woman painter's self-portrait circulated, survived in copies, and posthumously inspired painters' and connoisseurs' interest.[23]

The examples of Qu Bingyun (1767–1810) and Xi Peilan (1760– ca. 1829), the two women poets and painters who were among Yuan Mei's female disciples and who were close friends, reveal even more about these cultural trends in that they highlight the importance of the portraiture genre as a means of female bonding. Figures 2.04 and 2.05a are two extant portraits of Qu Bingyun painted by Xi Peilan. Figure 2.04, *Picture [of Qu Bingyun] Washing Her Hands with Dew Gathered from Roses* (Qiangweilu guanshou tu), features Qu standing in front of an exquisitely made wooden stand and washing her hands in a basin. The portrait demonstrates a relatively high degree of verisimilitude, as well as an intimate life scene from the inner quarters that is missing in the more formal portraits of women. It indicates that women painters of this time started to experiment with the practice of painting from life by drawing portraits of their female friends.[24]

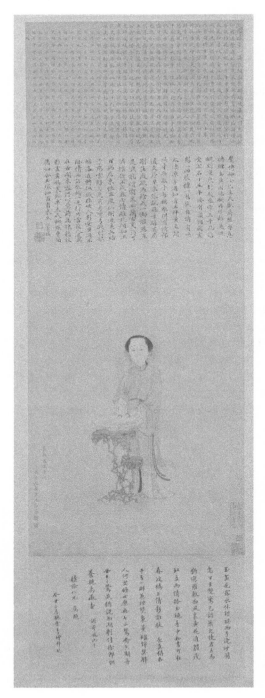

Figure 2.04. *Picture [of Qu Bingyun] Washing Her Hands with Dew Gathered from Roses*, by Xi Peilan. Reprinted by permission from the Palace Museum of Beijing.

Figure 2.05a, *Portrait of Lady Wanxian [Qu Bingyun]* (Wanxian furen xiaoxiang), is a half-length portrait in wood-block print found in the front matter of Qu's personal collection, *Collection from the Tower of Hidden Jade* (Yunyulou ji). The portrait bears a title inscribed by Xi Peilan and is followed by a eulogy that Qu composed for herself.[25] Qu's facial expression, hairstyle, and attire in this portrait resemble those in Figure 2.04, suggesting that the two portraits may have been based on the same draft. However, in this instance Qu can be said to have joined Xi in constructing her visual image by composing a eulogy for herself, in which she defines the major feature of her portrait as "melancholy" and attributes such melancholy to the literary canon *Sorrows in Parting* (Lisao) by tracing her ancestral lineage to the great poet Qu Yuan (340?–278? BCE; see Figure 2.05b).

These two portraits of Qu arose out of a larger picture of the two women painters' intense interest in the portraiture genre and their participation in the production of each other's visual images. Evidence can be found in a number of inscriptions from both women's personal collections:

From Qu Bingyun:
"[Inscription for] *Picture of [Myself] Looking into the Mirror*" (Duijing tu)
"[Inscription for] *Portrait of Daohua [Xi Peilan] in Receding Chill*" (Daohua xiaohan xiaoying)
"To the melody of Jinchandao, [Inscription for] *Portrait of Daohua Holding a Flower* (Jinchandao, Daohua nianhua xiaoying)[26]

From Xi Peilan:
"Inscription for My Portrait, Featuring Me Standing with My Back toward the Flowers" (Ziti *Beihua xiaoying*)
"Written in Gratitude to Qu Wanxian's Inscription on My Portrait, Using Her Original Rhymes" (Xie Qu Wanxian huiti xiaoying jici yuanyun)
"Inscription for *Picture of Qu Wanxian Holding a Plum Blossom*" (Ti *Qu Wanxian Nianmei tu*)[27]

In addition, Qu's personal collection incorporates around twenty-seven titles of inscriptions for women's portraits or autobiographical paintings, while Xi's personal collection incorporates around thirty of these titles. This body of texts offers valuable insight into the hitherto little known world of women, in which their portraits were frequently executed for a variety of occasions and in which women painters like Qu and Xi constantly received requests to paint and to

Figure 2.05a.   *Portrait of Lady Wanxian*, by Xi Peilan.
Source: Qu, *Yunyulou ji*, "author portrait and eulogy."

inscribe portraits for friends, family relatives, and their various social connections. Textual records like these highlight the importance of women's personal collections as a useful source for the excavation of evidence of women's portraits and autobiographical paintings.[28] A preliminary search in the digital library of Ming-Qing Women's Writings yields the data presented in Table 2.01.

No doubt we need to delve into the texts themselves in order to find out exactly which of these data are related to women's portraits. Nevertheless, even a preliminary search can provide a sense of women's active engagement with the cultural trends related to portraiture. Given that these data are generated by only ninety women's personal collections out of the over nine hundred titles included in Hu Wen-kai's source book, we can expect to locate even more of these records as more personal collections become accessible.

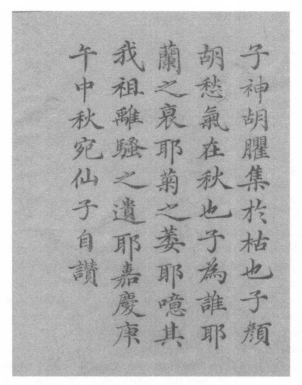

Figure 2.05b. "Eulogy for My Portrait," by Qu
Bingyun. Source: Qu, *Yunyulou ji*, "author por-
trait and eulogy." Reprinted by permission from the
National Library of China.

IMAGES AND TEXTS IN "SEMIOTIC CONTINUUMS"

Textual inscriptions are an indicator of the extent of women's interest
in portraiture and, whether inscribed on the painting itself or for the
painting beyond its material boundary, play a crucial role in shaping
the meanings of the images and in defining the circumstances of their
production and circulation. This is true especially because China has
a long artistic tradition of valuing texts associated with painting.[29]
Together the image and text form a semiotic continuum, echoing and
reinforcing each other and sometimes creating a dynamic interplay
that enriches and complicates the messages of the painting.[30]

Picture of [Mother and Son] Taking a Boat Back Home (Guizhou
anshi tu), is a painting in the personal collection of the woman poet

TABLE 2.01   Women's inscriptions for paintings potentially related to portraits

Key words	Number of entries
Portraits (*xiang, xiaozhao, xiaoying, xiezhao, xiezhen, huazhao*)	220
Paintings (*tu*)	1409
Inscriptions or paintings by oneself (*ziti, zixie, zihui*)	216
Self-/eulogies (*xiangzan, zizan*)	10

Source: http://digital.library.mcgill.ca/mingqing/english. Accessed June, 2014.

Gan Lirou (1743–1819).[31] Gan's son, Xu Xintian (ca. 1774–1853), resigned his position as county magistrate of Nanling, Anhui, in 1818, and together with his mother took a boat back to their home in Fengxin, Jiangxi. Gan composed a long poem on the boat to express her feelings about the journey.[32] After reading the poem Xu commissioned a painting to portray the journey. He then included the painting and the poem in an album (*tuce*), which he circulated among his social connections.[33] Inscriptions by twenty-nine authors were eventually incorporated into Gan's personal collection.

The painting portrays the vast expanse of a river by using large blank spaces dotted with tiny boats and sails. The lack of waves suggests calm weather and smooth-flowing water. A piece of land dense with trees and houses (indicating a village) covers the upper left side of the painting, balanced by a few treetops and marshes on the lower right side. A human figure walks from the boat to the stairs leading up to the houses. A few other human figures appear on a boat near the lower left corner. All human figures appear in minimal proportions, reminding us of those in Zhang Bao's *Asking for Directions in Lake Pi* (Figure 2.01a). Yet while Zhang's painting creates the effect of a lively discussion where the four boats meet, the painting in Gan's collection puts the boats at a distance from one another. Its predominant effect is a peaceful journey on calm and smooth water through expanses of natural scenery. The painting is headed by a title and followed by an inscription, which highlights Xu's filial feelings, the nice weather, the swiftness of the boat, and the mother and son who are like immortals in sceneries of unearthly beauty.

As the inspiration to Xu's commissioning of the painting, Gan's long poem provides crucial clues to the messages of the painting. In the poem Gan first retraces Xu's childhood, particularly his loss of his father, and his filial piety for his father as well as his ancestors. She then elaborates on her motherly feelings and her worry that Xu has shouldered too many responsibilities as county magistrate. During his ten years in office Xu devoted himself to protecting his people, reduced crimes, ensured the continuation of taxation, and never made improper gains from his position. Having thus glorified Xu's achievements and integrity as an official, Gan abruptly turns to the fact that he decided to resign, allegedly due to the eye problem she was suffering. She expresses her delight that Xu was able to retreat from "political storms" and urges him to return to a simple life in the countryside. She ends her poem by stating that, although Xu has not yet repaid the kindness of the court, he will leave his fate to the heavens. This lengthy poem is fraught with political tensions and indicates Gan's intention to glorify or vindicate her son's reputation as an official. Whatever truth lay behind Xu's resignation, Gan's poem reveals the inner peace of the subjects as opposed to the "political storms" from which Xu decided to retreat.

The painting and the poem fit into Gan's personal collection as a form of auto/biographical material at a specific stage of her life and her relation to her son. The inscriptions following the poem carry on a lively conversation among elite society, confirming and further expanding some of the encoded messages of the painting—particularly Gan as an exemplary mother (chaste widow) who raised her son to be a virtuous official, and Xu's political achievements and moral integrity. The semiotic continuum composed of images and texts are a site of active social assertion and involve the viewers' participation in constructing the image through textual responses.[34]

More straightforward examples of the semiotic continuums of paintings can be found in a chronological autobiography by Zeng Jifen (1852–1942), a daughter of the distinguished Qing official and general Zeng Guofan (1811–72). Zeng Jifen incorporated a sequence of sixteen paintings into her autobiography for the explicit purpose of modeling the "ancients' practice of incorporating pictures and texts concurrently [guren tushu bingxing zhiyi]."[35] The paintings cast her in her family relations: as a daughter who received "family instructions" (jiaxun) from her father and learned domestic skills from her mother; as a wife and mother who performed a variety of domestic duties and educated her children; and, when she achieved the matriarchal status accorded by old age, as the head in family meetings (jiating jihui).[36] These paintings provide a clue to Zeng's life course, which she recorded in the ensuing texts as entries of major events and incidents in chronological order. The traditional female virtues they illustrate are also cited by Zeng in an appended essay to address the challenges confronting China in a new age.[37]

Women's use of traditional female virtues to address a national crisis is the focus of chapter 4. I note here that the ancients Zeng refers to are in fact none other than her contemporaries or earlier generations who frequently combined images and texts for self-representation. Tracing the texts in this sense offers a useful means of *reconstructing* both the contents and contexts of paintings that failed to overcome the vagaries of time. This approach is especially pertinent to my present discussion because it helps circumvent the paucity of surviving samples of women's portraits and autobiographical paintings.

CHEN YUNLIAN (CA. NINETEENTH CENTURY): A LIFE IN EIGHT PAINTINGS

Chen Yunlian was from the county of Jiangyin, Jiangsu. She was active as a poet and painter around the Daoguang (1821–50) and Xianfeng (1851–61) reigns. She was married to Zuo Chen (ca. nineteenth century), who hailed from the illustrious Zuo lineage of Yanghu and who served in the salt administration in Tianjin. The couple had a daughter, Zuo Baiyu (1820–56), who was also known as a poet and painter and was recorded as a filial daughter and daughter-in-law who earned a court reward for cutting flesh from her own body to serve as medicine for her ill parents and in-laws.[38]

Selections of Chen Yunlian's poetic works entered prominent Qing dynasty anthologies of poetry, such as *Remarks on Poetry of Notable Women* (Mingyuan shihua), *The Dynasty's Records of Song Lyrics from Changzhou* (Guochao Changzhou cilu), *Selections of Song Lyrics by Gentry Women* (Guixiu cichao), and *Another Sequel to the Correct Beginnings for Gentry Women* (Guixiu zhengshi zaixu ji).[39] Her personal collection of poetry, *Poetry Drafts from the Pavilion of True Fragrance* (Xinfangge shicao), appeared in print in two editions in 1851 and 1859.

Although no records of Chen can be located in traditional treatises of Chinese painting, there is little doubt about her reputation as an eminent woman painter. The entry about her in *Remarks on Poetry of Notable Women* emphasizes her versatile skills: "The collection of Muqing [courtesy name of Chen Yunlian] abounds in fine pieces of work. . . . Muqing's poetry, calligraphy, and painting are all exceptionally fine, and her learning of history is profound."[40] The entry in *Selections of Song Lyrics by Gentry Women* quotes her brother Chen Zuwang, who said that she made a living by selling her paintings since her husband could barely provide for them, and that, as a professional painter, she earned acclaim from "dukes and ministers far and near."[41] The woman poet Pan Suxin (ca. nineteenth century), moreover, noted the connection between Chen's literary and painting activities, namely, that she "always had the habit of composing a new poem whenever she completed a fine painting."[42] It is unsurprising, then, that Chen's personal collection of poetry keeps meticulous records of her painting career. It reveals that she received an overwhelming number of commissions, which caused her physical exhaustion.[43] It also includes a fact that she was especially proud of. In 1848 the imperial painting academy dispatched messengers to visit her for the purpose of collecting samples of her paintings for the court painters to model—clearly her fame as a painter had by this time spread throughout Beijing and Tianjin.[44]

A portion of Chen's poetic works yield rich information about her personal vicissitudes as a refugee during the First Opium War (1840–42) and the Taiping Rebellion. Chen had no hesitation in voicing her frustration over the restrictions imposed on women, especially during this time of great chaos.[45] I have written elsewhere on Chen's personal collection of poetry—particularly her works on the theme of illness—as an extensive autobiography marked by a phenomenal degree of self-consciousness as well as practical motives.[46] Chen is also crucial to my present discussion because the eight prose inscriptions preserved in her collection provide direct evidence that she painted a sequence of autobiographical paintings. These prose inscriptions are attached to the end of the 1859 edition of her collection and are titled "My Own Inscriptions for the Eight Pictures Attached to *Poetry Drafts from the Pavilion of True Fragrance*" (Fuke Xinfangge ziti batu). Each of the inscriptions is headed by a four-character title of the corresponding picture in the following sequence:

琴瑟合鳴	Harmonious Concert of Zither and Lute
蕉下評詩	Judging Poetry under the Banana Tree
月下聯句	Linking Verses under the Moon
風雪籲天	Praying to Heaven in Wind and Snow
寫韻謀生	Writing Rhymes to Earn a Living
刲股療病	Treating Illness by Slicing Flesh from My Arm
目不交睫	Nursing without Blinking My Eyes
秋窗風雨	Winds and Rains at the Autumnal Window

Figure 2.06. Chen Yunlian, "My Own Inscriptions for the Eight Pictures Attached to *Poetry Drafts from the Pavilion of True Fragrance*," first page, in *Xinfangge shicao*, 5.7a. Reprinted by permission from the National Library of China.

There is textual evidence that Chen executed an autobiographical painting at an earlier time. A poem from the first *juan* of her collection is titled "My Own Inscription for *Picture of Brushes and Ink in Harmonious Singing*, Composed as Linked Verses with My Husband" (Ziti *Hanmo heming tu* xiewai lianju).[47] In the linked verses the couple stage themselves as an ideal "companionate couple" who find great delight in their joint composition of poetry. They highlight their refined tastes and their profound affection for each other (as suggested by the very title of the picture). The last line of the poem expresses Chen's wish that their affections will last "for a hundred years."[48]

Chen's earlier painting might have fit seamlessly into the beginning of her sequence of autobiographical paintings. The phrase "in harmonious singing/concert" (*heming*), for example, appears simultaneously in the title of this earlier painting and in that of the first painting in the sequence. Also, in her inscription for the third painting in the sequence, Chen directly refers to this earlier painting and recaptures

the circumstances of its execution. However, the sequence of paintings is marked by a radically different tone:

HARMONIOUS CONCERT OF ZITHER AND LUTE

I married into the Zuo family at the age of twenty-one. . . . At the
time, my husband and I were the kind of couple who truly deserved
to be compared to the zither and lute in harmonious concert. To com-
pare the present with the past, aren't they as different as heaven and
earth? This is what the first picture is about.[49]

Chen's sequence of inscriptions therefore starts with an ominous message that threatens to subvert the message of her earlier painting. In
her second inscription she recalls her "bliss" (*zhile*) at sharing brush
and ink with her husband as only a vague memory from a past life.[50]
In her third inscription the very thought of the *Picture of Brushes
and Ink in Harmonious Singing* gives rise to an impulse to burn her
brushes and abandon her inkstone.[51] In short, Chen refers to her idealized marriage only from the standpoint of a much later time, when
her relationship with her husband seems to have irrevocably changed.

Starting with her fourth inscription Chen is bent on creating an
"exemplary" profile for herself out of various facets of her devotion
to her husband. In the process she also guides the audience through
the tensions in her marriage, providing clues to what led to her radical
change of tone. The fourth inscription, "Praying to Heaven in Wind
and Snow," exposes Zuo Chen's "demonic obstacles [*mozhang*],"
namely, his obsession with sensual pleasures. Chen claims that she
prays to heaven every night while Zuo is on his journeys, despite the
wind and the snow, for the purpose of clearing such demonic obstacles for him.[52] The fifth inscription, "Writing Rhymes to Earn a Living," spotlights Chen as the financial pillar of her family. She states
with resentment that it falls on her alone to toil for a living, to the
extent that, "no matter in cold weather or hot," she is always engaged
in executing paintings and inscribing them. Only thanks to the money
she makes from her paintings, she emphasizes, does her family manage to survive. At the end of the inscription her anger bursts forth,
and she exclaims, "What an idiot I was then!"[53] Consequently, the
affectionate husband in her earlier painting turns out to be no more
than a profligate and a parasite on her.

Aside from exposing the less than ideal side of Chen's marriage,
the fifth inscription echoes the wealth of information in her poetry
collection regarding how she made her living. Chen favors the

metaphor "field of inkstone [*yantian*]"; for example, she relieves her husband's worry that their household has run out of food by assuring him that she has "rented the field of inkstone" (i.e., her paintings yield income).[54] She expresses her bitterness that she has to "till" this field in order to purchase grain even when her wrist has grown weak with her overwhelming workload.[55] She refutes the idea that an official post brings good income and states bluntly that it is always the "field of inkstone" that yields income.[56] And she condemns her husband's abandonment of her by reminding him that, when his money bag goes empty, she relies on the "field of inkstone" to pull them through financial straits.[57] Echoing her repeated contributions to the household economy is her enumeration of commissions that are sapping her energy and damaging her eyes and wrist.[58] Even a very quick look at the numerous poetic inscriptions incorporated in Chen's collection will therefore make it clear that these are by no means casual exchanges of courtesies between friends. Rather they bear witness to how Chen executed paintings by commission;[59] how she responded to a painting or a poem by someone's "request" (*zhu*) or "order" (*ming*);[60] and how she produced popular "decorative paintings," which probably went directly to painting shops.[61]

Reading the inscription within this larger context offers insights into a woman painter's active involvement in the commerce of art and her perception of her economic roles. What is crucial, moreover, is the fact that Chen fit her outright condemnation of her husband's failure—along with her own financial success and her pivotal role in the household economy—into a story glorifying herself as an exemplary wife. Her moral claim was a strategy of gaining leverage in what seemed to be a bitter fight following the bankruptcy of her formerly idealized marriage. This strategy most clearly characterizes her sixth and seventh inscriptions, which feature her devoted service to her husband when he is dangerously ill:

TREATING ILLNESS BY SLICING FLESH FROM MY ARM

During the spring of the year Renyin [1842], my husband and I fell dangerously ill simultaneously. Unable to find a cure [for my husband], the doctors did not see any hope of his recovery. I myself was so weak that I was all skin and bones. Yet my heart was broken when I saw [how ill he was]. So I told my maid to get me a pair of scissors in secret, and sliced flesh from my upper left arm to feed him as medicine. *This was how he managed to survive* [my emphasis]. This is what the sixth picture is about.[62]

NURSING WITHOUT BLINKING MY EYES

On the first day of the Seventh month of the year Bingwu [1846], my husband had a lesion at the base of his skull that penetrated toward one in his mouth. Also, he developed an ulcer on his back. In a few days, the pus erupted and the wound expanded to a foot in width. I stayed up all night without sleeping, sitting beside him, watching him, nursing his wound and driving away the flies for him—I kept up all this every day for half a year. In the Ninth Month, he had lesions in his mouth too. I knelt on my knees and lifted up my face to blow medicine into his mouth with a straw, and his pus, blood, mucus and saliva directly flowed into my mouth. It was not until the next spring that he recovered. So I painted this picture. If he sees it, maybe he would also be touched at heart—or not? This is what the seventh picture is about.[63]

A first-time reader of these texts may be struck by their candid tone, their graphic details, and their potentially subversive contents. These vivid depictions of what Chen suffered make it easy for readers to reconstruct the missing visual images. Furthermore, popular images of exemplary women can be easily located as Chen's source of inspiration. The Ming illustrated edition of *Biographies of Exemplary Women* includes three instances of women's self-mutilation for the purpose of saving either a dying husband or a dying mother-in-law.[64] Figure 2.07 features the "chaste and filial woman Fan" (*jiexiao* Fanshi) cutting flesh from her own body to serve as medicine for her ill husband.

The affinity between Chen's self-portrayal and popular images of exemplary women can also be seen in her indebtedness to the language of these popular tales:

THE CHASTE AND FILIAL WOMAN FAN

Shiqi [Fan's husband] fell ill . . . and Fan served him day and night without blinking her eyes. [This she did] for three months. [Shiqi's situation] turned worse. . . . [Fan] burned incense and prayed to heaven during mornings and evenings, hoping that [heaven] would take her life away instead of her master's. In secret she cut flesh from her arm to serve as medicine [for her husband], *and, as expected, [her husband] recovered* [my emphasis].[65]

THE WIFE OF HAN TAICHU

Woman Liu, the wife of Han Taichu, originated from the county of Xinle, Zhending [Hebei]. . . . After Liu's mother-in-law fell to the ground and hurt her waist, Liu stabbed her own arm and let the blood drop into the soup before she served it [to her mother-in-law].

Figure 2.07. *The Chaste and Filial Woman Fan.* Source: Liu, *Lienü zhuan,* reprinted from the Zhibuzuzhai Cangban, 15.26 a–b. Courtesy of the University of Hong Kong Library.

> *Thus [Liu's mother-in-law] recovered* [my emphasis]. . . . Two years later, Liu's mother-in-law had a stroke and was trapped in bed. It was summertime and steaming hot. For a day and a night Liu drove away the flies and mosquitoes without slacking her attention. When maggots appeared on the pillow and the bed mats, Liu bit them and they did not appear again. *Subsequently, Liu's mother-in-law recovered* [my emphasis].[66]

Widely circulating as a moral guide for women during the eighteenth and nineteenth centuries, this edition of *Biographies of Exemplary Women* fed the imagination of a contemporary female readership and led these women to "interpolate their experiences with the dramatic moments in other women's lives."[67] Chen's case is testimony to the influence that these popular moral tales had on a gentry woman. Yet while these tales never offered the women's side of the stories, in Chen's case we hear for the first time a woman telling in profuse detail what prompted her to mutilate her own body, how exactly she proceeded, how extremely hideous her experience of nursing her ill husband was, and what effects her unqualified sacrifices made on him. The message, in short, is that she has been through much suffering to save her husband's life and that it is to her that he owes his life—just as in the cases of Fan and Liu. (See my emphases in the quotations above for the alleged cause-and-effect relationship between the women's sacrifices and the recovery of their family members.)

Again, as in the fifth inscription, Chen's message has a significant twist. Her exemplary stories attest to the changed picture of her marital relationship and in this sense are integrated into her condemnation of her husband's lack of gratitude to her. It is based on this very practical use of female exemplarity that Chen is able to launch her vehement attack on her husband in her last inscription: Zuo started to indulge in debaucheries as soon as he was posted in Zhongzhou (Henan) in the year Xinhai (1851) and left her to a life of loneliness and suffering in their home in Tianjin.[68]

Aside from this dramatic story of how affections turned bitter, Chen discloses in her final note a variety of factors concerning the execution of her paintings, including her motivation, her intended audience, and the physical existence of the paintings and their preservation:

> The above eight pictures are about my life from my wedding day to the present. So many thoughts well up in me while I think of the past. This is why I had [the pictures] mounted and preserved in bamboo cases for later generations to see. By this means I can also keep a record of what I have experienced in life, and show that I am not without meritorious service to the Zuo lineage.[69]

Chen's case further prompts the question of genre. She paid meticulous attention to the organization of her personal collection and used these voluminous poetic works to tell her life story. By incorporating a new volume of poetry into the 1859 edition of her collection, she exposed her idealized marriage represented in the 1851 edition to be nothing more than a veneer, underneath which lay the story of affections turning bitter.[70] Why repeat the story by choosing another genre?

An obvious answer is that these eight autobiographical paintings and their inscriptions serve to capture the high points of an extensive life story. Instead of delving into a profusion of details, as Chen's poetry collection does, these high points provide a straightforward clue to the main plot of the story. They help the audience to avoid the gaps, pitfalls, or distractions that they might encounter in the process of reading through the poetry collection and to arrive safely and efficiently at the intended conclusion. In addition, Chen's choice of genre no doubt reflects the influence of the golden age of visual art. The combined use of images and texts lends vividness and force to the stories, the effect of which may not be achieved by a single genre.

Most important, Chen's choice of genre must be understood as an act of appropriating the moral weight originally carried by portraits (i.e., portraits as visual records of exemplary lives), as well as the genre's association with publicity (i.e., portraits as a means of publicizing exemplary lives for people to emulate). By portraying herself into an exemplary woman, she gained immense leverage over her husband who betrayed her affections and could potentially influence the judgment of an elite audience.

Unfortunately no evidence can be located for either the circulation of Chen's autobiographical paintings or elite society's reactions to these paintings. The silence on this vehement attack by a gentry woman against her husband may reveal precisely the subversive nature of the attack, despite its disguise of female exemplarity.

ZUO XIJIA (1831–1894): LEADING A BOAT THROUGH REBELS AND RAGING TORRENTS

Zuo Xijia hailed from the illustrious Zuo family of Yanghu. A biographical source reveals that Chen Yunlian was her affinal aunt (*shimu*).[71] She was known as a distinguished woman poet, painter, and calligrapher. Her voluminous personal collection, *Poetry Drafts from the House of Immortals Chanting in the Chilly Season* (Lengyinxianguan shigao) includes eight *juan* of poetry, one *juan* of song lyrics, one *juan* of prose, and an appendix of inscriptions. Selections of her poetic works entered the Qing dynasty anthologies of women's poetry and collections of poetry commentaries, including *Joint Prints of Song Lyrics by Gentry Women, from the Small Studio Made of Bamboo* (Xiaotanluan shi huike guixiu ci), *Poetry as Commentary on Poetry, Written in the Small Black Pavilion* (Xiaodaixuan lunshi shi), *Another Sequel to the Correct Beginnings for Gentry Women*, and *Remarks on Song Lyrics by Gentry Women* (Guixiu cihua). Zuo also had an entry in a collection of poetic works by prominent painters from the Qing period.[72]

Zuo was recorded as an exemplary woman by the local gazetteer of Huayang (Chengdu), Sichuan. Her exemplary life story can be retrieved from that source and from the numerous biographical accounts written in her honor.[73] She was a granddaughter of Zuo Fu (*jinshi* 1793), who served as governor of Hunan, and was a daughter of Zuo Ang (*juren* 1840), who served consecutively as subprefectural magistrate of Fengyang, Anhui, and assistant directorate in the Court of Judicial Review in the capital. Zuo Fu had wide literary renown and was connected with the leading poets and scholars of his time. Zuo Xijia had five brothers and seven sisters, among whom she was the sixth to be born. She lost her mother at the age of eight,[74] after which she stayed in her uncle's home for a short period before she joined her father in the capital. There she earned her reputation as a filial daughter due to her devoted service to her father and step-mother, Lady Yun. It was recorded that when Zuo Ang was danger-ously ill, Zuo Xijia pulled him from the verge of death by cutting flesh from her own body to serve as medicine for him. Soon afterward her two older sisters, Xihui and Xixuan, joined her in the capital. The three of them were lauded as the "filial daughters of the Zuo family." Xihui and Xixuan too were distinguished by their literary and artis-tic achievements.

In 1851 Zuo Xijia married Zeng Yong (1813–62), who was eigh-teen years older than she and served then in the Board of Revenue. Zeng was from a family of very limited means in the countryside of Chengdu. He had been married twice, and his former wives had passed away. Zuo treated his son, Guangxi, as her eldest son. She gave birth to three sons (Guangxu, Guangmin, and Guangwen) and six daughters. Two of her daughters died young.

After marrying, Zuo earned acclaim for her management of fam-ily finances since Zeng's earnings were barely enough to cover their living expenses. She personally performed all housework and con-stantly gave Zeng wise counsel. Most remarkably she was always able to set aside funds from their meager income to support her parents-in-law, who were living in the outskirts of Chengdu. When Zeng was appointed prefect of Ji'an, Jiangxi, Zuo went with him to his post, an area that suffered frequent attacks from the Taiping rebels. Zuo helped Zeng set up charities for the refugees, then pooled funds to help him establish a militia. With her help Zeng was able to defeat the rebels several times.

But the rebels soon retook the area. Zeng accepted the invitation of the General Zeng Guofan to help with military affairs in Anqing, Anhui. He died in the military camps there in 1862 due to illness caused by overwork.[75] Hearing the tragic news, Zuo tried twice to commit suicide but was rescued by her relatives. She then made up her mind to have Zeng properly buried in his native home and to serve her parents-in-law in his place. In 1863 she took her young children and Zeng's coffin on a long journey on the Yangzi River. She led the boat safely through the rebel ships that controlled large parts of the river and managed to survive the dangerous shoal. Numerous biographical sources and inscriptions point to the painting that she executed on the boat to record her experience at the shoal, *Picture [of Myself] Taking a Single Boat to Enter Sichuan* (Guzhou ruShu tu). Although this painting has not survived, a substantial corpus of inscriptions for the painting (by thirty-eight authors) is preserved in her personal collection. This body of texts stand as proof of the enthusiastic responses she inspired from elite society through her artistic self-representation. This painting and its circulation is the focus of my discussion of Zuo.

Finally, in early 1864, Zuo arrived in Zeng's native home. There she provided for her parents-in-law and raised her children, mainly by "putting up a price list to sell [her] paintings [xuan'ge yuhua]." Her renown as a painter and calligrapher spread throughout the local art market of Chengdu and eventually reached Japan and Korea. Her painting skills were compared to those of the Qing leading women painters Chen Shu and Yun Bing (ca. eighteenth–nineteenth century). Commissions poured in from "distinguished dukes and ministers," and it is even said that the extreme popularity of her artistic works caused the price of painting paper to soar.[76] In addition her sola flowers, that is, handmade flowers from the pith of certain plants, and other artworks became so popular in the local handicrafts market that those wanting to place orders filled the paths to her house. Her success as an artist seemed to significantly improve her financial situation: aside from covering the living expenses of her big family and paying off the fees incurred by the marriages of her children, her earnings from selling her paintings also enabled her to engage actively in charity works, which further enhanced her reputation in the local society of Chengdu.

Over the years Zuo spared no effort in supervising her sons' education. She moved her home twice just so that her sons would have better educational opportunities. She also hired outstanding scholars to be their instructors. Guangxu, her second son, was assigned to the post of country magistrate in Dingxiang, Shanxi, as a reward from the court in light of the contributions his father had made to the state.[77] Her other sons distinguished themselves in studies and established their careers in the government. Zuo also personally trained her daughters in a range of artistic and literary skills. As a result they grew up to enjoy wide renown as poets and artists. Her fifth daughter, Zeng Yan, was recorded by the local gazetteer of Huayang as a distinguished calligrapher.[78] Her second daughter, Zeng Yi (1852–1927), in time published voluminous poetic works and writings on medicine and women's learning.[79]

In the spring of 1881 Zuo joined her son Guangxu in Dingxiang, where she spent the rest of her life. In 1891 she collected her writings and had them printed.[80] She also organized Zeng's poetic works in chronological order and had them printed along with her own collection.[81] Guangxu had her two volumes of *Family Instructions* (Jiaxun), along with a family letter instructing him on political matters, printed around the same time.[82] He also made an application on Zuo's part for a court reward, which was approved.[83]

This sketch of Zuo's life provides general background to the multiple textual records shaping the meanings of her autobiographical painting, *Picture [of Myself] Taking a Single Boat to Enter Sichuan*.

The River Journey

A lengthy inscription by Zuo provides an immediate textual context for the painting. It can be further situated within *[Poetry] Chanted for Juanshi* (Juanshi yin), which Zuo used to describe her journey on the perilous Yangzi River.[84] I here summarize Zuo's travel as recounted in her own writings:

On the Twenty-fifth Day of the Double Eighth Month in the year of Renxu (1862), I received a letter that my husband was severely ill on his post in Anqing. At the time, our eldest son lived in Sichuan. The rest of our children—three sons and five daughters—lived with me in a relative's home in Ganzhou (Jiangxi). The eldest was only ten. I hired a boat the next day and, all by myself, went on a journey to pay my husband a visit. It was not an easy journey; my boat was deterred by strong winds at Poyang Lake, and my misgivings knew no bounds.[85] After the boat finally moved on, I traveled for another twenty days on the waterways of Jiangxi. On the Eleventh Day of the Ninth Month, however, tragic news arrived: my husband had passed away on the Second Day of the Double Eighth Month. Not knowing that I was on my way to Anqing, General Zeng Guofan had ordered that my husband's coffin be sent to Yuzhang (Nanchang, Jiangxi).[86] Heartbroken and in tears, I wrote a letter on the boat to inform my husband's family in Sichuan of his death. Because I could not bear to (and did not know how to) tell my parents-in-law, I addressed the letter to my husband's elder brother instead.[87]

    Later I managed to meet the boat sent by General Zeng Guofan and went on to take my husband's coffin to Ji'an, where my uncle

Zuo Shengsan served as an official. There I composed an elegy and painted a portrait for my husband, which I intended to use at his funeral.[88] Soon afterward I fell ill. While I was ill I painted a self-portrait. When I picked up the brush and looked into the mirror, I was struck by my emaciated and grief-stricken appearance.[89]

Afterward I went back to Yuzhang. In a few months I made up my mind to take my husband's coffin back to Sichuan so that he could be buried in his native home. Also on my mind were the burials of his younger brother and nephew, both of whom had passed away a year before in Yuzhang. I decided to have them buried in Sichuan too. Having learned of my plan, my uncle Zuo Shengsan wrote me a letter and suggested that I postpone my journey to a later time. I declined and selected an auspicious date for the burials. I took my children with me to arrive in Ji'an first. In the Eighth Month of 1863, I hired a boat to depart from Ji'an and went to Yuzhang to pick up the other two coffins. Thereafter my boat carried three coffins, my eight young children, and myself to enter the perilous waterways leading to Sichuan.[90]

When my boat arrived at Huangzhou, Hubei, I and those with me plunged headlong into the havoc of rebels, soldiers, and fleeing refugees. As soon as the rebels ravaged the area and left it in great terror, the government troops came up along the Yangzi River in ships to declare their protection of the people. Such protection, it turned out, meant extortion. While everyone else on the boat was shuddering before the swords of the soldiers, I stayed calm. I first pointed to the funerary banners on my boat and explained to the soldiers the purpose of my trip. Then I made it clear to them that I would rather die by their swords than compromise my integrity (yi). Finally I hinted at the connections of my family and threatened to see their commander in chief. At these words the soldiers fled in a rush and went on to extort people on the other boats next to mine. I was appalled by the lack of discipline in the government troops and believed that this was the very origin of the catastrophe that I and other people were suffering.[91]

My boat moved on and reached the most hazardous part of my journey, the Three Gorges. At night I had my boat moored by the Wu Gorge, unaware that in the caves between the cliffs of the gorge were hidden over twenty bandits. When a boatman, alarmed and terrified, informed me of their presence, I decided to preclude their threats. I took out my sword and sat with great composure. Having calmed down those around me by my own example, I ordered the boatmen to light up the boat with torches and to bang the gongs till the noise echoed between the cliffs. By creating this illusion of strong defense, I succeeded in scaring the bandits away at dawn.[92]

The danger of the gorges consisted not only of the bandits but the damaging waves, which had toppled innumerable boats and had made Sichuan a secluded land since ancient times. In the Winter (Eleventh) Month of 1863, my boat reached one of the most dangerous parts of the Yangzi River, the Chayu Shoal in the county of Qianwei (Leshan, Sichuan). Carried away by the torrents raging between the cliffs, my boat hit the reef that stuck out of the water and was nearly crushed. In my despair I composed a dirge and poured wine into the torrents as a means of appeasing the spirits. The winds ceased instantly and the waters calmed down. Having thus survived by what could only be a divine intervention, I executed a painting on the boat and named it *Picture of [Myself] Taking a Single Boat to Enter Sichuan.* I inscribed the painting with a preface and a poem.[93]

Finally, on the Ninth Day of the First Month in 1864, my boat arrived at Chengdu. Instead of heading directly to my husband's home, I arranged that the boat stayed outside the city for the night for fear that the terrible news I had for my parents-in-law would disrupt their birthday celebrations. Yet I had to break the news to them when I arrived at my husband's home the next day. Seeing their heartrending grief, I promised to make every effort to shoulder the familial duties and provide for the family in the place of my deceased husband.[94]

This personal testimony documents a gentry woman's ordeals in travel in times of chaos. The journey took her 150 days on dangerous waterways; she had in her care three coffins and eight young children and had no one to resort to but herself. (Note that the boatmen were of no help in times of crisis and needed her to calm them down.) This remarkable story as told by Zuo herself surpasses any other biographical sources in creating her exemplary profile, as she goes into great detail to highlight her resourcefulness, heroic courage, devotion to her deceased husband, and filial feelings toward her parents-in-law. It also provides the crucial context for the painting *Picture of [Myself] Taking a Single Boat to Enter Sichuan.* That is, the painting is integral to—and greatly dramatizes—Zuo's representation of herself as a devoted wife who took upon herself the mission of leading a boat through unimaginable hazards in order to have her deceased husband properly buried.[95]

The Painting

A closer look at selections from Zuo's inscription on her painting sheds further light on the rich messages she desired to convey (see Figure 2.08):

I remember the years while I stayed with my husband in Beijing, where he held office, since I first started to serve him in 1851. We had deep respect for each other even in poverty, and always followed each other's wishes. In 1859, he received orders to serve as the prefect in Jiangxi province. . . . (His integrity earned him great political renown in Ji'an.)

Figure 2.08. "My Own Inscription for *Picture of Myself Taking a Boat to Enter Sichuan*," by Zuo Xijia, first page, in *Lengyinxianguan shigao*, 4.4b. Reprinted by permission from the National Library of China.

In 1861, in deep sorrow we had to say farewell to each other, and it was at this time that we parted forever. As the general [Zeng Guofan] eagerly recruited talent [into his army against the Taiping rebels], my husband abandoned his brushes and took out his sword to join the army. (Commander-in-Chief Zeng and Provincial Military Commander Bao had sent letters to my husband to invite him to help with military affairs in Anqing.)[96] He put his life at great risk in the battlefield, and there was not a single battle that he did not win. (During the seven months while he served in the military camps in Anqing, he recovered nine counties from the rebels, including Qingyang and Shidai.) His overwork caused illness, and no medicine had an effect on him. During the worst moments of his illness, he was still shouting out from the pillow [as if in battle], and, in his writings from his deathbed, he was still expressing his concern for the emperor and for his parents. Alas! This loyal heart turned into a pool of martyr's blood.[97]

... How sad! I wanted to find his traces in the land of the dead, yet who would pity these unburied bones? To drag on in this mortal world, I had to live by a lonely lamp. I did not know whether I should live or die, and neither option seemed to offer a way out [of my dilemma]. As I read the letter [my husband] had written to me on his deathbed, I was in such great distress that I wanted to follow him to death, and I wished that we would be reunited in another life. [Yet] I saw our children playing and crying by my side, and they were at such tender ages. I also thought of my white-haired parents-in-law, who had already gone through so many afflictions.

... [On my way to Sichuan,] the cliffs rose high, and the torrents were raging. I wept bitterly by the side of three coffins (my husband's younger brother and nephew had both died this year), and I was so anguished that even the plants [by the river] seemed to grieve for me.[98] By the compassionate power [of the deities], the boat carried us through the waves, and dragons returned to the deep of the water. (When we reached the Chayu Shoal, our boat was damaged by the scattered reefs and was about to sink. I poured wine into the water and sang a dirge. In an instant, the winds ceased and the waters calmed as if by divine intervention.)

[Thus] I floated on the waters, having no idea where to land. Hundreds of thoughts were burning inside me, and I saw nothing but darkness ahead. Therefore, I painted my portrait, wrote this preface, and sang the [following] song, so as to record my experience.[99]

...

天空濛兮無情，	The sky appeared gloomy and cruel,
日慘澹兮失色。	The sun, dismal and pale.
山糾紛兮塞衢術，	The mountains lay as if in chaos and blocked the roads,
水澎湃兮懸絕壁。	The waters raged between the towering cliffs.
石筍磷磷森劍戟，	The reefs stuck out like swords and spears,
伏蛟掉尾巴水裂。	The underlying dragons, turning their tails, ripped open the Ba River.
篙師撟舌魂膽驚，	The boatman gasped and shuddered,
獨我撫棺腸寸折。	I alone wept bitterly by the coffins.
...	
遺書懷中字不滅，	I held the letter [of my husband] in my bosom, its words not having vanished;
心香誓慰君之靈。	I swore to myself that I will appease his soul [by fulfilling his deathbed wish].[100]

This lengthy quotation can be read as a detailed statement of the circumstances that prompted Zuo to execute her painting. It can be divided into three sections that convey different levels of meanings. First, she briefly delineates the life experiences of Zeng Yong, with a focus on his achievements as the prefect of Ji'an and the military counsel of Zeng Guofan. She specifically attributes his death to his unsparing efforts in fighting the rebels and, by this means, glorifies him as a loyal official who died a martyr's death.

Second, Zuo highlights her own dilemma following her husband's death. Just like some of the women I have discussed previously, Zuo represents herself as being torn between her wish to follow her husband to death and her responsibilities to her remaining family. It is the latter concern, she emphasizes, that forced her to give up the idea of being "reunited" with her husband in another life. Tremendous responsibilities confronted her, including burying her husband against all odds, raising her nine young children, and providing for her aged parents-in-law. These responsibilities fell mostly on her, probably because the three deaths in a row left few others in the family to share the burden with her.

Third, Zuo's vivid description of her near-fatal experience at the shoal conveys her great emotional distress and the direness of her situation. Her almost obsessive attention to the visual impact of her words makes it possible to reconstruct the painting's major compositional elements: a grim background of towering cliffs, raging torrents, and sharp reefs. The background color is "gloomy," with overcast skies and a pale sun. In the foreground should be the boat, crashing onto the reefs. The boatman has lost control and is in great fear. The heroine—Zuo—weeps by the side of the coffins, heartbroken, yet still holding onto her husband's letters in her bosom.

Circulation of the Painting

There is evidence that this painting circulated for a long time, at several locations, and among different groups of social elites. It first circulated among a few local luminaries in Chengdu before 1876.[101] During the Winter Month of 1876 Guangxu went to the capital to study at the National University. He took the painting with him and circulated it as an album of approximately one foot on four sides (*chifu*) among a large number of officials there.[102] After he assumed office in Dingxiang (before 1880) and took Zuo to live with him, he further circulated the painting among his social connections there.[103]

The concept of portraiture as social events is especially pertinent to Zuo's case. The concept carries two levels of meanings: first, the portraiture act always involved issues of intended audience and appeared as a site of active cultural or social assertions; second, the viewers participated in constructing the image through textual responses, thus engaging in ongoing conversations with both the subject of the portrait and other viewers as a way of reaffirming group affiliation.[104] Zuo's autobiographical painting became a site of intense social assertion as it conveyed a rich variety of messages to expanding elite audiences and, in the process, affirmed the family's affiliation with these various groups of social elites.

During the earliest stage of the painting's circulation in Chengdu, Zuo found a few eminent authors to inscribe her painting, including Wu Tang (1813–76), the governor-general of Sichuan from 1867 to 1875; Wang Degu (1815–?), the provincial administration commissioner of Sichuan from 1869 to 1875; and Zhao Wulian (1814–94), a woman poet from Jiangsu who married and lived in Chengdu.[105] In order to reconstruct this early stage of the painting's circulation, it is crucial to situate the inscriptions into the broader context of Zuo's life in Chengdu.

We should first recall that Zuo arrived in the countryside of Chengdu in early 1864. She was a thirty-three-year-old widow with eight young children. From this time onward—until 1881, when she joined her son Guangxu in Shanxi—she was solely responsible for providing for her family. Her poetic works from this time refer to her incessant toil. She does mention an older brother of Zeng, who lived with Zeng's parents; however, this brother was not much help. A few of Zuo's biographers hint at the familial tensions she faced during this time. One, for example, reveals that Zuo had never met Zeng's family in Chengdu during her twelve years of marriage with him—an important fact that Zuo herself never mentions and that was passed over by her other biographers. Consequently when she went to live with her parents-in-law, she served them as if she were their "new daughter-in-law [xinfu]."[106] She handled her relationship with her sister-in-law carefully, treating the latter with patience while offering her sincere advice.[107] After her parents-in-law died, Zeng's older brother proposed dividing the household properties. Zuo tried to stop him but failed. She then willingly took her share of thatch and some barren land and let him have the better properties. Following the household division, a drought destroyed her hope of living on her share of the land and forced her to seek other means of making a living. Her wish that her sons would establish their careers became especially acute.[108] Every night she gathered together her nine children and personally supervised her sons' studies and her daughters' needlework. She was so strict that, whenever she found any of them slackening attention, she would burst into tears and beat her chest.[109]

From these accounts emphasizing Zuo's admirable qualities with which she treated her in-laws and raised her children, we gain a sense of the enormous pressure she lived under as she started her life in Chengdu. In particular, the new wife's entry into a household of strangers—which was inevitable in virilocal marriage—was rather delayed in her case. This fact suggests that all the challenges usually confronting a new wife must have been fresh to her at this time: She did seem to have delicate relationships with her in-laws, especially with Zeng's older brother.[110] Further complicating the situation were the financial tensions that she had to face as a widow who brought her eight children into this family. It is important to recall that she had not been able to save much from Zeng's income. It had not been abundant in the first place, the fact of which led a few of her biographers to marvel at her capable management of the family finances—especially the fact that she was able to set aside a share from this income for her parents-in-law. Moreover Zeng's family had very limited means and lived in a humble cottage in the countryside.[111] Now that the share from his income was cut off, the arrival of Zuo with her eight young children no doubt further worsened the family's financial straits. Only in this context can we make sense of the insistence of Zeng's older brother on household division. As I elaborate in chapter 3, the cohabitants of a household during this time shared the household wealth, which was under the control of the most senior patrilineal descendant, usually the father. Household division was by definition the equal division of household wealth among the sons—in most cases following the death of the father.[112] Through household division Zeng's older brother was relieved of the financial burden incurred by Zuo and her children. And, at least from the accounts above, it is clear that he took advantage of Zuo's helpless situation and took the better share for his own family.

A poem Zuo wrote shortly after she started her life in Chengdu indicates exactly these familial tensions. It is the second of two poems titled "Miscellaneous Lines Written to Express My feelings" (Ganhuai zayong):

門內全恩義，   Within the household there should be nothing but
                affection and loyalty,
忍言公與私？   How can I bear to talk about [which things] belong to all
                and which are my own?[113]

解衣呈長姒，	I took down my robe and gave it to my elder sister-in-law;
畫荻教孤兒。	With nothing to teach my orphans, I used a straw to draw characters on the ground.[114]
燈識炎涼味，	The lamp knows the taste of human capriciousness;
機縈婉轉絲。	On the spinning wheel roll the silk threads [that resemble my endless thoughts].
牢愁向誰語？	To whom can I tell about my pent-up sorrow?
毫素寄微辭。	I can only rely on my brush to vent my veiled criticism.[115]

Zuo's criticism is not as "veiled" as she claims. It is clearly targeted at those in the Zeng household (*mennei*) who have lost their "affection and loyalty" toward the other household members and pursue only their selfish interests. By contrast, Zuo represents herself as adhering to these values, even giving her own robe to her sister-in-law. The fact that she highlights her unselfishness toward her sister-in-law indicates that the latter had much to do with the tensions surrounding *gong* and *si*—which I have translated, according to the context, as "which things belong to all and which are my own." This fact sheds light on the household division. That is, the division of the household properties was precisely the division of the *gong* (i.e., common) properties of the household into the *si* (i.e., personal) properties of the sons (and the sons' families). The intention to divide household properties on the part of Zeng Yong's elder brother, as well as the wife of this brother, was already clear at the moment when Zuo Xijia wrote her poem.

Moreover the poem depicts the extreme poverty Zuo lived in and her struggle to make ends meet. However, it was the "capriciousness" with which she was treated that caused her greater sorrow. The phrase *yanliang*, which I translate as "capriciousness," indicates the radically changing attitudes of people around her. Even more important, the phrase suggests the snobbishness associated with such changing attitudes; that is, she was treated differently because she had lost her former status and fortune. By personifying the lamp and referring to its knowledge of human capriciousness, Zuo is in fact asserting that she herself—while weaving by the lamp—has tasted the changing attitudes of Zeng's family due to her lost fortune. She further highlights her helplessness by stating that she has no one to share her sorrow and that all she can do is vent her criticism in writing.

Clearly Zuo was making a painful transition when she tried to settle down in Chengdu. Left with even humbler means following the household division, how could she and her children survive? She soon exhausted what was left of her jewelry.[116] The poetic works that she wrote in the following years document the range of her productive activities. As much as they keep a record of her incessant toil, they also demonstrate her resourcefulness in dealing with her situation as a widow who was left on her own to provide for her nine children. These productive activities include sericulture, textile production, embroidery, cutting colored papers into flowers (*jiancai*), making sola flowers, and selling her works of calligraphy and painting.[117] She also set up a family studio to produce silk, embroidery, handicrafts, and artworks. She taught her daughters these various skills and trained them to produce the works with her.[118]

In Zuo's poetic works of this time, these activities figured as more than cultural symbols—for example, textile production as an age-old symbol for female virtue and artistic endeavors as symbols of cultural refinement.[119] Instead she describes them as explicitly economic activities: a fine painting of flowers was executed for the purpose of bringing in some rice to save the family from starving; paper flowers were cut to make a modest profit (*yibo weili*); the unceasing weaving was directly attributed to poverty—hence Zuo's portrayal of the "poor woman" clearly designates her economic efforts as a virtue.[120] In short, Zuo resorted to every skill she was in possession of to survive, and she had no qualms about describing her efforts.

Soon after the household division, however, Zuo picked up a number of important connections of her natal family. Just as her paintings started to circulate through the local art market, a fan she painted led to her introduction to the outstanding scholar Tang Qiushi, who originated from Yanghu and who earned the *jinshi* degree in the same year as her father, Zuo Ang. Tang was then residing in Chengdu and did not realize that Zuo Xijia lived so close by until he saw her painted fan. He in turn introduced her to his wife, Chen Jiwan, and his two cousins, Zhao Peiyun and Zhao Wulian.[121] These women were highly literate and soon became close friends with Zuo. They paid her visits and exchanged poetry with her frequently. Both Zhao Peiyun and Zhao Wulian had married in Chengdu and had been widowed at a young age. By this time they had earned the title of "Grand Ladies" due to their sons' successful careers. They were also friends with poets and scholars and had published their own collections of poetry.[122] Zhao Wulian was the woman who inscribed Zuo's autobiographical painting.

Tang led Zuo to another important connection of her natal family, the Miaos. Tang was then the mentor of Miao Quansun (1844–1919), whom Zuo referred to as a cousin. Zuo had been especially close to Miao's wife, Zhuang Yingru, and they now resumed their friendship. Zuo also resumed her ties with Miao Zhongying, the father of Miao Quansun, whom she referred to as her uncle; Grand Lady Xue, mother of Miao Quansun; and Zhuang Biru, sister of Zhuang Yingru.[123] The Zhuang sisters excelled in painting. Together with the Zhao sisters, they gave Zuo much support. Zuo later organized a poetry society with this group of literate women.[124]

In 1872 and later Zuo picked up a few former connections of Zeng Yong, including Governor-General Wu Tang, Provincial Administration Commissioner Wang Degu, and the censor Wu Chunhai. Wu Tang and Wang Degu earned the *jinshi* degree in the same year as Zeng. They treasured her paintings, and it was around this time that Zuo established her reputation as an artist who "caused the price of painting paper to soar."[125] They were among the authors who inscribed her autobiographical painting. Wu Chunhai originated from the county of Tongliang, Sichuan, and was a former colleague of Zeng in the capital. Zuo developed close ties with him and married her fourth daughter, Shujun, to his son, Wu Zhongying.[126] In addition, as Zuo's other daughters came of age, their marriages also seemed to become a means of making or affirming the family's social connections.[127]

Zuo moved her home twice in 1872. In the autumn she moved to Jincheng (literally, the City of Brocade), a few *li* (half kilometer) south to the urban center of Chengdu. In addition to the fact that it was close to local government schools, the area was known for a broad array of commercial products, especially brocade (for which it was named), textiles, fans, and handicrafts.[128] Although it was a convenient location for Zuo to sell her artworks and the products of her family studio—where she worked more and more—her financial situation did not improve, and she soon became tired of the bustle of the urban area. In the winter she moved a few *li* farther south, to an area by the Stream of Washing Flowers (Huanhua xi), alternatively named the Pond of a Hundred Flowers (Baihua tan; see Figs. 2.09a and 2.09b).[129]

This area is known for the beauty of its scenery. More important, it carried the cultural heritage of the great Tang poet Du Fu (712–70), who spent several years there taking refuge from war. The Qing government constructed a grand memorial hall for Du Fu by the stream in 1793. Zuo settled in her new home just by the side of

Figure 2.09a.   Stream of Washing Flowers (Huanhuaxi), Chengdu. Photo by
Fang Liu, 2015.

the memorial hall. She further appropriated this cultural heritage
by organizing the Poetry Society by the Stream of Washing Flowers (Huanhua shishe) and referring to herself as a "neighbor" of Du
Fu.[130] The elites favored the area and wrote profusely about it since
Du's time; it contained a plethora of historical sites and renowned
gardens, making it much more culturally refined than the commercial center.[131] It was during her residence of nearly a decade there,
rather than in the commercial center, that Zuo's fame as a woman
artist peaked and she was able to pay for her children's education
and marriages, purchase land and houses, and engage in charity
works.[132] These facts suggest that a woman painter's livelihood, like
her male counterpart's, depended no less on her connections to elite
culture than on commercial factors.[133]

    This sketch of Zuo's life in Chengdu reveals much about the cir-
cumstances under which she started to circulate her autobiographical
painting. That is, she did so while eking out a living and, at the same
time, trying to establish her social networks. The few authors who
viewed and inscribed her painting were key figures in local elite society, including virtually the most powerful officials in Sichuan, and an
established and widely connected woman poet. The importance of
their support cannot be dismissed, especially if we take into account
the painful transition Zuo made and the helpless situation she was
in when she started her life in Chengdu. In circulating her painting

Figure 2.09b.   A traditional-style house, named Depths by the Stream of Washing Flowers (Huanhua Shenchu), Chengdu. Photo by Fang Liu, 2015.

among these people she was conveying her remarkable story to them and hence winning their sympathy and support.

A look at these inscriptions immediately indicates the authors' reception of Zuo's intended messages. Both the governor-general and the provincial administration commissioner compared her to the most celebrated female moral exemplars in history: the chaste woman from the ode "Cypress Boat" (Bozhou) in the *Book of Odes* (Shijing) and the woman of Qi and the woman of Lu from *Biographies of Exemplary Women*. Zhao Wulian predicted that Zuo would soon win extraordinary honor from the court.[134] Additional support came in the form of gifts or financial aids from these social connections, no doubt helping to relieve some of Zuo's pressing financial concerns. For example, when Wu Tang left his post in 1875, Zuo expressed her gratitude to his generosity; every year (for the past few years) he would send her a share of what he saved from his salary to help her "orphans."[135]

Given the influence of these authors, Zuo's painting may have reached a wider audience than these few textual records suggest. A local elite woman named Wei Xiaolan, for example, asked Zuo to execute a painting to record her own experience of traveling in chaotic times in order to return home. The painting was titled *Picture [of Wei Xiaolan] Returning to Sichuan* (GuiShu tu).[136] Wei's clear intention to imitate the theme of Zuo's painting suggests that she had at least some knowledge of the painting. Zhao Wulian was probably not the only elite woman who had the chance to view Zuo's painting, given that Zuo was closely associated with a group of these elite women.

Without any definitive evidence, however, I do not intend to speculate on how wide an impact Zuo's painting made on local elite society. Rather the question is this: If the circulation of her painting was part of her effort at gaining support from her social connections, what in particular did she have in mind?

Regaining Family Status: Vindicating the Husband and Advancing the Son's Career

A further context reveals much about what was weighing on Zuo's mind during these years. In 1872 the censor Wu Chunhai took his mother on a home visit in Sichuan. He commissioned a painting, *Picture of the Green-and-White-Colored Horse Leading the Carriage* (Congma daoyu tu), to depict the grandeur of his visit and to highlight his filial feelings toward his mother. He showed the painting to Zuo and asked for her inscription. It was the beginning of a close relationship between Zuo and Wu; in fact she probably betrothed her fourth daughter to his son around this time.[137]

At Wu's request Zuo composed a lengthy poem of 133 lines for the inscription, attaching to it a preface and thirteen notes.[138] It fits uncomfortably with the celebratory mood of the painting; Zuo refers to Wu's visit in only eight lines and uses the remainder of the poem to glorify her husband's military achievements and her own devoted service to his family following his death. She ends her poem by explicitly stating that she has other purposes in mind than Wu's visit:

| 十年幽憤向誰啼？ | To whom can I tell in tears about my ten years of deep anguish? |
| 聊借此圖寫哀曲。 | I am merely using this picture to write a sorrowful song [for myself].[139] |

This most ill-fitting "sorrowful song" inspired three other inscriptions. The first, written by none other than Wu himself, starts with a line that describes Zuo's inscription as "using the topic for other purposes [jieti fahui]." Another author, Qin Huan, also refers to Zuo's "unstated intentions [kuxin]," which "would take a truly discerning eye to find."[140]

What were Zuo's unstated intentions? A closer look at this lengthy inscription leads to an unexpected discovery about the vicissitudes of Zeng Yong's career. Shortly after he assumed office in Ji'an, the Taiping rebels again laid siege to the city. Having suffered repeated attacks from the rebels, people fled and left behind a deserted city. Consequently Zeng's urgent requests for aid were easily turned down by his superior. He finally received orders to guard the city with some reinforcements. However, he had no idea that the two military directors who brought the reinforcements, Lu Desheng and Li Jinyang, had made a secret pact with the rebels. They convinced him to lead a small militia out of the city at night and promised to guard the deserted city by themselves. Zeng and his militia were on the road for only a few miles when they heard the horns by the south gate: Lu and Li had opened the gate and the rebels had swarmed in.

In great regret and shame, Zeng tried to commit suicide but was rescued by his aides. He then led his militia to attack the rebels by surprise and successfully recovered the city. Lu and Li shamelessly claimed the victory for themselves. Zeng's superior did not look closely into the matter and therefore did not know the truth. It was not until the end of the year that Lu and Li were found out and executed. Zeng was wrongly dismissed from office and did not have the chance to vindicate himself. A few of Zuo's lines refer particularly to these wrongs as well as Zeng's unswerving loyalty to the court:

不願水清白石現，	His wish was not that the whole incident would finally come to light;
但願甲兵一洗四海同。	Rather, his only wish was that armored troops [of the court] would sweep across the four seas and reunite [the lost land].
鞠躬就部議，	He bowed his head to receive impeachment from the Board [of War],
敢言明主棄。	And made a bold statement that he was abandoned by the wise emperor.
事君未克忠，	Since he was unable to complete his loyal service to the emperor,
擬遂養親志。	He planned to fulfill his wish of serving his parents.[141]

It was at this moment that Zeng Yong received the invitation of Zeng Guofan to serve in Anqing. He put aside his filial concerns for his parents and joined the leadership of Zeng Guofan's army. The rest of his story is already known: he had great military success in Anqing, but soon died of illness there. Zuo ended his story with the following line: "In vain his loyal heart turned into a pool of martyr's blood!"[142]

It is now time to recall that this line first appeared in Zuo's lengthy inscription for her autobiographical painting. In my earlier reading of that inscription, I noted her intention to glorify her husband as a loyal official who died a martyr's death. Given what we have just learned about Zeng's downfall, this line requires a more complicated reading. The phrase *bixue* not only refers to the blood of the martyr but also alludes to the wrongs inflicted on the martyr.[143] Zuo's use of the phrase "in vain" indicates unambiguously that Zeng died unappreciated, without vindicating himself. Therefore, both here and early on, Zuo's apparent "digression" into Zeng's life story was in fact driven by her agenda of making a case for him by glorifying his unappreciated loyalty and achievements.

A further exploration of this part of Zeng's life reveals the complexities surrounding his vindication. His biography in the local gazetteer of Huayang suggests the tension between him and his superior—probably Yuke (?–1865), who was then the governor of Jiangxi.[144] Such tension not only cast a shadow over Zeng's career but also created obstacles to his vindication later.[145] For example, even after the two military directors who had tricked him were found out and executed, his superior showed no intention of restoring his official title. Moreover his superior even tried to prevent him from joining Zeng Guofan's army. Only when Zeng Guofan put some pressure on the matter was Zeng Yong finally transferred.[146]

Zeng Guofan, on the other hand, clearly intended to make a case for Zeng Yong and was already hoping that he would be able to restore Zeng Yong's official title when he arranged for Zeng Yong's transfer. About a year following the transfer, Zeng Guofan made an appeal to the court for this purpose based on Zeng Yong's military achievements. However, his efforts were not successful because Zeng Yong soon died of illness. The local gazetteer of Huayang only tersely records that Zeng Yong was vindicated posthumously: "The court learned of the matter, and issued an order that an extra pension be given [to Zeng Yong's family] according to the rules befitting those who died of illness in military camps, that [Zeng] be awarded posthumously the title of Chamberlain for the Court of the Imperial Stud, and that one of his sons be assigned to the post of county magistrate due to his achievements."[147] The entry gives the impression that Zeng was vindicated soon after his death. A funerary epitaph authored by Zuo in his honor is attached to the end of the entry, and it generates the same impression. (It appears that Zeng's biography in the local gazetteer of Huayang drew most of its material from this epitaph.)[148] Nevertheless an earlier text by Zuo indicates that Zeng's vindication was a more complicated process than the local gazetteer suggests. This earlier text, a eulogy for Zeng's portrait, is found in Zuo's small volume of prose, *Preserved Prose* (Wencun).[149] Despite the caption that bears Zeng's posthumous title, its contents yield various clues that it was written shortly after his death in 1862. In other words, the posthumous title was added to the caption at a later time.[150] This text reveals that Zeng Guofan did not successfully have Zeng Yong's official title restored at the time because someone thwarted his efforts; as a result Zeng Yong's achievements did not reach the ears of the emperor ("zhong huo nizhi, nanda tiancong").[151] This crucial fact about the forces working against the early efforts of Zeng's vindication may indeed explain why Zuo needed to make a case for him.

We now have a sense of Zuo's sustained efforts to vindicate Zeng. She first attributed his dismissal from office as the fault of his superiors in her eulogy for his portrait (around 1862). Then she glorified his "loyal heart" and his "martyr's death" in her inscription for her autobiographical painting (1863). Her circulation of her painting among the few key figures in local elite society of Chengdu no doubt helped convey Zeng's unappreciated achievements to this audience (as much as it conveyed her own exemplary profile). A second look at the inscriptions authored by Governor-General Wu Tang and Provincial Administration Commissioner Wang Degu indeed confirms their reception of Zuo's message: both glorify Zeng's achievements and mourn his unfulfilled ambitions. Wang particularly highlights Zeng's "loyalty and faithfulness [zhongxin]."[152] In 1872 Zuo tried once again to vindicate Zeng in her inscription for Wu Chunhai's painting, this time going into even greater detail about the intrigues Zeng had suffered and the faults of his superior. Note that she does not mention the court's recognition of Zeng's achievements; instead she refers to her ten years of "deep anguish [youfen]"—a more precise translation of which would be "deep anger," namely, her deeply repressed anger at the wrongful charges against Zeng. Two of her notes further disclose her "unstated intention" in having Zeng's story reach Wu Chunhai. That is, Wu was involved in several projects to promote the moral reputation of Sichuan, including compiling biographies of eminent officials and moral exemplars and petitioning the court to glorify chaste widows and filial daughters and daughters-in-law. He was also collaborating with Governor-General Wu Tang in establishing local schools.[153] Zuo's inscription is an explicit appeal to Wu Chunhai and the powerful figures he was collaborating with.

I suspect therefore that the obstacles to Zeng's vindication were not removed until a much later time—around 1876, when Guangxu went to the National University after the court's recognition of Zeng's achievements—and that they were removed only because of Zuo's persistent efforts to convey his unappreciated achievements to the powerful connections she managed to make. The local gazetteer and a number of other biographical accounts of Zeng generate confusion in that they refer only vaguely to his vindication, without specifying either the lapse in time or the complexities involved.

These complicated messages that Zuo encoded into her painting become legible only in the larger context of her ongoing campaign to vindicate her late husband. The painting's circulation after 1876 bore testimony to how these messages reached a wider elite audience—now that her son Guangxu could act as her proxy in making the connections in the capital. Many of the poetic inscriptions that the painting inspired during this time are striking in their sheer length (e.g., over one hundred lines), which is itself indicative of the painting's impact, as well as the authors' efforts to capture its rich variety of messages. Some authors recapitulate the vicissitudes of Zeng's career, highlighting precisely what Zuo chose to highlight: his loyalty to the court, the intrigues he suffered, and the blindness of his superior. Other authors marvel at Zuo's heroic courage in protecting the body of this "loyal official" and his offspring, adding graphic details to the vastness of the raging torrents and how she overcame them, and eagerly claiming a court reward for her based on her heroic acts. Still others attribute her survival at the shoal to "heaven's sympathy," claiming that the deities took her side because even they were moved by what this loyal official and his widow had suffered. Yet other authors express their delight that the wrongs were finally corrected and that the sons were starting to distinguish themselves in studies and ready to glorify their family again.[154] In short, it is clear from even a cursory look that Zuo's painting truly created a stir among a number of officials in the capital.

Most of all, behind the son's visits to those officials—introducing himself by referring to former family ties, opening the album and showing the painting inside, and requesting inscriptions[155]—there was always the presence of the mother. Zuo already had her sons' future in mind in seeking Wu Chunhai's attention in 1872. She told him her deep worry about her sons' lack of connection with the outside world.[156] In the winter of 1876, as she saw Guangxu finally venturing into the outside world, she sensed his anxiety about the uncertainties ahead and composed ten poems *in his voice*.[157] The following lines indicate that Guangxu was still far from securing an official position despite the fact that he now had the chance to study in the National University due to the court's recognition of his father's achievements:

驅車入燕市，	As I lead my carriage into the city of Yan,[158]
風塵安所托？	Where am I going to settle in the wind and dust of the city?
投刺少知名，	When I send out my cards, few would know my name,
父執半寥落。	Friends of my father have half fallen out of contact.
寥落戀親故，	With few connections and with nothing left in my bags,
囊空悲羈旅。	I would miss my family and deplore my protracted journey.
漂母千古情，	Who would be as kind as Mother Piao from thousands of years ago
臨流向誰語？	To tell me her encouraging words by the river?[159]

As a few recent studies show, the system of granting titles to the son due to the father's contribution had by this time expanded to such an extent—especially due to the great number of officials who lost their lives in putting down the Taiping rebellion—that the number of qualified candidates far exceeded the available positions. After fulfilling the required period of study in the National University, the candidates would then wait for an assignment from the Board of Personnel. The eventual assignment, if any, was contingent on a variety of factors, the least important being the candidate's merit.[160] It was precisely such uncertainty that prompted Zuo's anxiety (albeit in the voice of her son), especially regarding how little support was available to Guangxu. The circulation of her painting, then, would solve precisely this problem, helping Guangxu to pick up the lost connections of his family, to introduce himself and his extraordinary family history to these officials, and hence to win their support.[161]

Guangxu successfully obtained a post and circulated the painting among the connections he made on his post in Jiangxi. The inscriptions from this later time continued the process of publicizing the rich messages encoded in the painting—now among a different group of social elites. A number of these inscriptions honor Zuo's sixtieth birthday in 1891. In that year she personally put together her own personal collection and that of her late husband and, with the help of her son Guangxu and her son-in-law Lin Shangchen, had both collections printed.[162] The circulation of her painting at this moment no doubt served to create more publicity for this grand celebration of her exemplary life story and the family's extraordinary history. All this publicity served in turn as a prelude to the court reward that Guangxu eventually obtained for her.[163]

Here at last a woman's artistic self-representation joined forces with more familiar cultural trends of the time and turned into a family project. The son grew up to assume the mission of regaining his family's former status. It was he who made contacts and who literally opened the album to broader elite audiences. As he embarked on his mission, however, it was his mother who had a precise idea of what challenges were awaiting him and how he should overcome them. Her painting served as his stepping stone to the social networks that had long been lost to his family. In the long run, as he advanced on his career path, he found chances to further publicize the richly encoded painting as a means of enhancing his family's reputation. Just as the famous instance of Chen Shu illustrated, a woman's visual image featuring her virtue was meant to be circulated and thus to garner social honor for her and her family. Zuo Xijia's painting bore witness to a dynamic process by which her own exemplary life story as well as a range of complicated messages she had encoded into her visual image helped affirm her family's affiliation with various groups of social elites—besides serving more imminent aims, such as vindicating her husband and advancing her son's career.

CONCLUSION

Textual records from the Qing period attest to the prominence of women's portraits and paintings as a visual means of self-representation. While the massive data yielded by a preliminary search suggest a broad field for further investigation, the focus here is the theme of female exemplarity as it was integrated into women's visual self-representations. The two major case studies offer useful points for comparison.

Chen Yunlian's inscriptions for her eight autobiographical paintings yield a wealth of information that makes it possible to reconstruct the content of the paintings, their encoded messages and intended audience, and their original form and preservation. These textual records reveal the paintings' close affinity with the widely circulating images of exemplary women, particularly in light of Chen's enactment of dramatic moments of bodily suffering. On the other hand, these same texts reveal the subversive nature of Chen's claim to female exemplarity. Precisely by glorifying her suffering, she gained immense leverage over her husband who had betrayed her. Her vehement condemnation of his lack of gratitude for her sacrifice might not have made her much of an exemplary woman to her contemporaries—the fact of which can be sensed in elite society's complete silence over her paintings, unlike the zeal that this society otherwise had for the paintings featuring female virtue. Nevertheless, her case demonstrates most clearly how a woman *laid down her own terms* of how exemplary she was and how she appropriated the moral authority accorded by female exemplarity for her personal agenda.

Chen can be viewed as an extreme case, given her exposure of her failed marriage. Zuo Xijia, by contrast, indicated no such family scandal or taboo but rather echoed familiar cultural trends of the time, such as the use of women's portraits to enhance family reputation. And yet Zuo's case is complicated by other contexts. The rich messages that she encoded into her painting become legible only when situated in the larger picture of her life as a widow and a professional painter in Chengdu, especially her ongoing efforts to regain her family's former status over these years. The circulation of her painting among various groups of social elites served the purposes of conveying its richly encoded messages to these audiences and winning their support at crucial moments. As much as it joined familiar cultural trends in glorifying the family's extraordinary history, the painting also bore witness to how a woman used her artistic self-representation to exert control over both her own life and the fate of her family. In this sense both Chen and Zuo tailored the theme of female exemplarity to their personal needs—despite the fact that Zuo's painting did gain much publicity (as originally associated with paintings of exemplary lives), while Chen's paintings did not.

Moreover the way the two women asserted their contributions to their families suggests intriguing links between women's moral claims and their economic activities. Chen chose to phrase part of her contribution to her family in explicitly monetary terms. Her case unveils how a woman's economic roles changed her perception of her importance to her family and, in particular, her relation to her husband (i.e., that he was "indebted" to her). Zuo too characterized as her virtue a woman's economic activities in saving her family from privations and felt no qualms about describing how she resorted to every skill she had to make a living. What has to be left out of the case study of Zuo—due to limited textual evidence—is how the circulation of her autobiographical painting might have created a form of social currency for her. The painting incited enthusiastic responses from a few key figures in local elite society, and her rising competitiveness as a professional painter paralleled the expansion of her social connections. A further exploration of how Zuo Xijia's artistic self-representation served as her stepping stone to social reputation may provide a sense of the dynamics wherein a variety of factors in her rising career—moral, social, and financial—interacted with each other.

CHAPTER 3

Staging Family Drama
Genealogical Writing as Ritual Authority

Genealogical writing grew primarily out of the ritual needs of the lineage. These writings delineate family histories with lists of descendants and ancestors' biographies, establish the order of the ancestral worship, specify the ritual procedures and the types of offerings to be made, assign duties to the family or lineage members, and even discuss such practical topics as the family or lineage fields that yielded income to cover the expenses of the ritual. In short, it is a genre of writing that directly addresses the question of how ancestral worship should be performed and sustained.[1]

Much has been said about the development of local lineages and the increasing importance attached to ancestral worship by these lineages during the late imperial period, especially in areas along the Yangzi River.[2] It was the duty of the lineage head to determine affairs concerning lineage ancestral rites. In fact the Ming legal code of 1397 defined the duty of a lineage head solely in this respect, and the Qing laws, while expanding the responsibilities of the lineage head, kept this heritage from the Ming code intact.[3] The core of the lineage head's duty, consequently, was to commission writings to specify the terms for ancestral rites. Authors of these writings usually included local luminaries from the lineage, such as those who held *jinshi* degrees or official titles or those with an eminent literary or scholarly reputation.[4] Women were usually excluded from the compilation of genealogies, and hence from the ritual authority inherent in these writings.

Women were not excluded from ancestral worship per se, but their roles were limited and largely of an assisting nature. In rituals

performed in the family, for example, the wife was expected to prepare offerings of food and clean the sacrificial utensils. She was also
expected to assist her husband in managing the procedures of the
ritual, but it was her husband who played the leading role.[5] This fact
remained generally unchanged across great expanses of time, from
the Song period till the Qing.[6] In certain areas women were even pro-
hibited from the lineage ancestral shrine, although they attended to
the domestic ancestral altar.[7] No wonder, therefore, that few records
can be found for women's involvement in the compilation of writings
that laid down the rules governing ancestral rites. Thus any evidence
for such involvement can reveal much about women's appropriation
of the enormous ritual authority that they were originally excluded
from.

WOMEN'S ENGAGEMENT WITH GENEALOGICAL WRITING

I mentioned in chapter 2 a short preface that Zuo Xijia authored for
her husband's lineage genealogy. The quotation below indicates her
involvement in the compilation of the genealogy:

PREFACE TO THE ZENG LINEAGE GENEALOGY

The Zeng lineage descended from the Yellow Emperor. . . . [The lineage members] spread in all directions and lived in Shandong, Guangdong, Sichuan, and areas along the Yangzi River. Thousands of lines
descended from the same ancestor—[the Zeng lineage] can indeed be
said to be a prosperous lineage! Ever since our ancestor Mr. Guanwan entered Sichuan, [the Zeng lineage] has lasted here for over a
hundred years, and has produced lines of descendants. The lineage
genealogy, however, has long ceased to develop, and therefore needs
to be compiled afresh. Now [I] have followed its old format and
delineated [the lines of descendants in the Zeng lineage], in order to
pass it on to the later generations.[8]

The genealogy itself, however, has not survived, leaving no evidence
of the actual extent of Zuo's involvement in its compilation. This
is precisely why the instance of Yuan Jingrong (1786–ca.1852), the
female protagonist in the following discussion, stands out as a unique
case deserving of close inquiry. A more detailed introduction to Yuan
Jingrong's life and works is included below. Here I begin by discussing several issues that make her case significant. First of all, her case
includes the most extensive records found to date regarding wom-
en's engagement with genealogy writing. Although a few samples of

potentially related writings, such as family biography (*jiazhuan*), survive in works by female authors,[9] Yuan's personal collection provides
direct evidence for a woman's compilation of genealogies for her husband's family and lineage. The surviving writings reveal how she laid
down the rules governing ancestral rites and appropriated the authority attached to the rites.

Second, a close analysis of Yuan's writings reveals that they served
more than purely ritual purposes. While expressing her respect and
filial feelings for her husband's ancestors, Yuan also carefully weaves
into her narrative a family drama characterized by the rapid rise in the
family's status and the ensuing tensions, ambiguities, and dramatic
shifts in family relationships. Much of the drama, as she describes it,
was related to the power dynamics within the family. An examination
of these family dramas therefore sheds light on the power structure of
the "patriarchal family" in times of transition (i.e., when the identity
of the "patriarch" was in question) and also reveals much about how
a woman might be able to fill the power vacuum left by the deaths of
the patriarchs and succeed in resolving the family disputes according
to her own wishes.

Third, the family drama was as much about power as about the
family's material means, since the family's rapid rise in status was
accompanied by disputes regarding the control of its increasing
wealth. The central role played by Yuan in the management of the
household finances provides a fascinating case study in the pointed
vagueness in women's material lives. Recent studies have shown that,
despite the abundance of historical records that describe women's role
as family financial managers, there is a conspicuous lack of records
discussing the precise way in which they managed their own wealth—
their dowry assets, for example, and their virtuous use of these assets
for the benefit of their husbands' lineages. Indeed, one of the virtues
of the exemplary Confucian wife lay in her ability to conceal monetary transactions even while using them to ensure the household's survival and success.[10] By shifting the focus to women's own writings, we
may circumvent this vagueness and reach an understanding of their
precise roles in the household economy.

YUAN JINGRONG AND HER GENEALOGY WRITINGS

Yuan Jingrong was born in Huating (Shanghai), Jiangsu. Biographical
entries about her can be found in *Poetry as Commentary on Poetry,*

Written in the Small Black Pavilion and *Another Sequel to the Correct Beginnings for Gentry Women*.[11] Both entries refer to her as a woman poet. Her personal collection comprises two volumes, entitled *Poetry Drafts from the Studio of Yuequ [courtesy name of Yuan Jingrong]* (Yuequxuan shicao), and *Biographies and Brief Records from the Studio of Yuequ* (Yuequxuan zhuanshulue).[12]

Biographical facts about Yuan Jingrong can mainly be found in the prefaces and epilogues—all of a eulogizing nature—that are attached to the two volumes.[13] She was the daughter of Yuan Houtang, a county official in Jiangsu, and a cherished grandchild of Yuan Botian, who served in a number of important official posts, including as provincial administration commissioner of Jiangxi. Like many other gentry women of her time, Yuan Jingrong benefited from a tradition of family learning (*jiaxue*) and, as a girl, received an education in poetry and classical prose from her father. Her grandfather personally arranged for her marriage to Wu Jie (1782–1836), a young scholar from Kuaiji (Shaoxing, Zhejiang) who was known as a "precocious talent."[14] Wu later served as the vice minister of rites.

From the scant biographical information available about the early years of Yuan Jingrong's married life, we can gather that she diligently performed the wifely role as soon as she entered the Wu household. It seems that her husband was from a much less affluent background. Yuan accepted the reduced financial circumstances and devoted herself to household work, in which she supposedly engaged day and night without appearing disheartened.[15] She was also happy to pawn her dowry to enable Wu to study, was said to "deal with privation as if it were abundance [*chu buzu ruo youyu*]," and was reluctant to reveal her situation to the messengers sent by her grandfather for fear that he would be concerned.[16]

Yuan's marriage was marked by a significant change of fortune after Wu passed a series of civil service examinations. He was first awarded the *juren* degree in 1808, then passed the *jinshi* in 1814 and was assigned to a post in the Hanlin Academy in 1817.[17] The subsequent two decades witnessed his successful career path. After filling a number of provincial posts, he was promoted to capital magistrate in 1833, and in 1834 he assumed the post of vice minister of rites to supervise state education and civil service examinations.[18] As Yuan later recalled, from 1833 on, the rapidity with which Wu was promoted was unparalleled.[19] In his capacity as vice minister of rites he was highly influential among the younger generations of officials. A number of his disciples held offices in the capital and in the provinces. The most illustrious among them was Shen Zhaolin (1801–62), who later served as grand secretary, minister of revenue and of war, and grand minister of state.

The eulogizing accounts of Yuan included in her personal collections underscore this significant change in her life as further illustration of her virtue and laud her unrelenting efforts to perform her wifely duties both before and after Wu's rise to power. She continued to devote herself to the care of the elderly and the young in her household, to personally perform all housework, and to meticulously manage the household accounts so that Wu was free from all such worries.[20] The eulogizing accounts therefore attribute Wu's outstanding career to Yuan, namely, to "aid from the inner quarters [*neizhu*]."[21]

Yuan's exemplary profile culminates with her achievements in the wake of the deaths of Wu in 1836 and, several years later, his father. The eulogizing accounts about her focus on her ability to manage their funerals according to the appropriate rites and, more significant, to deal with the familial chaos generated by the deaths. Shen Zhaolin, for example, states, "After the Vice Minister passed away, it was urgent that his household matters be dealt with. Her Ladyship put herself to these matters with the utmost care, neither submitting to the powerful nor humiliating the weak. Even men would find it difficult to go through what she experienced and dealt with. Yet all her acts were appropriate, and her measures clear."[22] We may wonder exactly what household matters Yuan dealt with to win herself such acclaim, since managing the funerals alone would not seem to involve the many difficulties Shen hints at. The preface authored by Zhuang Zhongfang (1780–1857, a well-known scholar and bibliophile) provides more detailed information in this respect (see Figure 3.01 for the first page of the original preface, preceded by the title page of Yuan's collection):

> My second son Zhuang Xiao married the daughter of Vice Minister Wu Meiliang [style name of Wu Jie] of Kuaiji. He brought from Kuaiji the *Family Biographies of the Wu* and the *Agreement on Ancestral Rites*—both authored by Lady Yuan, the mother of his wife—and asked for my opinion. Having read these works, I exclaimed: "How greatly people's achievements can vary! It normally falls on the scholars and officials to compile genealogies and to allocate land for ancestral rites, duties of which ordinary men are not capable—let alone those from the inner quarters. Meiliang had once thought of writing biographies for his ancestors and of allocating land for ancestral rites,

Figure 3.01. Title page and first page of Zhuang Zhongfang's preface to Yuan Jingrong's personal collection, *Yuequxuan zhuanshulue*. Reprinted by permission from the National Library of China.

yet had barely found the chance to start before he passed away. While mourning the deaths of her father-in-law and her husband, as well as lamenting the fact that her son had lost his fatherly protection, Her Ladyship traveled thousands of miles to have them [Wu Jie and his father] buried in their native place. Instead of taking the land left [by Wu Jie] to be her own property, she set it aside for the ancestral rites. Moreover, she authored biographies for Mr. Minhui and those who came after [in the Wu lineage] in order to fulfill her husband's unac-complished wish and to let them [the Wu ancestors] be remembered for a long time to come. Indeed, even scholars and officials might refrain from attempting these tasks out of their sense of modesty, yet Her Ladyship resolutely put herself to them and accomplished them in such an orderly fashion. Were she a man and an official in the court, who knows what grand achievements she could accomplish?[23]

And from Zhuang Xiao's epilogue:

I have once read the volume of *Biographies and Brief Records* authored by my mother-in-law. [From the volume I can see how] she recounted the virtues of the [Wu] ancestors, set aside land for [Wu] ancestral rites, managed funerals and sacrifices, valued the [Wu] kin and created harmony in the [Wu] lineage, diligently performed the roles of both a filial daughter-in-law and a loving mother, and set up the example for the later generations through her own words and behaviors. She can be said to have attained all the three ideals of "establishing one's virtue, one's deeds, and one's words." How many officials nowadays can earn themselves such praise and feel that they truly deserve it?[24]

Yuan's main accomplishments, then, were her management of affairs related to ancestral rites, including her authorship of biographies for her husband's ancestors, and her setting aside land for ancestral rites. *Biographies and Brief Records* keeps a more detailed record of her efforts:

1. Leading the Wu clan in restoring the lineage ancestral hall and hence in restoring the lineage's suspended ancestral rites.[25]

2. Authoring two books for ancestral rites (*jisibu*) for her husband's lineage branch, focusing on ancestral rites for those from the seventh generation to the tenth and on ancestral rites for those from the eleventh to the twelfth generations.[26]

3. Authoring a book for ancestral rites for her husband's household, fifteen biographies for those to be included in the household ancestral rites, and an account book for the land that yielded rent income to cover the expenses of the household ancestral rites.[27]

4. Setting aside funds and land for the above three categories of ancestral rites.[28]

It does not take long to realize, however, that Yuan was overstepping her authority. Even as her eulogizers laud her achievements in these areas, to the extent of claiming that she put men to shame, they also suggest that her achievements belong to the male sphere. Zhuang Zhongfang makes this point clear by identifying the compilation of genealogies and the allocation of land for ancestral rites as the duties of "scholars and officials." His statement that "even scholars and officials might refrain from attempting these tasks out of their sense of modesty" suggests the boldness of Yuan's acts. Zhuang Xiao, in commenting that Yuan had attained the three ideals of "establishing one's virtue, one's deeds, and one's words," implies that she had accomplished what a Confucian gentleman, not an exemplary Confucian wife, was expected to achieve.

An inquiry into Yuan's own writings will resolve this apparent contradiction. Instead of examining them item by item, I begin by reconstructing a family history from their contents. This history diverges from the framework established by the eulogizing accounts in that it starts with an unconventional marriage. In fact it is the nature of Yuan's marriage that provides the key to much of the ensuing family drama.

AN UXORILOCAL MARRIAGE

Yuan's biographers laud her virtuous use of her dowry. In *Biographies and Brief Records*, she herself highlights this point whenever she refers to the early years of her marriage to Wu. She frequently describes the extreme poverty with which she was confronted: "The stove was always empty of firewood and the bottles and bags empty of any stored food"; "Without grain to make food, [our family] was on the verge of starving to death."[29] At critical junctures it was always she who came to the rescue by pawning her wedding clothes to buy food. Beyond seeing to the basic needs of the family, she also "pulled hairpins out of [her] hair and went through all [her] trunks to look for things [to pawn or sell] in order to enable [Wu] to study."[30]

These descriptions go well beyond that which is stated in the eulogizing accounts about her. Yuan represents Wu's family as utterly destitute and portrays her dowry as the family's sole source of income. *Biographies and Brief Records* also differs from the eulogizing accounts in that Yuan discusses her relationship with her natal family. Her grandfather Yuan Botian continued to assist her financially after her marriage and also provided generous financial aid to both Wu Jie and his father, Wu Yonghe.[31] Furthermore, after Yuan Jingrong's wedding ceremony, Yuan Botian invited Wu Jie to stay in his official abode to facilitate his studies. When Wu Jie took a teaching job in a local school, Yuan Botian offered to take care of his family by inviting Yuan Jingrong and Wu Yonghe to join him at his official abode.[32] Yuan Botian's generosity also extended to Wu Jie's relatives. Soon after Yuan Jingrong and Wu Yonghe arrived at Yuan Botian's official abode in Jiangxi, Yuan Botian learned that Wu Jie's uncle, Wu Yongqing, had been assigned to a post as county magistrate in Jiangxi, yet was short of travel funds. Yuan Botian not only offered to cover these expenses but even purchased a house for Wu Yongqing. He then made arrangements for Wu Yonghe to join Wu Yongqing in the new house and provided both men with monthly stipends, in addition to supplies of rice and firewood. Meanwhile, Yuan

Jingrong continued to stay in Yuan Botian's official abode and sent frequent gifts and daily supplies to her father-in-law.[33]

Therefore, in contrast to the eulogizing accounts that describe how Yuan Jingrong hid her financial situation from her grandfather, she and her husband's family were, in reality, supported by her natal family. Most important, for over one year after the wedding, and for extended periods afterward, the marriage was uxorilocal.[34] This aspect of her marriage easily slips our attention as a result of the standard language of wifely exemplarity adopted by both Yuan and her eulogizers, all of whom claim that she began to perform her wifely duties as soon as she "entered" her husband's family. Only when we spot the word *zhui* ("an uxorilocal marriage") in her writings do we realize that her marriage was in fact arranged the other way around:

> In the year Xinyou [1801], [Wu Jie] competed for the position of a tribute student. At the time my grandfather Mr. Botian supervised the provincial level of civil service examination for the Circuit of Hangzhou and Jiaxing, Zhejiang. Wu Jie was handsome and delicate in appearance and refined in demeanor. . . . Mr. Botian turned to the people around him and commented: "What an outstanding youth—he can be compared to the most precious dish on a banquet! He would be a good match for the daughter [of a good family]. It is a pity that he is already married." For a long time he went on with his praises. During the Twelfth Month of this year, Wu Jie's original wife, Lady Yuan, passed away. During the spring of the following year, Renxu [1802], he came to visit [my grandfather's] office. Mr. Botian . . . hired a go-between [to propose marriage to the Wu household] and arranged that I be engaged [to Wu Jie]. Then he invited [Wu Jie] to study in his official abode and hired an erudite scholar to be Wu Jie's instructor. The next year, Guihai [1803], saw the completion of the wedding ceremony of *an uxorilocal marriage* [my emphasis].[35]

In short, Yuan did not "enter" the Wu household to perform her wifely duties. Rather Wu Jie married into the Yuan household by having "an uxorilocal marriage." Although the eulogizers are unanimous in their silence regarding this fact, uxorilocal marriages were in fact not uncommon during this time, particularly in the Yangzi delta. Powerful families tended to arrange uxorilocal marriages for their daughters as a "social mobility strategy"—a means of recruiting talented young scholars to enhance the families' chances for success in degree competition and, hence, to perpetuate their elite status. Their concern with family status prompted them to take an active interest in the education of their uxorilocal sons-in-law.[36]

Yuan Botian's eagerness in arranging the marriage was therefore
motivated by more than simply his fondness for Wu Jie's appearance
or demeanor. The following entry from the local gazetteer of Kuaiji
is illuminating: "Wu Jie's courtesy name was Zhuoshi, and his style
name was Meiliang. In his tender years he was exceptionally talented
and was known as a child prodigy. He entered the county school when
he was fourteen [in 1796]. At the time, Grand Secretary Ruan Yuntai [Ruan Yuan] was paying an official visit to Zhejiang and, when
he met Wu Jie, he was deeply impressed by the boy's talent."[37] The
entry goes on to describe the way Grand Secretary Ruan Yuan (1764–
1849) tested Wu Jie's talent, asking the young man to compose, on
the spot, a poem on a given subject. Wu's immediate response won
Ruan's approval. The same account can be found in Yuan Jingrong's
biography of Wu, which adds that Wu's composition led Ruan to pre-
dict that he had a brilliant future ahead of him.[38]

It was Wu's exceptional talent, then, that drew the attention of
Yuan Botian. It is even probable that Yuan Botian had already heard
of Wu's reputation as a prodigy before he met the young man at the
exam. Since Yuan Jingrong had a younger brother, Kejia,[39] Yuan
Botian did not seek out Wu as his grandson-in-law out of a concern
over the continuation of his patriline. Rather, probably fearing a
potential decline in his family's status over time (his son, Yuan Houtang, had only reached the level of county magistrate), Yuan Botian
was eager to seek ways to improve the family's chances for future success. His active involvement in Wu's education, which started even
before Wu's marriage to his granddaughter, also indicates his concern
with the civil service competition.

In terms of the present discussion, the most crucial issue is not
the uxorilocal marriage itself as much as its consequences. We might
well wonder how Wu's uxorilocal marriage would affect the family
dynamics in the wake of his rise to power.

A CHANGE IN FAMILY FORTUNES

To approach an understanding of this issue, it is necessary to first consider the flexible nature of uxorilocal marriages among the Qing literati. In contrast to the prevailing situation among lower social groups,
among the Qing literati little stigma was attached to uxorilocal marriage. This was, first of all, because the uxorilocal couple were not
required to change the surname of their children. This meant that

the husband in an uxorilocal marriage had the freedom to decide the patriline of his offspring. He was also able to determine, or at least influence, the affairs of his own patriline. In addition the duration of uxorilocal residence was normally short, lasting only several years before the couple switched to a virilocal residence.[40]

Beginning in the Yuan period, legal codes mandated that both families involved in an uxorilocal marriage sign a contract to specify its terms. Once the uxorilocally married man satisfied the time requirement, he was free to return to his own patriline, and the marriage would be regarded as exactly the same as virilocal marriages. The contract should serve to clarify patriline and property issues, such as which patriline the uxorilocally married man and his offspring belonged to, whether he was entitled to properties of his own family or his wife's, and which household had claim to what he earned.[41] Yet in practice uxorilocal marriages among the Qing literati were so flexible that they often did not involve a contractual agreement.[42]

In the case of Wu Jie's marriage to Yuan Jingrong, there is no evidence of the existence of such a contract. It also appears that the couple constantly changed their residence, so their marriage was neither uxorilocal nor virilocal in the strict sense. A little over a year after their wedding, the couple moved out of Yuan Botian's official abode and into the Wu household in Kuaiji. But since Wu Jie frequently traveled and sometimes returned to live in Yuan Botian's official abode, Yuan Jingrong constantly moved back and forth between the Wu household in Kuaiji, her grandfather's official abode, and Wu Jie's county-level posts. Wu Jie's father also moved several times, first to Yuan Botian's official abode, then to the house that Yuan Botian purchased for Wu Yongqing, and, after Wu Jie assumed his post in the Hanlin Academy, to Beijing. In the following years, when Wu Jie was assigned to a number of posts in Hunan, Sichuan, Guizhou, and Guangdong, Yuan Jingrong moved even more frequently, sometimes residing in Wu's various official abodes, sometimes in Kuaiji, and sometimes traveling to meet her father-in-law, who would join Wu and her. This means that Wu's father also moved between Kuaiji and Wu's official posts. It was not until nineteen years after her wedding that Yuan Jingrong finally settled down with Wu in Beijing, when he served first as the capital magistrate and, soon after, as the vice minister of rites. It seems, however, that there were still times when she or Wu's father moved between Kuaiji and Beijing.[43] Here is a brief chronology of Yuan's changes of residence:

1803: Yuan Jingrong marries Wu Jie.

1803–4: The couple reside in Yuan Botian's official abode in
Zhejiang.

1804: The couple join the Wu family in Kuaiji for three months
before returning to Zhejiang; later they rejoin the Wu family.

1807: Wu Jie takes a teaching job in Beijing; Yuan Jingrong stays in
Kuaiji.

1809: Yuan Jingrong and Wu Yonghe join Yuan Botian at his official
abode in Jiangxi; Yuan Botian arranges for Wu Yonghe to stay
with Wu Yongqing in a new house, while Yuan Jingrong stays
with Yuan Botian.

1811: Wu Jie returns from Beijing to Jiangxi and stays in Yuan
Botian's official abode for four months; when Yuan Botian is
assigned to a post in Beijing, Wu Jie becomes secretary to an
official in Jiangxi and Yuan Jingrong joins Wu Yonghe and Wu
Yongqing in their new house in Jiangxi; when Yuan Botian is
reassigned to Jiangxi, Wu Jie and Yuan Jingrong again stay in his
official abode.

1814: Wu Jie is awarded the *jinshi* degree and assigned to a post
in Beijing; on leave in autumn he visits Yuan Jingrong and Wu
Yonghe in Jiangxi.

1817: Wu Jie is assigned to a post in the Hanlin Academy; in the
winter Yuan Jingrong and Wu Yonghe join him in Beijing.

1817–33: Wu Jie serves on various posts in Hunan, Sichuan,
Guizhou, and Guangdong, and Yuan Jingrong moves constantly
between his official abodes and Kuaiji.[44]

1833: Wu Jie is appointed capital magistrate, and Yuan Jingrong and
Wu Yonghe join him in Beijing.

1834: Wu Yonghe moves to Kuaiji.

1835: Yuan Jingrong and her two sons visit Wu Yonghe in Kuaiji.

1836: Wu Jie dies; Yuan Jingrong and Wu Yonghe return to Beijing.

1837: Wu Yonghe moves to Kuaiji; Yuan Jingrong and her two sons
stay in Beijing.[45]

It was the extreme flexibility of their marriage that led to a high
degree of ambiguity in Yuan Jingrong and Wu Jie's family relationships. Most important, while all of the eulogizing accounts of Yuan

represent her as a devoted household manager, we might, in the light
of the above discussion, wonder which household she was managing.
Yuan's own description of who had authority over household management directly contradicts the eulogizing accounts:

> [During those times when I lived in Kuaiji,] to begin with, there were
> no decent household belongings. My late father-in-law was in charge
> of all household matters. I always asked for his permission when-
> ever there was anything to be dealt with and dared not ask too many
> questions. He would not tell me anything either. . . . Although [after
> my husband started to hold office] our financial situation improved
> and we started to purchase land and properties, my late father-in-law
> still maintained sole control over the family finances [duzi zhucai].
> Some of the Wu kinsmen, thinking that he would back them up,
> gained control over these assets. Although I wanted to make inquiries
> [regarding the assets], in the end I dared not. Even when we lived in
> the official abodes of my husband, my late father-in-law took control
> of all incomes and expenditures. All I could do was fulfill my filial
> duty as his daughter-in-law.[46]

Yuan conveys several messages here. First, despite her well-doc-
umented and frequent changes of residence between her natal and
marital families, she portrays a more conventional familial structure,
with her father-in-law at the top, enjoying the authority of the patriarch, while she plays the role of a filial and obedient daughter-in-
law. However, she is also subtly questioning that structure and her
father-in-law's authority, in particular in regard to his management of
the family fortune. Twice she emphasizes the fact that she dared not
inquire about the family finances, even when she wanted to do so. She
also suggests that the family wealth was derived solely from Wu Jie's
income; she emphasizes again that the Wu household was originally
destitute. Finally, her open criticism of the Wu kinsmen—namely,
that they relied on Wu Yonghe's power to exert control over the assets
(zhangshi bachi)—clearly states that they have no just claim to these
assets. The passage also criticizes Wu Yonghe because, according to
Yuan, it was due to his monopolization of the household management
that the family lost control of its wealth. In short, Yuan's passage is
primarily concerned with establishing who is justified in exerting control over the family wealth.

In a typical household during this time, the power structure was
straightforward. The most senior patrilineal descendant, the patriarch, occupied the position at the top of the hierarchy, with his sons
and their families occupying, successively, the lower rungs. The sons

were heads of their own households, but, before the family underwent household division (the equal division of the father's properties
among his sons),[47] these households were subsumed under one large
household headed by the patriarch. The guiding principle for this large
household was "cohabitation and common properties" (*tongju gongcai*),[48] meaning that household members who lived together exercised
shared management of the household properties (*jiachan*) that were
handed down by the previous generations of the family. The patriarch
held supreme power over the household properties.[49] According to
the Qing legal code, any junior member who took possession of the
household wealth without the consent of the patriarch was subject to
punishment.[50]

These straightforward rules, however, cannot be applied in this
case. The ambiguity lies primarily in Wu Jie's status: Which patriline
did he belong to? Since there was no contract specifying the duration
of his uxorilocal marriage, there are two possibilities. One is that he
never officially returned to his own patriline. In this case neither Wu
Yonghe nor the Wu kinsmen had any claim to Wu Jie's earnings from
his official posts. In records of a legal case from the Yuan period, for
example, the brothers of an uxorilocally married man failed to lay
claim to his properties in the process of household division.[51] The
other possibility is that, from a certain point on, Wu Jie returned
to his own patriline, though perhaps without an official contract. In
this case ambiguity arises regarding the principle of cohabitation and
common properties. Even excluding the periods during which Yuan
resided with her natal family, she still lived with various households
in different locations, as opposed to a single "Wu household" with a
stable number of cohabitants. In other words, since the main family
members—Wu Yonghe (and sometimes his concubines as well), Wu
Jie, and Yuan Jingrong (and sometimes their children)—were constantly on the move, the principle of cohabitation did not apply. The
principle of common properties was also not applicable to their situation, since, as Yuan makes clear, no household property had been
passed down to Wu Yonghe in the first place. Consequently Wu Yonghe's right to exclusive control of the family wealth was thrown into
question.

Yuan's use of the term *yingyang* (to have one's parents to stay in
one's household in order to provide for them) to qualify Wu Yonghe's
financial situation is also illuminating.[52] The term should apply to situations after household division. The Qing legal code mandated that,

when dividing household properties, arrangements should be made
to support the parents. The consequence of household division was
therefore that the father no longer enjoyed supreme power over all
household properties. Rather, a share should be left for the parents
to live on; alternatively they should be provided for by the sons.[53]
Although there were no household properties to divide in Wu Jie's
case, Yuan asserts that he and his natal family lived in different locations and had control over a different number of properties. To apply
yingyang to Wu Yonghe is equal to saying that he was invited to stay
in Wu Jie's household—just like a parent who is supported by his son
after household division—and that he should not hold supreme power
over household properties.

Simply because of the attention that Yuan draws to Wu Jie's salaries from official posts, we can sense her anxiety regarding who would
control the newly earned wealth. With Wu's rise to power came a vis-
ible change in the family's source of income. This change also marks
a corresponding shift in the focus of Yuan's writings; she no longer
emphasizes her virtuous use of her dowry and the support from her
natal family and instead concentrates on Wu's salary, or *lianfeng*. The
use of the character *lian* emphasizes his integrity, implying that he did
not earn his income by corrupt means. Significantly the term *lian* may
also be associated with the subsidy system for Qing officials. Scholars
have noted that, although salaries for Qing officials were much lower
than during previous dynasties, the Qing government developed a
system of "subsidy to cultivate integrity" (*yanglian yin*) as a means of
preventing the corruption associated with low salaries. The subsidy
for higher-ranking officials could be as high as twenty thousand taels
of silver per year.[54]

Although Yuan does not specify the exact amount of Wu's salary, she does imply its abundance. For example, she recounts an episode in which Wu used two thousand taels of his own income to help
the grain suppliers in Hunan when he was posted there.[55] According
to Yuan, he also covered all of his family's living expenses and purchased a house for his father, in addition to the land and properties
in his native home.[56] He even extended his support to his uncle Wu
Yongqing, a fact that Yuan mentions several times, for example, "Mr.
Lizhai [style name of Wu Yongqing] was compassionate in nature and
was always happy to lend his help to other people. Plus, he had a
big family to provide for and his income was barely enough to cover
his expenses. His debts therefore amounted to thousands of taels of

silver. . . . When he escorted some loads of paint to the capital, my
late husband paid off all his debts."[57] Elsewhere she reveals that Wu
Jie not only solved his uncle's financial problems but in fact saved him
from ruin. It turns out that, when Wu Yongqing escorted the paint to
the capital, the government found that a portion of the official funds
in his charge was missing. Wu Jie intervened and saved Wu Yongqing from being impeached. He then used his own income to cover
the missing funds for which Wu Yongqing was held responsible.[58] It
is unclear whether Wu Yongqing had embezzled the funds to pay his
debts or these missing funds were in fact the "debts" that Yuan refers
to. In any case, according to Yuan, Wu Jie saved his uncle as well as
his entire family from scandal.

Moreover, after Wu Yongqing died, Wu Jie paid for all of the
funeral and burial expenses, to the extent that he also purchased a
piece of land on which to build the tomb.[59] Yuan uses this fact to glorify Wu Jie's devotion, saying that he "valued his family roots and
cared for his kin [dunben xuqin]."[60] Yet elsewhere her tone is critical:
"The late uncle of my husband had many children and grandchildren,
and it would seem that his funeral and burial would not need to rely
on other people's help. On the contrary, however, it fell on my late
husband alone to handle all of these matters."[61] Yuan is clearly criti-
cizing the "many children and grandchildren" who failed to take care
of Wu Yongqing's burial.[62] She also takes pains to emphasize that
there was nothing that Wu Jie would not do to take care of his kin
and that he did so relying only on his salary. Therefore she makes the
case that neither his father nor his kin had the right to lay claim to his
properties after all he had done for them.

THE FIGHT OVER INHERITANCE

Wu Jie died in 1836, at the age of fifty-four. Of his four sons, only
his twins by his concubine Cao survived. These two young boys were
thus the sole heirs to the family fortune. As their legal mother, Yuan
should have enjoyed custodial rights over the household properties.[63]
However, she soon found that there was nothing left over which she
could exert her rights:

> I was ill when news of my husband's death reached his native home
> in Kuaiji. Upon hearing the news, I grieved so much that I lost con-
> sciousness. . . . [When I arrived at the capital,] I wept by the side
> of his coffin and was determined to follow him in death. I realized,

however, that my father-in-law was eighty years old and that my sons were only four. It was up to me to serve the elderly and raise the young. Therefore, together with my father-in-law, I took account of what my husband had saved. In his trunks there were only documents, books, and clothes; no funds were left. We went through his account books and found that, during the past twenty-odd years, during which he had served in official posts everywhere from Sichuan to the capital, he had continued to send all that he saved from his salaries to my father-in-law. He kept a careful record of exactly when and from where [he sent the money], and [it is clear from the records that] he had saved no funds at all for himself. He can indeed be qualified as one who was filial to his parents and who was able to cultivate his [virtuous] intent!

I then tried to devise a plan for providing for my father-in-law and my sons. I arranged a meeting with my husband's disciples, told them about my concerns, and asked for their advice. They all said: " . . . For the present, it is better that, for convenience' sake, the household members live separately in the south and in the north. When sons of our mentor grow up, they can come up with a long-term plan. Since our mentor's father is advanced in years and is not used to living in the north, it would be better if he return to the south and live on the properties there. Besides, he has a concubine and a younger son at home to serve him. As for your ladyship, the best plan would be for you to stay in the capital to raise your sons. We will all send you living supplies to repay the kindness of our mentor . . . ." I thought that this was good advice. Grand Secretaries Pan Zhixuan and Ruan Yuntai and Censor-in-Chief of the Left Yao Bo'ang were my husband's mentors. They also considered this good advice and spoke to me about it. Thus I made up my mind.

The next year, Dingyou [1837], my father-in-law returned to Kuaiji, while I stayed in the capital and hired an instructor for my sons. I relied on the aid from my husband's disciples to cover all my living expenses.[64]

At this point Yuan does not mention the issue of inheritance. The emotions she expresses are those that would be considered appropriate for a woman in her situation. However, her direct discussion of the financial difficulties she faced after Wu's death is also prompted by her filial piety and motherly concerns. Contrary to the praiseful descriptions of her meticulous household management found in the eulogizing accounts about her, she discloses that she was unable to find out about the accounts until after Wu's death. According to her own account, she was left destitute, unsure of how she could "serve the elderly and raise the young." Moreover there is a pointed contradiction between her expression of her filial concerns and her claim that all of the family wealth had, in fact, gone to her father-in-law. Upon reading her account, we realize that Wu Yonghe not only exercised exclusive control over the properties in Kuaiji but had also been receiving all of Wu Jie's savings. Yuan even provides specific evidence to support her claim that Wu Jie had given his savings to Wu Yonghe, stating that Wu Jie had "kept a careful record of exactly when and from where" he sent the money. Elsewhere she restates this fact by emphasizing that Wu Jie "had never in private given anything [from his salaries] to his wife and children [*congwu siji qinu zhe*]."[65] And she persists with her question: Since Wu Jie had left nothing at all to her, what could she possibly use to provide for her father-in-law now?

What is crucial here is not just the tension laid bare by these contradictory statements but also that they explain the temporary arrangements concerning household division. Although these arrangements were never made official, the next year the household was divided as follows: Wu Yonghe returned to Kuaiji to live on the family properties with his concubine and younger son, while Yuan stayed in her Beijing home with her sons, as well as Wu Jie's concubine Cao (whom she does not mention here).[66] To prove that these arrangements were entirely to the benefit of her father-in-law, Yuan provides a meticulous list of the donations from Wu Jie's disciples, on which she relied to cover all of her living expenses:

> [Wu Jie's disciples who held office in] the two provinces of Zhili and Sichuan offered small donations here and there which together reached the considerable amount of over six thousand taels of silver. Some of these donations were used to purchase properties, and some were put in banks to yield interest. All of the bonds and deeds are currently held by [Wu's] disciple Peng Yuwen, who currently serves as the Tianjin Circuit Intendant. At the initiative of the disciple Zhang Xigeng, who earned his *jinshi* degree in the Bingshen [1836] Civil Service Examination, the candidates who earned their degrees in 1836 together donated six hundred taels of silver. These donations were put in a bank to earn a monthly interest, which served to cover [my] living expenses. Afterwards, [Zhang] withdrew them from the bank to purchase properties for me. At New Year's or other festivals, disciples in the capital, as well as those in the provinces, always sent me funds. Thus, I was able to stay in our home in Beijing, using the remaining years of my life to raise my orphaned sons.[67]

This detailed inventory of the donations and their investment provides valuable documentation of the support system that helped the elite deal with family crises. Even more relevant to the present discussion is the way Yuan unambiguously asserts that all of the remaining Wu household wealth had gone to her father-in-law, so that what she had at her disposal—including the properties purchased with the donations—had nothing to do with the Wu family wealth. She also implies that the present arrangements were only temporary and that Wu Jie's sons would assert their right of inheritance when they grew up.[68]

In 1838 one of Wu Jie's twin sons died, leaving this household with only one heir.[69] A series of Yuan's poems from early summer of 1841 indicate the emotional stress she was under during these years. Seeing a pair of swallows finding shelter in her house, she writes four poems to express her delight at seeing this propitious sign. Such delight soon gives way to self-pity as she relates her own life to the swallows busy building their nest. Her self-pity in turn leads her to write four more poems to mourn her late husband and her son who had died fifteen years before (i.e., Wu Enxi, whom she refers to as En'er). She uses the metaphor of a lonely swallow that has lost its companion to characterize her own situation, and expresses her grief at her son's death when she dreams of his last moments. When the swallows leave her house bound for the south in the autumn, she writes yet another four poems, this time lamenting her lack of freedom to follow them to her (natal) home. The reason for her lack of freedom, as she states in the lines that close this long sequence of poems, is that she is hindered by her duties of raising her "orphaned fledgling [guchu]"—namely, the only surviving heir of her husband.[70]

These emotional poems stand out from the majority of the pieces included in Yuan's collection of poetic works (a thin volume, which suggests that she did not resort to this means of self-expression very often). While her other poetic works from this period serve mainly socializing purposes,[71] her sequence of poems on swallows provides rare glimpses into her grief, self-pity, and lament over her situation. Most important, they reflect her anxieties about ensuring the legitimate rights of Wu Jie's heir and, by extension, her own custodial rights. It is particularly revealing that she should be mourning her son Enxi, who had died fifteen years before, instead of mourning the more recent death of the twin. Yuan had given birth to two sons: the elder, Wenxi, in the spring of 1819, and the younger, Enxi, in the eleventh lunar month of 1820.[72] Wenxi died only a few months after his birth. The birth of Enxi brought Wu and Yuan great joy. He was a particularly cherished child in the family and was exceptionally talented in his tender years. The couple gave him an alternative name, Huisheng (literally "born to be talented") precisely due to his precocious talent. Unfortunately Enxi died of a serious ulcer in his leg before he reached the age of eight, in the sixth lunar month of 1827. Yuan was heartbroken and never recovered entirely from the tragedy. In a biographical account she included in *Biographies and Brief Records*—titled, ironically, "A Biography for My Child Wenxi" (Wenxi tongzi zhuan)—she gives poignant voice to her memories of Enxi's life after only briefly mentioning Wenxi as her eldest son, writing lovingly of Enxi's numerous merits that made him a prodigy. She ends her account by stating that, during all those years after Enxi's death, she would always burst into tears whenever she took out a portrait of him and wonders why such a promising life had been cut short by illness.[73] She also included a funerary epitaph and a sequence of mourning poems that Qian Yiji (1783–1850), a former colleague of Wu Jie, had written for Enxi. Qian's writings glorify Enxi's promising talent as well as the filial piety and virtues he had already demonstrated as a young child.[74]

Surely Enxi would have solved the problems confronting Yuan if he had lived. He would have been twenty-one in 1841 and thus able to legitimately claim his inheritance. Given his precocious talent and filial piety, he would even have been able to head the household and preclude any dispute on the household properties in the wake of Wu Jie's death (he would have been sixteen in 1836). Yuan's mourning poems for Enxi in 1841 therefore reveal much about her anxieties regarding inheritance issues—anxieties worsened by the death of the twin.

In 1844 Wu Yonghe died in Kuaiji, and, about one month later, his younger son Wu Qiu also died. Yuan took the only surviving heir of Wu Jie, a boy of eleven, on a trip back to Kuaiji. Upon their arrival she was shocked by what she found:

> Without anyone to head the household, all of the remaining clothes and household wares had either been destroyed or had been sold by [my late father-in-law's concubine] woman Chen, so that not a single thing was left. My late father-in-law's tomb had also been opened by woman Chen and was left in ruins. At first I felt outraged, and then was filled with deep sorrow. In grief I sighed and said to myself: "Now that my husband is dead, and the orphan he left is but a child of tender age, whom can I count on but myself to bury my father-in-law? This matter [burial] can no longer be delayed." Therefore I sold my jewelry and pawned my clothes—indeed used up all that I had and went through all kinds of hardships to deal with the matter.[75]

A fight over inheritance had no doubt already started before Yuan and her son arrived. Elsewhere she reveals even more about this fight:

> I started to inquire about household matters, and the Wu kinsmen all put the blame on each other and said that they themselves knew nothing about such matters. When I asked what remained of the clothes, household wares, antiques, and heirlooms, I found that they had all been destroyed or sold by woman Chen, my late father-in-law's concubine; not a single thing remained. Then, I questioned the person who had managed household matters while my late father-in-law was alive and tried to obtain from him the account ledgers that recorded incomes and expenditures. The answer that I got was: "There are none." I then made a thorough search [of the house], and I only found the bonds and deeds for the land and mountain properties, and even these documents were incomplete and in utter disorder. I made every effort to sort them out. It was only after much trouble that I finally started to get a sense of the documents' initial order.[76]

To learn more about these bonds and deeds we need only refer to Yuan's inventory of the remaining family properties:

> My examination revealed that what remained [of the family properties] were merely: lake fields of thirty-seven *mu*, six *fen*, four *li* and four *hao*; mountain fields of fifteen *mu*, one *fen*, two *li* and eight *hao*; mountain land, for tombs, of two hundred and twenty-four *mu*, three *fen*, three *li* and six *hao*.[77] I then set aside an account book for each of the above categories and carefully kept these account books in a trunk for the reference of later generations. In regards to the mountain land for tombs, when I checked the original account books for rent incomes from the past years, I found that only a little over a hundred *mu* of the land [was accounted for], while the rest was not mentioned in the accounts. I again checked what had been omitted and added it to the accounts—altogether the land reached over two hundred *mu*. . . . However, what remained was but a small fraction of what had formerly been owned by the household. From this point forward, I have taken it upon myself to personally examine the rent incomes accruing from the lake fields, the mountain fields, and the mountain lands [for tombs] and set aside this new account book [i.e., *Meifang shouzu bu* (Account book for the rent incomes of Wu Jie's household)] to keep a meticulous record of them. [Indeed I know the figures by heart as if] I could hold them in my palm and point out their specific amounts [*liaoruo zhizhang*]. . . . There are still mountain lands labeled "Si" and "Wen," as well as fields labeled "Wei" and "Shou," for which the documents are not complete. . . . I am going to conduct further investigation [into this matter].[78]

It would seem that the purposes of Yuan's trip were not only to bury her father-in-law but also to take over the accounts for the family properties.[79] She was obstructed at every turn, however, by the Wu kin and the household servants, not to mention woman Chen, who had been quick to snatch whatever she could lay her hands on. As Yuan informs us, this woman Chen was one of Wu Yonghe's concubines and the mother of Wu Qiu.

At this point it is necessary to briefly consider the inheritance rights of concubines. The Qing code, in line with the legal codes of previous dynasties, defined the status of the concubine as subordinate to the principal wife in all aspects, including inheritance.[80] This explains Yuan's utter exclusion of Wu Jie's concubine Cao from the decision-making process. It was almost as if Cao existed only in her capacity as biological mother to Wu Jie's children. Regarding woman Chen's status, however, ambiguity soon arises. One of the innovations of the Qing legal code concerning the inheritance rights of the concubine was that, in the absence of the widowed wife, the widowed concubine could enjoy full custodial rights over her husband's properties as long as she did not remarry. The Qing code also expanded the widow's right to appoint an heir in the event that the household was left with no heir. In this aspect as well the widowed concubine could be treated just as if she had been the widowed wife, if the wife was deceased.[81] As legal cases from the Qing period illustrate, "a concubine often did assume the role of family matriarch after the wife's death and the role of *de facto* head of the household after her husband's death."[82] Was woman Chen acting in these capacities?

Given the ambiguity of Wu Jie's status, this may well have been the case. If Wu Jie were treated as an uxorilocally married son who never returned to his own patriline, he, and by extension his son, would be excluded from the inheritance of the Wu family wealth. Even though the wealth, as Yuan insists, came solely from Wu Jie's income, it was always under the de facto control of Wu Yonghe, as well as of the Wu kin. The arrangements that Yuan made following Wu Jie's death to a certain extent recognized this control. In this case woman Chen, as the sole widow of Wu Yonghe, was entitled by law to act as the household head and appoint an heir of her choice. She was also entitled to full custodial rights over the family wealth.[83]

Yuan clearly favors a different interpretation of the situation and represents woman Chen as a thief who stole the family wealth and even as a grave robber. Yuan's actions—such as conducting thorough searches of the house and sorting out what she found—bespeak her intention to take matters into her own hands. She intends to eliminate any ambiguity regarding Wu Jie's status by asserting that he had been an active member of his own patriline and had made every effort to take care of his own kin. Consequently his son is the rightful heir to the wealth that he alone had earned.[84] (See Figs. 3.02 and 3.03 for a list of the descendants in the Wu household and the possible chains of inheritance.)

Yuan's meticulous inventory in particular intimates her determination to assert her right to control the family wealth. By claiming a thorough knowledge of the family properties, down to the smallest fraction, she precludes any further "hiding" (*ni*) of assets by the Wu kin. At the same time, precisely by condemning the control of the properties by the Wu kin as an illegitimate act of "hiding," she asserts the legitimacy of her own control. And she announces her determination to conduct further investigations. Her statement that what she had recovered was but a small fraction of the family's original properties suggests that she was fighting for a fairly significant inheritance.

These overt criticisms differentiate Yuan's from the many genealogy writings by male authors during this time. Recent studies have delineated the great developments of genealogy writings during the Qing period and have shown how these writings helped create cohesion among lineages and indoctrinate kinship values and discipline among the lineage members. A distinctly moral tone often characterizes these writings, to the effect that the family and lineage histories as recounted by these writings are governed by the principles of benevolence and filial piety (*renxiao*) rather than the kind of family dispute laid bare by Yuan.[85]

THE SUPREME IMPORTANCE OF ANCESTRAL RITES

Let us return to the issue of ancestral rites, the importance of which cannot be overemphasized. Scholars have long recognized the centrality of ritual, and especially of ancestral rites, to the Confucian ideal of an orderly society. For example, ancestral rites served to create a hierarchical organization among the living, in addition to shaping conceptions of the relationship between the living and the dead.[86] Such hierarchical organization was crucial to rank and gender distinctions in society at large and also influenced how individuals perceived their relationships to each other within a close community,

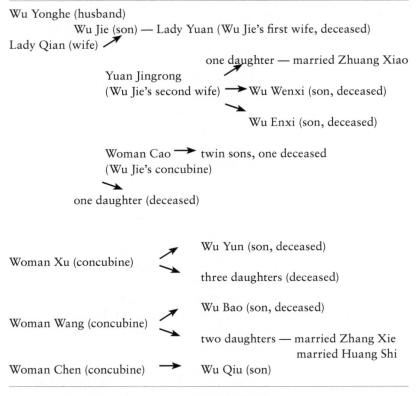

Figure 3.02.   Descendants of the Wu household.

such as a lineage. The sequence of ancestral rites assigned a proper role to each of the lineage members in the service of their common ancestors and hence defined both their status within the lineage and their relationship to each other. The direct equation between inclusion in the ancestral rites and lineage membership underlies the case of Wu Jie and his heir.[87]

It would of course be an oversimplification to attribute all of Yuan's commendable efforts to a practical desire to ensure her son's inheritance as opposed to her devotion to ritual propriety. Yet it is equally misguided to underestimate the way her emphasis on ancestral rites gained her leverage in her fight for inheritance. By assigning herself and, above all, Wu Jie's household (including Wu Jie himself and his heir) a proper place within the Wu lineage, she was able to erase any ambiguity regarding Wu Jie's status. To return to the very

1) Wu Jie had not returned to his own patriline:

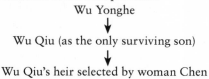

Wu Yonghe
↓
Wu Qiu (as the only surviving son)
↓
Wu Qiu's heir selected by woman Chen

2) Wu Jiu had returned to his own patriline, with Wu Yonghe serving as the household head:

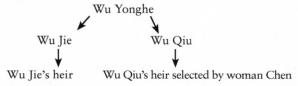

Wu Yonghe

Wu Jie   Wu Qiu
↓   ↓
Wu Jie's heir   Wu Qiu's heir selected by woman Chen

3) Wu Jie had returned to his own patriline, serving as the household head and the owner of all household properties:

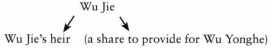

Wu Jie

Wu Jie's heir   (a share to provide for Wu Yonghe)

Figure 3.03.   Possibilities of Inheritance Sequence in the Wu household. The third possibility is the case Yuan argued for: that the share set aside to provide for Wu Yonghe should, after his death, be returned to Wu Jie's heir.

first sentence of *Biographies and Brief Records*: "*Our Wu lineage* [my emphasis] has lasted for nearly five hundred years, since, during the Hongwu reign of the former Ming dynasty, Mr. Zhonghe moved [his family] from the east of the Yangzi River to the Yue area."[88] In identifying the Wu lineage as "our Wu lineage," Yuan represents her marriage as being no different from a more conventional virilocal marriage wherein the wife became a member of the husband's lineage. Her claim of membership in the Wu clan implies her intention to clarify Wu Jie's status as a descendant of the Wu lineage. In fact she identifies herself precisely by identifying Wu Jie and by specifying his status in his own lineage branch: "Authored with reverence by née Yuan, [courtesy name] Jingrong, the second wife of the fourteenth-generation descendant, Wu Jie."[89]

In addition she states that it was all thanks to Wu Jie that the Wu ancestors were granted official titles by the court: "To note: Mr.

Duzhai [Wu Jie's great-grandfather] . . . was granted the title of 'Minister of Glory and Fortune' because of the official rank achieved by the master [Wu Jie]. . . . His [Mr. Duzhai's] wife, the Grand Lady Tang [Wu Jie's great-grandmother] . . . was granted the title of 'Lady of the First Rank' because of the official rank achieved by the master [Wu Jie]."[90] Yuan proceeds to list the titles that were granted to Wu Jie's grandparents and parents. The system of title-granting (*fengzeng*) can be traced back to the Tang dynasty and continued into later periods. Basically it was a system in which the forbearers of an official were granted titles as a means of glorifying his lineage.[91] If, as Yuan asserted, Wu Jie's lineage was glorified on his account, there should be no question of the legitimacy of his status within his own lineage.

Moreover, because ambiguity often arose concerning the offspring of the uxorilocally married man,[92] Yuan also takes care to clarify the status of Wu Jie's son:

> During the Eighth Month of the year Jiachen [1844], the fifteenth-generation descendant [missing characters] accompanied his mother to return to his native place in order to have his grandfather buried. After the burial was completed, during the Eleventh Month, he arranged a meeting with his kin by the order of his mother and discussed with them: "The purpose of establishing the lineage ancestral hall is to perform ancestral rites and to unite the kin."[93]

The logic here is that if Wu Jie's son could have a meeting with his kinsmen as the "fifteenth-generation descendant" of the Wu lineage to discuss the restoration of the lineage ancestral hall, there should be no question of his status as the only heir to Wu Jie.

Finally, by designating the household of Wu Jie as "Meiliang's [Wu Jie's] household" and establishing the sequence of household ancestral rites, Yuan confirms Wu Jie's status within the household:

> I authored volumes [for the two categories of ancestral rites for Wu Jie's lineage branch] and listed in detail [the source of funds for the rites]. There was only one branch left, namely, that of my late father-in-law, Mr. Meipo, and my late husband, Mr. Meiliang. Ancestral rites for this branch had not been decided upon, nor had the fields for the ancestral rites been allocated. . . . I dared not think in my own interest and donated all of the family's remaining fields—around a little over fifty-two *mu*—for this purpose. I reserved nothing at all for myself. *I changed the registered name of the fields to "Fields for the Ancestral Rites of Wu Meiliang's Household"* [my emphasis] so that the expenses arising from the ancestral rites for the branch of Mr. Meipo and Mr. Meiliang could be covered [by the rent income from

the fields]. . . . *Since the style name of my late husband was Meiliang, I have titled this volume, "Book of Ancestral Rites for Meiliang's Household"* [my emphasis].[94]

When laying out the ancestral rites for Wu Yonghe and Wu Jie's branch, Yuan refers to this branch specifically as "Wu Meiliang's household." Moreover she registered the fields under this name and used it as the title for her volume on household ancestral rites. It was Wu Jie, in short, whom she entered as the head of this household. Read in the context of the ongoing fight over inheritance, it can thus be inferred that Yuan meant to indicate that, first, as the household head, Wu Jie was entitled to supreme power over the household properties and that, second, after his death his properties should rightly go to his only surviving son. Although Wu Yonghe, as Wu Jie's father, is the subject of the first of the fifteen biographies that follow this excerpt, he is regarded as the parent for whom the son provided rather than the household head. The arrangements Yuan made in the wake of Wu Jie's death were solely intended to ensure that Wu Yonghe would continue to be provided for, with the assumption that Wu Jie's son would in the future announce his legitimate claim to the family wealth. It was exactly in this sense that Yuan condemned woman Chen as a thief. Her claim that Chen was able to plunder the wealth only because there was no one there to "head the household" precluded the possibility that, after Wu Yonghe's death, Chen would have been justified in acting as the household head.

This is of course very much Yuan's version of the story. Had woman Chen been literate and able to write her own story—or had anyone from the Wu kin chosen to write his or her own account— the family drama might have been cast in a completely different light. Some may even suspect that the story as told by Yuan is more likely about her pursuit of self-interest than a case of injustice overturned. Nevertheless it is not my intention to speculate on what really happened in this fight over inheritance, which may contradict Yuan's version of story. My interest instead lies in how Yuan chose to *represent* her role in the fight, especially how she found in genealogy writing an effective means of legitimizing her own perception of the family dispute. In other words, this case study concerns not so much the right or wrong of those involved in the family dispute as the female author's self-representation and the rhetorical strategies she used to her advantage.

A FURTHER POINT: THE ELITE SUPPORT SYSTEM

The elite support system mentioned earlier played a crucial role in helping Yuan deal with the crisis in the wake of Wu Jie's death. It organized donations for her, helped her with investments and property purchase, and advised her on arrangements for her sons and father-in-law. When she confronted the Wu clan, this support system may have exerted its influence again:

> Alas! How dare I not devote myself to the duties of burying the dead with discretion and of retracing the ancestors! . . . However, ever since I came back to Shaoxing, for several months I have been busy with the burials and the household matters. Although I dare not complain of my toil, I constantly feel that it is extremely hard to solve all of the problems [in the household] and to shoulder the responsibilities alone. Fortunately, Mr. Yang Juyuan, the Prefect of Shaoxing who was a disciple [of Wu Jie], extended his generous help to me. . . . There were innumerable occasions on which I relied on him to deal with the household matters of his former mentor. I feel truly grateful.[95]

Elsewhere Yuan reveals that "generous help" also came from other local officials who were among Wu Jie's former disciples.[96] It was these local officials who most probably backed her up in her ascent to authority among the Wu clan. It is hard to imagine, after all, that a widow accompanied only by an eleven-year-old boy could convince the Wu clan of her authority to determine their affairs, especially because her interests conflicted with theirs. As legal historians have argued, not all household disputes ended up in the courtroom. While legal cases from this period show that the courtroom may have been a preferred choice of lower social groups, the elite had their own ways of solving disputes and of providing support for each other in times of need.[97] Yuan was no doubt aware of the support that was available to her and knew exactly when and where to find it.

The rest of Yuan's life story can be supplemented by a few poetic works she wrote after she finished the burial matters in Kuaiji. She returned to Beijing in 1845.[98] She believed that the pair of swallows she had written about earlier had been following her to and fro between Kuaiji and Beijing throughout the years (or even decades). She again wrote five poems for them, praising their faithfulness to her despite the vicissitudes of her life, and comparing their hardships in traveling across thousands of miles to her own.[99] In the early summer of 1848 she adopted a five-year-old grandson named Qixun and expressed her wish that this boy would grow up to "expand my [the Wu] family and continue my [the Wu] family line."[100] This indicates that she was still very much concerned about establishing an heir to Wu Jie. A poem that she wrote sometime between 1845 and 1848 refers vaguely to her loss of her only surviving son.[101] It was imperative, then, that she find a new heir to the disputed household wealth.

During the same summer of 1848 Yuan sent her volume of poetry to her son-in-law, Zhuang Xiao, and requested his inscription.[102] While she was in Kuaiji, she showed her volume of genealogy writings to the prefect Yang Juyuan.[103] She also sent it to Zhuang Xiao in 1844, and he in turn sent it to Zhuang Zhongfang.[104] In the summer of 1848 both volumes circulated among a few of Yuan's family connections—including some of the powerful former disciples of Wu Jie, such as Shen Zhaolin—before they came out in print in the same year.[105] By this means Yuan conveyed her version of the family dispute to her elite connections and won their approval. Whether she eventually succeeded in securing her inheritance claims for her adopted grandson is beyond the scope of my discussion.

CONCLUSION

Unlike the genres discussed in the previous chapters, genealogy writing is not prevalent in women's personal collections. Neither is it explicitly autobiographical, given its predominant concern with ritual and with the lives of people as primarily constituents of a lineage's history. Despite its apparent lack of interest in personal history, however, this genre of writing opens a new window into women's self-empowerment strategies situated within a larger picture of family or lineage history.

Young women from elite families were often married to talented young scholars with great potential for future success as a social mobility strategy. In the event that the young man was lucky enough to fully realize his potential, as happened in Wu Jie's case, we would expect his wife to likewise experience the typical happy ending. That is, we would expect that the wives would be rewarded for their sacrifices and their unrelenting service to their husbands' families in good times and bad. However, as Yuan Jingrong's narrative suggests, even in cases with such happy endings the women still faced various challenges posed by the rapid rise in family status and the ensuing ambiguities and tensions.

Biographies and Brief Records exposes Yuan's skillful negotiation of the challenges confronting her. To a great extent the collection was itself a powerful strategy with which she dealt with these challenges. By authoring family histories and setting down in writing the rules governing the ancestral rites, she succeeded in resolving the greatest ambiguity in her family, namely, the status of her husband as an uxorilocally married man. Once her genealogy writings had successfully returned Wu Jie to the Wu lineage tree, she could then go on to solve the disputes surrounding the newly acquired family wealth in a way that was favorable to her husband's only heir. At the very least she could justify a claim to what had fallen into the hands of the Wu kin.

Yuan's fight for inheritance may not have ended before the collection was complete, judging from her determination to conduct further investigations and her continuing efforts to ensure an heir to the disputed family wealth. Yet she no doubt conveyed her version of the family dispute to her elite connections through the circulation and publication of her writings. Neither is there any doubt that she succeeded in establishing her reputation among these connections—not as a woman who became embroiled in tawdry fights over money and power but, on the contrary, as an exemplary wife who had devoted herself to her husband's family and lineage. Every word in *Biographies and Brief Records* emphasizes her unselfishness, her concerns with ritual, and her filial feelings toward the Wu ancestors. By employing the language of humility and virtue, she was able to preclude any accusations that she was overstepping her authority and instead win the support of her connections. In this sense this family drama testifies to one woman's extraordinary use of self-empowerment strategies, in particular her appeal to traditional conceptions of ritual propriety and female exemplarity—and all the moral authority sanctioned therein.

Enacting Guardians of Family Health

From Exemplary Wife to Reformer

Gentry women's access to medical knowledge can be attributed to the boom in commercial printing that made medical texts, along with encyclopedias and guidebooks for everyday use, widely available during the late imperial period.[1] These texts conferred medical authority and served as guides to practice. They were so ubiquitous that authors of their prefaces often complained that "ox carts are weighed down" by their volumes. In the case of *To Benefit Yin* (Jiyin gangmu), a popular late Ming medical treatise on female disorders (*fuke*), the audience was composed broadly of elite readers and commoners, including women.[2] The wide availability of medical books allowed literate women to develop medical knowledge as a domestic skill and to participate in the male-dominated medical system.[3] Gentry women from the Qing period used medical texts to help their friends and families and to distribute medicine for charitable purposes, and women paid to have medical texts on female disorders published.[4]

Since elite families with an interest in book collecting often had large collections of medical books in their private libraries, medical knowledge was easily absorbed into the family's learning and became part of the education that female family members received. We do not know the number of gentry women who obtained their medical expertise this way or the exact nature of their expertise, but the cases I discuss suggest that a gentry wife's daily chores often involved regulation of family health. Although the late Qing reformer Liang Qichao (1873–1929) deplored women's lack of practical learning—so much so that he reserved the label "new woman" for the first Chinese woman physician trained in Western medicine[5]—it is clear that medical knowledge was among the "daily basics" of gentry women's lives.

Several genres of writing preserve medical content: family letters, essays, and medical texts. "Exemplary wife" Chen Ershi (1785–1821) demonstrates that guarding family health was a daily routine for gentry wives; the woman physician, hygiene advocate, and reformer Zeng Yi (1852–1927) describes this wifely role as a source of inspiration for women of later generations to promote themselves as active agents in nation-building. The case of Wang Ying (1781–1842) serves as an interlude between the eras of these two women. Though around the same age as Chen, Wang lived to witness both the uprisings in China and the impending threats from abroad. Her interest in the common ground between medicine and statecraft therefore anticipated the incorporation of medicine into a national discourse at a slightly later time.

CHEN ERSHI: MEDICINE IN A GENTRY WIFE'S DAILY EXISTENCE

Chen Ershi was born to a gentry family in Hangzhou. Her father, Chen Shaoxiang, served as an official in the Board of Justice. She was married to Qian Yiji (1783–1850), who served consecutively in the Boards of Revenue, of Justice, and of Works and was also a well-known historian and bibliophile. Her eldest son, Qian Baohui, earned the honorific title "Filial and Upright" (*xiaolian*); he later collected a portion of Chen Ershi's writings and had them printed posthumously as her personal collection, *Posthumous Manuscripts from the Tower for Listening to the Wind through Pine Trees* (Tingsonglou yigao).[6] A few of her poems were also incorporated into the Qing anthologies of women's poetry, including *Correct Beginnings: Women's Poetry of Our August Dynasty* (Guochao guixiu zhengshi ji), *Selections of Song Lyrics by Gentry Women*, and *Poetry as Commentary on Poetry, Written in the Small Black Pavilion.*[7]

The entry on Chen Ershi in the local gazetteer of Hangzhou describes her as a woman distinguished by both her talent and her virtue. She studied the classics and history from an early age, excelled in poetry writing, and, after she was married, capably managed her household and personally educated her children.[8] She also had an important family heritage. Her great-great aunt on her husband's side, Chen Shu, was known for the *Picture [of Chen Shu] Spinning at Night and Teaching the Classics [to Her Son]*, which won imperial attention.[9] The writings that Chen Ershi authored in honor of Chen

Shu—including an epilogue to the latter's collection of paintings and a brief biography—show how highly she valued this family legacy of virtuous and accomplished women.[10]

A quick look at the titles of Chen Ershi's major works shows that she used that legacy to establish her own authority to instruct gentry wives on womanly duties and ritual propriety: *Precepts for My Daughters, Composed from the Tower for Listening to the Winds through Pine Trees* (Tingsonglou nüxun); *A Collection of Rites in the Inner Quarters* (Guimen jili); *A Collection of Wifely Duties* (Fuzhi jibian); and, *Charts for Empresses and Imperial Consorts of All Dynasties* (Lidai houfei biao). Although none of these works survived, their titles and a few of their prefaces appear in Chen's personal collection. Her preface to *A Collection of Wifely Duties*, for example, conveys her strong sense of moral authority. She passes harsh judgment on her contemporaries for their moral decline and specifies the purpose of her composition as reviving from the classics the appropriate rites for women:

> Gentleness and submission are particularly valuable among female virtues. . . . Yet due to the decline of the rites . . . whenever a woman and her sister-in-law dislike each other, they would engage in bitter disputes. Jealousy also prevails in the inner quarters. Out of jealousy a woman would prefer that the family line be cut off rather than acquire a concubine for her husband. This is all because she did not learn the proper behavior early enough in life. . . . I have therefore selected from the classics and history [teachings on wifely duties] and put them into categories, which are: respecting your parents-in-law, serving your husband, cultivating harmony in your relationship with your sisters-in-law, assisting in ancestral rites, [properly] treating your husband's concubines, instructing your children, and managing the maids and the servants.[11]

Abstract categories of wifely duties and high-minded moral principles, however, needed to be realized in the mundane details of everyday life and through the innumerable tasks that women handled in satisfying the daily needs of their families. In this sense Chen's family letters provide telling instances of how she personally fulfilled her wifely duties on a day-to-day basis.

The Quotidian Nature of Chen Ershi's Family Letters

Letters have long been a source of autobiography and biography in the Chinese literary tradition.[12] Recent studies on Chinese women's biographies also draw attention to letters as valuable records of women's lives.[13] Most of the family letters (*jiashu*) in Chen's personal collection—twenty-nine in total—were addressed to her husband, Qian Yiji, while he was away from their abode in Beijing to take care of his mother's funeral. These letters cover a period of approximately one year, from the Eighth lunar month of 1817 to the Seventh lunar month of 1818. They served as Chen's reports to her husband on daily household matters, informing him of how the household was being run in his absence. Precisely because of their quotidian nature, the letters provide intimate details of how a gentry woman performed her daily chores, details that are hard to find in other sources of women's writings such as poetry.

As these letters illustrate, the typical daily work of a gentry wife included the following: First, managing the accounts. This required not simply balancing income and expenses but also the much more complicated task of making ends meet, such as making decisions about what jewelry or household wares could go to the pawn shops, which part of the available funds should be used to cover living expenses and which part should be sent for Qian's needs, and how living expenses could be decreased. Chen's accounts go into such detail that they even mention how many winter coats were made for the children as well as the question of whether to use fire for heating in certain rooms.[14] Second, managing the maids and servants. This included assigning tasks, making sure that they do their jobs, and disciplining or expelling the unruly ones. In the event that valuables in the household went missing, Chen also needed to do a bit of detective work and decide which servant she should keep an eye on. Third, educating the children. Chen personally taught all of her children (two sons and two daughters), assigning readings according to their age and level of learning and meticulously recording their progress. She also compiled a collection of her lecture notes, titled *Noted in Random While I Taught the Classics to My Children* (Shoujing oubi). Many other matters that Chen had to deal with cannot be categorized. To name but a few: accidents that happened in house construction; a relative who was involved in litigation and needed help; a friend who came to ask for a loan; and disputes in the household that had to be resolved. As we can imagine, managing the household and creating harmony among the household members took not simply gentleness and submission on the part of the gentry wife but her patience, wisdom, energy, and, above all, practical skills.

Figure 4.01. The first page of Chen Ershi's collection of family letters, in *Tingsonglou yigao*, original page 3.1a. Reprinted by permission from the National Library of China.

Guarding Family Health

What most absorbed Chen's attention, however, was an even more basic need of the household members, namely, proper medical care. Given hygiene conditions and available medical treatments, it is not surprising that illness was a prevailing presence in the Qian household. A recent study of the Zhang family in Changzhou, for example, draws attention to a variety of diseases that posed constant threats to that family, ranging from mundane conditions to fatal epidemics, such as cholera, malaria, scarlet fever, typhoid, and measles.[15] In an age before vaccines and antibiotics, minor illnesses had the potential to rapidly become serious. Medical historians have also shown that people paid great attention to guarding their health throughout Chinese history. Consequently self-dosing based on available medical texts and techniques became a common phenomenon. There was a wide range of practices for "protecting life" (*weisheng*) and "nurturing life" (*yangsheng*).[16] This larger context explains why, judging from Chen's writings, the health of her household was a matter of intense concern to her and why she had to stay alert to even the slightest signs of its fluctuation. In her letters to her husband she constantly urges him not to worry—in itself highly indicative of the enormous pressure she was under. Table 4.01 lists the illnesses and their frequency of appearance in Chen's letters, providing a general picture of what she had to handle. (Bear in mind that these illnesses occurred within less than a year.)[17]

Over one-third of the contents of the letters concerns the measures that Chen took to treat these illnesses, including hiring the physicians, considering (and comparing) their prescriptions, discussing treatment methods with her husband, personally selecting medical formulas (from medical books), dealing with shortages of certain medicines (by concocting replacements), and taking precautions to guard the household against epidemics. Notably these measures never entered the category of wifely duties listed in Chen's preface to *A Collection of Wifely Duties*. It would seem that she simply assumed they were part of her everyday regulation of family health.

The following selection from Chen's letter dated the tenth day of the Sixth lunar month of 1818 throws more light on her working pattern, that is, how she had to watch over several health issues at once, including her own:

> It is extremely hot this year in the capital, and many epidemics broke out. A number of people in the household fell ill. Luckily, they recovered within one day or two. To my surprise, our third child has not had another onset of her eye illness—it must be that the folk prescription [that I found for her] has worked. The belly of A He is bloated, and he cries all the time—I wonder whether the following prescription would work for him? I cannot make up my mind on this. Please give me your instructions. A Ying has not been feeling very well since the start of the summer. . . . I am planning to ask Mr. Chungu [a physician] to see him again and to prescribe some energy-nourishing medicine [*buqi zhi yao*] for him. I . . . have not been affected by the measles epidemic, and have been taking my normal doses of pills. Please do not feel concerned. Since it is very hot in the south, please take good care of yourself.[18]

TABLE 4.01.   Illnesses in the Qian Household

Name of person	Name of illness	Number of appearances
Yishou (daughter)	unspecified	one
A He (son)	ulcer on back of the head	one
A He	egg-sized ulcer in the neck	two
A He	bloated belly and tendency to weep	one
A Ying (son)	unspecified	one
A Ying	weakness and lack of appetite	three
Cishou (daughter)	chronic eye problem	three
San xiaoxiao (the third young child)	ear problem	one
Si xiaoxiao (the fourth young child)	ulcer in the ear	one
A Ying, Yishou, A He	measles and fever	two
Concubine Cheng	unspecified mental problem	two
Chen Ershi	"Fire disorders"	one
Chen Ershi	hepatic disorder	one
Chen Ershi	typhoid	four
Chen Ershi	ulcers in the neck, gums, and ear	one
Qian Yiji	hemorrhoids	three
Qian Yiji	chronic coughing	two

Source: Data collected from Chen Ershi's family letters.

This inventory-like account makes it clear that handling health issues in the household was but a routine for Chen. Performing this routine, however, presumed that she had the relevant medical knowledge as well as common sense. She knew, for example, what folk medicine to use for the eye problem of one of her children. In deciding to seek the physician's help, she also had a general idea of what type of medicine her son A Ying would need. In the case of her other son, A He, we find her consulting her husband on a prescription that she had probably selected from available collections of medical formulas. This last fact also suggests that exchange of opinions on medicine was common between the couple, a point I pursue further.

The following four cases provide a sense of the knowledge in Chen's possession, each of them illuminating a particular aspect of how she incorporated medical knowledge into her routine of treating illness. Case 1, dated the twenty-eighth day of the Fifth lunar month of 1818, concerns choosing physicians:

> Ever since his minor illness early this month, Ying has been feeling fatigued, and has lost some of his appetite. I asked Mr. Wen [a physician] to diagnose him. After taking the doses of cold nourishments [*liangbu*] prescribed by Mr. Wen, Ying felt even worse. Yesterday, I took him to another physician, Mr. Chungu, who decided that he should not take cold doses because of the lack of harmony in his pulses. [Instead, Mr. Chungu gave] the following prescription: skin of trichosanthes, stir-fried with bran, three *qian*; bulbus fritillariae cirrhosae, one *qian* and a half; citrus aurantium, eight *fen*; poria, three *qian*; raw licorice, eight *fen*; coix seeds, stir-fried, three *qian*; burned grain shoots, stir-fried with earth, three *qian*; large white peony, one *qian* and a half; inula, two *qian*; wheat, one *liang*; jujube, two.[19] The doses worked very well. I am planning to take him to Mr. Chungu again tomorrow for follow-up.[20]

In making her choice between the two physicians, Chen did not just consider the factor of efficacy; her thorough account shows that she was also capable of addressing the different rationales underlying the physicians' prescriptions—for example, whether to use "cold doses" given the symptom of the pulse. Her full quotation of the second physician's prescription suggests that she was giving thought to the concoction of medicine itself and was again seeking her husband's opinion. As case 2 (date missing) demonstrates, she was capable of not only reading prescriptions but of revising them when certain components were unavailable:

> Mr. Chungu's prescription has worked very well on me. As I could not find Atractylodes macrocephala koidz, I revised the prescription by myself . . . and replaced the item with coix seeds. Having taken doses for a month, I am feeling well now, and both my sleep and my appetite are better than usual. My old symptoms have also been slightly reduced. These are the good effects [of the prescription].[21]

Case 3, dated the tenth day of the Eleventh lunar month of 1817, indicates that Chen sometimes made decisions independent of the physicians on what medicine to use. As in the previous two cases, her decision had positive effects:

> All have been well, except that our fourth child has got an ulcer in one of his ears. It has been causing him great pain. I have therefore chosen the following prescription for him: raw astragalus, two *qian*; licorice, eight *fen*; angelica, two *qian*; honeysuckle, eight *fen*; radix, two *qian*; rehmannia glutinosa libosch, two *qian*; mulberry leaves, two *qian*; skin of peony root, one *qian*; campanulaceae, three *fen*; ligusticum chuanxiong, three *fen*. I have given him two doses and his pain is gone. There is a scab forming on the ulcer. He is in good spirits now.[22]

Although Chen does not specify the source of this prescription—that is, whether she drafted it herself or chose it from prescriptions available to her—there is no doubt that she had confidence in her own ability to judge the appropriate measure to take. Case 4, dated the last day of the Tenth lunar month of 1817, provides the strongest evidence in this regard (see Figure 4.02):

> Cishou had eye problems frequently. I checked medical books and used a prescription to greatly reduce her hepatic Fire [*daxi ganhuo*]. It goes: peony root skin, stir-fried, one *qian*; frosted mulberry leaves, one *qian* and a half; white tribulus terrestris, fried, thorns removed, three *qian*; abalone calcined, three *qian*; bulbus fritillariae cirrhosae, five *fen*; north adenophora, three *qian*; poria, one *qian*; lotus leaf, one piece. She has taken five or six doses, and both the redness in her eyes and the pain are gone. The white nebula has also become thinner. She is in good spirits now. It turned out to be very effective. Now I am thinking of following up with her treatment and drafting a prescription to nourish her Yin and nurture her Liver [*ziyin yanggan*].[23]

Chen chose the appropriate treatment and decided the follow-up treatment based on the progress made. Most important, this case points unmistakably to the source of her medical knowledge, namely, the medical texts available to her. Although her writings do not indicate which specific medical texts she referred to, nor how they came into her possession, the sense of familiarity in her tone—that she mentions these texts only in passing, as a fact in her life—is in keeping with the wide availability of medical texts as a guide to practice during this time.[24]

Chen's access to medical texts is no doubt attributable to the fact that her husband was a well-known bibliophile and that the couple shared an interest in book collecting.[25] Since neither the Qian nor the Chen family was distinguished by a tradition of physicians, the

Figure 4.02. The original page for Chen Ershi's prescription for treatment of eye pain and redness, in *Tingsonglou yigao*, original page 3.7a. Reprinted by permission from the National Library of China.

couple's private collection of medical texts was more likely a hobby than a family vocation. This common interest in medicine can indeed explain the lengthy descriptions of prescriptions and treatments in Chen's letters: the couple shared a certain amount of medical knowledge and engaged in frequent conversations on the topic. In her elaborate accounts of the health issues in the household, Chen was both giving her husband an update on the household matters—as the letters were meant to do—and seeking his counsel on treatments.[26]

If we further relate the couple's collection of medical texts to the general trend of book collecting among the elite during this time, it might well be that this was not an isolated instance but a small part of a broader picture of gentry women's access to medical knowledge.

A Broader Picture of Women's Access to Medical Knowledge

Scholars have identified the Qing period as the height of book collecting in premodern China. Several facts attest to the scope of these
trends: the number of bibliophiles on record during the Qing period
exceeds that of all previous dynasties together; private libraries
expanded during this time from their former centers in the Yangzi
delta to all across the country, including such remote areas as Yun-
nan, Gansu, and Sichuan; and the books that entered private libraries covered an extremely broad range of topics, among which medical
texts were a familiar presence.[27] With book collecting becoming one
of the distinctive features of Qing elite culture widely emulated by
gentry families, any type of knowledge conveyed by the books had the
potential of becoming popularized among the families who owned
the books.

Furthermore, by the late Ming period the boundary between "literati physicians" and physicians by vocation had largely disappeared.
The flourishing of commercial printing gave rise to a medical and cultural elite composed of scholars and physicians who mingled socially
and drew from a common pool of medical knowledge available in the
widely circulating medical books. These books ranged from medical
classics to case histories, treatises of family medical traditions, collections of prescriptions, pharmacy texts, easy-to-consult handbooks,
and medical texts printed for charitable purposes. The selling point
of the extremely popular medical treatise *To Benefit Yin* was that
"not only physicians but . . . ordinary gentlemen can put a copy on
the shelf for household use."[28] This diffused nature of medical knowledge during the late Ming became even more pronounced during the
Qing period because of the continued growth in commercial printing
and book collecting. Medical historians in fact specify "self-training"
based on private collections of medical books as one of the major
forms of medical training during the Qing period (along with training
by family vocation, in government-run schools, and in private schools
established by famous physicians).[29] Given the increasing educational
opportunities and hence literacy for women in gentry families during this time, it is safe to presume that it was commonplace for these
women to refer to medical books whenever they needed to.

My focus here is not women in medical lineages—such as the "cul-
tured daughters" of physicians who assisted their fathers in medical
scholarship or practice[30]—but a much broader category of women in

gentry families who used medical knowledge as a domestic skill (see Figure 4.03). By "a much broader category" I by no means want to overstate the number of women who could be considered medical experts since we lack statistics of how many self-trained women physicians were produced during the Qing period. Instead, I am more interested in those gentry wives who did not claim the status of physicians and who left very few written records of their medical knowledge and yet could obtain at least a fair degree of such knowledge from available texts. Yi-Li Wu attributes the dearth of extant medical works by women to the probability that women lacked "networks" to help them preserve or reproduce their works.[31] The life of Chen Ershi, on the other hand, indicates that a gentry wife's interest in medicine most likely arose out of her practical need to care for her family rather than a desire to establish a medical reputation through published works.

Wang Zhenyi (1768–97), a distinguished woman scholar and poet of a slightly earlier time,[32] testifies in two contradictory statements to this broader picture of women's medical knowledge. On the one hand, Wang bemoaned the fact that anyone who had access to medical books could now easily dispense medical advice and that such abuse of medical knowledge "killed people" instead of saving their lives. Although her father was well versed in medicine and she herself had the chance to read widely in medical texts and to engage in discussions with her father, she always refrained from treating her own illness since she did not want to boast of her limited knowledge as others did.[33] On the other hand, however, Wang also complained that there were so many "quacks" that she had to speak up once in a while. She offered to closely examine the prescription that a physician had given her female cousin Liu Jirong. After checking Liu's pulse and referring to a number of medical texts on female disorders, Wang condemned the physician for using "medicine of a wolf's or a tiger's nature [langhu zhi ji]" that was utterly unfit for the "fragile frames of women in the inner quarters," and urged Liu to forward her opinion to someone in the Liu family who also knew about medicine.[34]

In Wang's ambivalence the diffusion of medical knowledge figured as a double-edged sword. When used indiscreetly such knowledge had disastrous consequences, yet when used wisely it rectified the mistakes made by quacks. Even more pertinent here is the presence of women in this picture. As a gentry woman who obtained medical knowledge from her family learning—by both reading widely in the medical texts owned by her family and by engaging

Figure 4.03.   *Picture of Women Making Medicine [in a Qing Gentry House-hold]*, in Zeng, *Chongde laoren bashi ziding nianpu*, frontmatter, painting no. 10. As an illustration for Zeng's chronological autobiography regarding how she performed her domestic duties, the painting stands as proof of gentry women's use of medicine for domestic caregiving during the Qing and early Republican periods. Courtesy of the University of Hong Kong Library.

in discussions with her knowledgeable father—Wang had the confidence to engage with the medical discourse of her time and to dispense her advice to a family relative.

As recent studies conjecture, the extent of gentry women's medical education at home during the Ming and Qing periods may be greatly underestimated since, for the elite, "literary and medical learning

were traditionally seen as two compatible intellectual pursuits."[35]
A late Qing official, for example, compiled a collection of easy-to-
remember verses about basic medical principles and urged readers to
use these verses to acquaint their daughters with knowledge that was
"useful" to women's fulfillment of their wifely roles.[36] This example
confirms what I have just described about the wifely duties of Chen
Ershi, but it is as relevant to the following discussion of the question
of what composed "useful" knowledge for women of the late Qing
period. Before delving into the case of the late Qing female physician Zeng Yi, however, it is useful to look at a case that serves as an
interlude.

WANG YING (1781–1842): "ON THE COMMON GROUND BETWEEN MEDICINE AND STATECRAFT"

Wang Ying hailed from a family of scholars in the county of She,
Anhui, and in her tender years moved with her family to Yangzhou.
She received a fine education at home in the classics as well as in
poetry writing and painting. At the age of twenty-one she married
into a family of salt merchants in Yangzhou. Her husband died in
1816. She then raised their son, Cheng Bao (1805–60), on her own.
Despite declined family means, Wang insisted that Cheng pursue his
studies instead of following the advice of his kin to learn the salt trade.
She designed a strict curriculum for him and personally supervised his
education. Afterward Cheng pursued a successful career path. Following Wang's death in 1842, he collected her works and had them
printed as her personal collections of poetry and prose, *Collection
of Poetry from Ya'an's [courtesy name of Wang Ying] Study Room*
(Ya'an shuwu shiji) and *Collection of Prose from Ya'an's Study Room*
(Ya'an shuwu wenji). These writings ensured Wang a place in official
history as an eminent woman writer and an exemplary mother.[37]

Wang's writings are extremely rich; I focus on her medical expertise as demonstrated by a few of her essays included in her collection of
prose. The following five titles are explicitly related to medicine; the last
two in particular indicate her access to published medical texts:

"On the Common Ground between Medicine and Statecraft" (Yi
yu zheng tong lun)[38]

"On Medicine" (Yi shuo)[39]

"Five Issues about the Study of Medicine" (Xi yi wushi)[40]

"Written after *Additional Annotations to The Bronze Cabinet,
Authored by the Famous Physician Mr. Li Zhensheng*" (Shu
mingyi Li Zhensheng xiansheng *Jingui buzhu* hou)[41]

"Written after the Prescription, 'A Drink to Clear the *Qi*," in *Miscellaneous Words on Distinguishing between Plagues*, Authored by
Mr. Li" (Shu Li xiansheng *Bianyi suoyan* "Qingqiyin" fang hou)[42]

A closer look at these essays suggests that Wang attained her expertise by reading the medical classics. "On Medicine," for example,
opens with the following passage:

> Just as no one in the world could become a Confucian scholar with-
> out reading the five classics and the four masters' books, no one could
> become a physician without reading *Basic Questions* [Su(wen)], *Acu-
> puncture* [Ling(shu)], *[Treatise on] Cold Damage* [Shanghan (lun)],
> and *The Bronze Cabinet*. Ever since the Han and Tang periods, medi-
> cal books [have reached such great abundance that they] filled the
> storage rooms and weighed down ox carts. Book-collecting families
> are fond of searching for the abstruse [medical] books. Because their
> tastes are too broad, they cannot focus [on the canons]. There are
> hardly any families who are free from this mistake. This is so because
> [people from these families] model themselves upon the quacks, who,
> in order to hide their inadequacy, treat only the head if [the patient]
> has a headache, and only the foot if [the patient] has pains in the
> foot. This is a result of their lack of a profound understanding of the
> [medical] books.[43]

As with the example of Wang Zhenyi, here we witness anxiety about
the prevalence of medical texts and the distrust of the "quacks." Yet
contrary to what Wang Zhenyi perceived as the danger of applying
the widely available medical knowledge to the treatment of illness,
Wang Ying proposed that the training of the physician should start
first and foremost with the medical classics, a process that was comparable to the training of the scholar with the Confucian classics. The
real danger, as she perceived it, consisted in the indiscriminate use of
medical texts. Precisely because these texts were in great abundance,
one needed to reach "a profound understanding" of what constituted
the canons.

Notable here is Wang Ying's claim to authority in delineating the
canonical tradition of medicine and in cautioning against digression from it. Such authority, as she suggested, arose out of her thorough mastery of medical texts. When she advised a female relative on
the study of medicine, she described two ways of attaining medical

expertise: reading as broadly as possible in medicine, to the point that one learned how to use medical texts wisely and discriminately; alternatively reading only those medical canons she designated. Either way one would become a superior physician.[44] In other words, it was through reading—whether reading broadly or reading with a clear focus—that one would eventually obtain command of medical knowledge and complete one's training as a physician.

Wang's significance lies not only in her example as a woman with access to medical knowledge but in the link between her interest in medicine and her political stance. The use of medicine as a political metaphor can be traced to Han Fei's (ca. 281–233 BCE) famous tale about the genius physician Bianque meeting Duke Huan, in which the duke's inattention to his illness while it was still curable allowed it to grow out of control and eventually cost his life. The political lesson that Han drew from the story, that "a sage should always take early precautions," was widely cited during the ensuing ages.[45] The Song prime minister Fan Zhongyan's (989–1052) aphorism "If you cannot become a good prime minister, you can become a good doctor [buwei liangxiang, bianwei liangyi]" was based on the premise of close affinity between medicine and politics.[46] A few of Wang's essays elaborate on such affinity. "Five Issues about the Study of Medicine" and "Ten Principles of Being an Official" (Juguan shize), for example, reflect her intention to pair studying medicine with acting as an official.[47] "On the Common Ground between Medicine and Statecraft" is typical in this respect:

> Bianque knew where the illness originated from as soon as he felt the pulse [of his patient]. Quacks, [by contrast,] know nothing about the fibers underneath the skin that the pulse goes through, nor about the components of the *qi* in the blood. Puncturing at the wrong spots [on the body] does no good in curing the illness and merely damages the skin.[48] Those who govern the state want to eliminate the evil and violent acts, yet are unable to do so. I presume that this is because they have not learned the marvelous art of Bianque and have therefore failed to fulfill their duties.
>
> The scholar Jia [Yi] [200–168 BCE] was good at feeling pulses, yet not at making prescriptions. The scholar Dong [Zhongshu] [179–104 BCE] was good at making prescriptions, yet he never spoke of the pulse. When Duke Zhou [ca. 1100 BCE–?) was in the Qi and Lu states, he predicted which states were to become strong and which to become weak, and whether the land was to be in good political order or in turmoil. His predictions proved to be true even after a thousand years. He can be said to be the person who truly knew about pulses.

When Mencius helped to govern the Qi and Liang states, his political measures were recorded in meticulous detail. He can be said to be the person who truly knew how to make prescriptions.

The good governors of the states during the ancient times never used the superior skills of the artisan Shi to destroy the body of [the state that can be compared to] the Tai Mountain. Neither did they exhaustively use the power of the warriors Ben and Yu to damage the nature of thousands of people.[49] This was what they relied on to guard the vitality [of the state]. . . . [The physician's duties] are to prevent [the system of the body] from being obstructed and to decide what strategies should be used [to fight the illness]. [The physician] reduces or increases the nourishments for the body according to the nature of the sick person, just as the governor of the state dispenses rewards or punishments [according to the acts of the person concerned].

The sage based his judgments on what the people liked in order to encourage good deeds, and on what the people hated in order to eliminate evil acts. When he [properly] rewarded a person, those under heaven followed the example; when he [properly] punished a person, those under heaven felt afraid [to commit similar offenses]. Therefore, the rewards he conferred did not violate the proper order, and the punishments he dispensed did not go beyond proper limit. . . . Being a good prime minister and being a good doctor—how could they be two different matters?[50]

In short, what Wang perceived as the "common ground" between medicine and statecraft lay in the fact that both the physician and the governor of the state needed to follow the nature of the people in choosing their strategies to "guard the vitality" of the body—whether it was the human body or the "body" of the state. By alluding to Fan Zhongyan's aphorism at the end of her essay, Wang asserts a direct equation between the duties of the physician and those of the governor of the state.

Wang went even further than elaborating on an old aphorism. Though undated,[51] the essay's political criticisms aligned it with a number of political essays that she wrote at a later stage of her life. "Ten Principles of Being an Official" (dated 1836), for example, demonstrates her thorough knowledge of the challenges confronting an official in a time of unrest and lays out the measures that he should resort to in order to deal with these challenges. Among Wang's major concerns are the poverty-stricken people who turned into bandits; the social evils of prostitution, gambling, opium abuse, and gangs; the huge number of lawsuits and the complexities involved; the need to strengthen the *baojia* system to protect people from disasters and crimes;[52] the use of community covenant (*xiangyue*), literary societies (*wenhui*), and charity schools (*yixue*) to "cultivate" the people and reduce social evils; and the corrupt bureaucratic system and the discretion that an official should use to avoid the pitfalls in this system. Some of the dangers that she refers to are typical of the mid-nineteenth century, namely, bandits, opium, and social unrest.

In "An Account of My Joy at Hearing about the Ban of Opium" (Xiwen jin yapianyan ji), Wang writes extensively on the harm that opium had done to people and the social instability it had caused in her native She county. She attributes the abuse of opium to the vicious intentions of foreign countries (*waiyang*) and expresses great joy at the news that the government finally added troops to the major port cities to cut off the lines of the opium trade. She twice emphasizes that, although a gentry woman like her stayed within the inner quarters and lacked a thorough knowledge of politics, she had been alerted by the dire consequences of opium abuse and had long hoped that the emperor and his officials would have the resolution to eliminate it.[53]

Also on Wang's mind were the danger of "bandits" and the strategies for precluding such danger. "An Account of How I Heard Lady Cao Weiru, My Sister-in-Law, Talking about Military Tactics" (Wen Weiru dasao Cao ruren tanbing ji) recounts her discussion with her sister-in-law about the heritage of the great strategist Sunzi (ca. 535– ca. 470 BCE). This remarkable essay is a rare example of gentry women's political concerns and their interest in military tactics as they became increasingly alerted by the crisis of their time.[54] It was these imminent concerns that prompted Wang to reflect on the art of governing the state as compared to that of guarding the human body. In this sense she anticipated the case of Zeng Yi, who would soon develop this parallel into a national scheme.

ZENG YI (1852–1927): MEDICINE, WOMEN, AND THE NATION

Zeng Yi was the second daughter of Zuo Xijia, the woman painter examined in chapter 2. Her older brother, Zeng Guangxu, represented her as a young prodigy whose talent always won applause from their father, Zeng Yong, and who spent days and nights exploring Zeng Yong's collections of books when the family lived in Ji'an, Jiangxi.[55] Recall that Zeng Yong died in the military camps in Anqing in 1862, when Zeng Yi was ten years old, and her mother traveled across dangerous parts of the Yangzi River to take her and her siblings back to Chengdu. There Zeng Yi learned from her mother a wide range of subjects and skills, including poetry writing, calligraphy, painting, needlework, history, and the classics. When she was fifteen she was able to help her mother teach needlework to her younger sisters, and poetry writing and the classics to her younger brothers. In time she became celebrated all over Sichuan for her literary and artistic achievements. She was especially famous for creating extraordinary embroidered replicas of her own paintings of scenery, flowers, and birds.[56] Her poetic works too won her great acclaim.[57]

Zeng Yi remained close to her mother and her siblings. Her lengthy autobiographical poem, "Remembering the Past" (Yixi pian), idealized the years she spent in Chengdu as a golden time of love among her family. Her perspectives differed significantly from her mother's in that financial straits, a predominant concern for her mother throughout these years, figured at best marginally in Zeng's memory. Instead she highlighted the affection her mother had for them and the care she and her siblings had for each other. Particularly fresh in her memory was a period following 1872, after her family moved to a house by the Stream of Washing Flowers. There she found delight in the beautiful scenery by the stream and enjoyed immensely her poetic exchanges with her siblings as they participated in the poetry society organized by their mother. This idealized time of family life ended when her brothers left home to pursue their careers (e.g., Zeng Guangxu went to Beijing in 1876). It was with both sorrow, when parting with her brothers, and great pride for her family that Zeng Yi wrote about her brothers successfully establishing their careers and glorifying their family.[58] She stayed in close contact with her siblings in the ensuing years.

Zeng was married to her cousin Yuan Xuechang, who was the son of Zuo Xijia's older sister Zuo Xixuan (1829–ca. 1891). The marriage was first arranged to be uxorilocal. The couple shared intense interest in epigraphy and a range of other intellectual pursuits. Together they conducted close inquiries into their collections of rubbings "from dawn till dusk."[59]

A recent study on the family relations of Zuo Xijia and Zeng Yi provides a clearer timeline for Zeng's married life. She was married to Yuan in 1875, at the age of twenty-three. The couple stayed in Chengdu for three years, and, during this time, Zeng gave birth to two sons, Lizhen and Lizhun. In 1878 Yuan took Zeng back to his home in Fujian, where they stayed for two years. That year Zeng gave birth to her third son, Lijie. During her stay in Fujian she became very close to her mother-in-law and aunt, Zuo Xixuan. In 1881 she went with Yuan to Jiangxi. The next year she gave birth to her fourth son, Liheng. Sometime between 1882 and 1887 she had a fifth son, who died soon after being born. In 1887 and 1890 she gave birth to two more sons, Lixian and Lichen. In addition Yuan had four sons and two daughters by his concubines Yang and Fan. Zeng raised and educated these children just as she did her own sons.[60]

In 1896 Zeng Yi was reunited with her brother Zeng Guangxu. After serving a period of mourning for Zuo Xijia, who died earlier that year, Zeng Guangxu was assigned to a post in Jiangxi, which was close to where Yuan held office. By this time several of Zeng Yi's sons had distinguished themselves in studies and earned official posts. In the spring of 1903 she followed Yuan to a post in Gansu, and Zeng Guangxu assumed a post in Hubei. Later that year she sent her collection of poetic works to Zeng Guangxu for his inscription. She modeled her collection after her mother's by organizing her poetic works in chronological order and by dividing these works into three volumes, which recaptured her three life stages. The first volume, *Collection of [Poetic Works Written by the Stream of] Washing Flowers* (Huanhua ji), incorporated her works from the time when she lived in Chengdu. The second, *Collection for the Singing Phoenixes* (Mingluan ji), recaptured her travels with her husband when they moved from Sichuan to Fujian and then from Fujian to Jiangxi. The third, *Collection for the Flying Swans* (Feihong ji), focused on her life in Jiangxi, where she followed her husband to several posts. She also included a volume of song lyrics.[61]

In 1905 Zeng put together her four volumes of poetry and song lyrics to be printed along with a collection of poetic works by Zuo Xixuan. Between 1903 and 1906 she had compiled two other volumes of writings, titled *Treatise on Medicine* (Yixue pian) and *Treatise on Women's Learning* (Nüxue pian). In 1906 and 1907 she used her family connections to reach a few distinguished officials who encouraged the import of the Western educational system and who led in establishing new-style schools in China. These included Duanfang (1861–1911), the governor-general of Jiangsu, Anhui, and Jiangxi; Zhang Baixi (1847–1907), the minister of personnel who was supervising state education; and Wu Qingdi (1848–1924), the provincial education commissioner in Sichuan and Hunan. These founders of new-style schools in China wrote with great enthusiasm on Zeng's treatises on medicine and women's learning in their prefaces to these volumes. In 1907 Zeng added an appendix to her volume on women's learning, titled *Records of Doing the Cooking* (Zhongkui lu). She had all these works printed together with her earlier volumes of poetry and song lyrics under the title *Collection from the Studio of Ancient Joy* (Guhuanshi ji).[62] This voluminous collection bore testimony to her transformation from the earlier generations of the talented and erudite women—as represented by her mother—into a new generation of women reformers.

A recent study makes the case that Zeng embodied the changes happening to women's identity as the "talented women" during the late Qing period, particularly in relation to changes of the overarching metaphor of illness in the Chinese cultural mentality.[63] Here I focus on Zeng's medical expertise and her incorporation of such expertise into her redefinition of women's roles in response to the political and national crises of her time. Her treatises on medicine and women's learning illustrate how medicine, as a form of female domestic caregiving, was incorporated into China's modernization scheme.

Treatises share the same concern of national strengthening based on a distinctly medical approach. *Treatise on Medicine* is composed of numerous essays and prescriptions that deal separately with four categories of ailments: seasonal epidemics and febrile ailments, including warm disease (*wenbing*), cold damage (*shanghan*), and wind damage (*shangfeng*); miscellaneous diseases (*zazheng*); female disorders; and children's diseases. *Treatise on Women's Learning* is a collection of essays that address the question of "what women should learn," as defined by their roles as wife, mother, and daughter-in-law. It is divided into nine chapters: "Getting Married," "The Husband and Wife," "Giving Birth to a Child," "Nurturing the Infant," "Educating the Child in the Cradle," "Educating the Young Child," "Caring for the Elderly," "Family Economics," and "Hygiene." These chapters transform much of the medical knowledge provided by *Treatise on Medicine* into the basis for "what women should learn." For example, the numerous prescriptions Zeng uses for female disorders and children's diseases in *Treatise on Medicine* are precisely what she urges women to learn in chapters 2 and 3 of *Treatise on Women's Learning*, where she elaborates on how to protect the health of the pregnant woman and how to raise healthy children. Her discussion of women's duty to guard family "hygiene" and the well-being of family members in other parts of *Treatise on Women's Learning* presumes that women should have the relevant medical knowledge. Before delving into these writings, it is useful to look briefly at Zeng's background of family learning, from which she drew her inspiration for her scheme of national strengthening.

Family Learning and Self-Training in Medicine

Zeng characterized her background of learning as that of "receiving instructions from [her] mother [cheng muxun]."[64] She spoke of this tradition of learning in her family with great pride, and it was not only literary or artistic talent that she claimed to have inherited from her family. Rather she drew attention to the luster that both her mother, Zuo Xijia, and her aunt and mother-in-law, Zuo Xixuan, had brought to her family by their exemplary conduct, which she referred to in general terms as chastity and filial piety. More specifically she also referred to a variety of practical skills they used—and taught her to use—in household management, including "specialized categories of learning such as the principles of educating children and regulating hygiene, and also easy-to-learn skills such as needlework and cooking."[65]

I will discuss in detail the transformation of the term *hygiene* and its changing significance to the discourse of national deficiency during the late Qing period, particularly how Zeng's reformist ideas figured in this discourse. Here I first propose that, as Zeng's background of learning indicates, medical knowledge used to regulate family hygiene could be part of the education that the mother gave to the daughter as a practical skill of household management. Implicit in this aspect of the *muxun* tradition was the assumption that guarding family health, like the "womanly work" of needlework and cooking, was a wifely duty that a gentry woman should be trained to handle even before marriage.

Aside from receiving her education from her mother, there was a significant experience in Zeng's life that sheds light on her learning. At the age of fifteen she started to suffer from an illness that lasted for five years. Several times she suffered high fevers and was on the verge of death, all because of the wrong treatment of "quacks." Only by referring to the large collection of medical books owned by her family did she manage to prescribe for herself and to eventually recover. Because of that experience Zeng developed a strong interest in medicine and for the next thirty some years read broadly in medical works, including classical medical texts, case histories by famous physicians, and collections of prescriptions. By the time she published *Treatise on Medicine* she had collected hundreds of prescriptions—including some she created—that had proven themselves to be efficacious in her actual practice. The purpose of her publication was to ensure that "everyone from a family of educated background would know about medicine and would therefore not be beguiled by the quacks."[66]

Zeng thus achieved the status of a medical expert primarily through self-training, testifying to the expansion of book collecting to more remote areas, such as Sichuan, during the Qing period and the consequent popularization of medical knowledge among gentry families. Conversely, precisely because of these trends, Zeng could expect her own medical works to reach "everyone from a family of educated background."

Zeng demonstrates the same distrust of "quacks" harbored by Wang Zhenyi and Wang Ying, which arose out of her personal experience of being ill and led her to privilege medicine as part of elite family learning. However, she did not share Wang Zhenyi's anxiety about the diffused nature of medical knowledge but rather relied on medical texts as a means of benefiting a broad readership. Such reliance on the popularization of medicine—particularly among women—constitutes the core of Zeng's reformist scheme.

"What Women Should Learn": Women as Guardians of Family Health

In her preface to *Treatise on Women's Learning*, Zeng relates in detail what prompted her to reflect on the question of "what women should learn" in order to serve their country. This is also where her reference to her own background of learning can be situated in its original context:

> I, [Zeng] Yi, received instructions from my mother when I was young. I always had an interest in the studies of epigraphy and poetry, as well as in such [practical] skills as painting, needlework, and cooking. After I reached fifteen, I suffered from a disease for five years. [Since then,] I have read broadly in the *Inner Canon* and *Basic Questions*, and have explored the principles of medicine and the techniques of hygiene. After I got married, I crossed big rivers and numerous waterways, and traveled in the provinces in the Southeast. At the time, the boycott of trade with overseas countries was broken, and the central land was experiencing great turmoil. As I quietly observed

the great shifts that China's governing power went through, and how the dozens of foreign powers plotted together to seize China's territory, I became deeply concerned, and racked my brain for a plan of national strengthening . . . .

Since the war of the Gengzi [1900], [China] has undergone gradual changes, and reforms have been rapidly implemented: The political system of the state is being improved; education is being popularized; the minds of the people are being enlightened; and industries are growing stronger. The people of China are finally starting to learn about the ways by which joint efforts of the crowd can enlighten the people, and by which the fittest can survive. We have a great population of female fellow citizens: Why don't the two hundred million women together compete [with men] to fulfill their heaven-assigned duties? Such as: educating the children and sharing responsibilities [with their husbands], which would lay the foundation for the growth of national citizens; using their diligence and frugality to bring about the well-being of their households, which would be the key to their management of their households; and [learning] medicine and hygiene to guard family health, which would be what the [Chinese] race relies on to grow stronger. Every time I read such poems as "The Soldier's Chariot" [Xiaorong] and "No Clothes" [Wuyi],[67] I would secretly sigh over the fact that, essentially, it was not just men but, rather, women that the Qin state relied on to turn into the strongest state of the time . . . .

However, [among women of China today] the rich pursue an extravagant lifestyle, and the poor are ill-informed and ignorant. Inside their families, they are unable to perform their household duties, and, outside their families, they are no help to the hardships of the time. As they do not know how to treat the diseases of their children, how can the Chinese race grow stronger? As they do not know how to educate their children, how can education be popularized? Those few women who know something about "new learning" only know it superficially and pick up from the West such terms as "free marriage," "equal rights," and "independence." They model the West in food and clothing. They weep as they talk enthusiastically about current events, and all you hear is how the foreign powers are seizing China's territories. However, they are ignorant of even what their own duties are and do not perform their duties diligently. This is called the mistake of "going beyond the limit is as bad as falling short [guo you buji zhishi]." . . .

I am not a talented person. Fortunately, both my mother and my aunt and mother-in-law were distinguished by their talent and virtue. They were erudite scholars of the classics and history, and were at the same time known for their illustrious virtues of chastity and filial piety. The complete *Collection from the House for Chanting in the Cold Season* authored by my mother has long been circulating in the world. Now I have just had the poetry collection of my aunt and mother-in-law, *Poetry Collection from the House of Green Phoenix Trees and Red Banana [Flowers]* [Biwuhongjiaoguan shiji], and that of my own, the four volumes of *Collection of Poetry and Song Lyrics from the Studio of Ancient Joy*, printed. [However,] I realize that the learning of poetry was of no help to the hardships of the time. . . . I have therefore selected from what I in the past had benefited from the teachings of my mother and my aunt and mother-in-law and had practiced personally to write this treatise on women's learning. Used outside the family, it can help to promote patriotism; used within, it can help to create harmony in the household.[68] [It includes] both specialized categories of learning such as the principles of educating children and regulating hygiene, and easy-to-learn skills such as needlework and cooking. . . . It can be used as family instructions or precepts for daughters, or as textbooks for women as well. If the conservatives think that it is over-stated and abhor it, and if the [radical] reformers dismiss it as trivial and ridicule it—to the extent that there are ones who deride my position as being neutral—I would still be happy to face their attacks.[69]

What Zeng describes is now a familiar story, namely, rapidly declining state power and control in the face of foreign invasions and efforts at reform in response to this great crisis. Her approach to the national scheme of self-strengthening, however, presents a less known aspect of the story. Recent scholarship has shed much light on late Qing visions of a dichotomy between the "old" and the "new," one of which hinged on the equation of a tradition of "talented women" with weakened national fiber. A number of reformers, headed by Liang Qichao and his coterie, urged women to abandon their frivolous literary pursuits such as poetry writing and master instead useful knowledge that would qualify them for their new roles in nation-building.[70] This radical "erasure of talented women" led to the rejection of the entire tradition of women's learning.[71] Liang's famous essay, "On Women's Education," outlines an exciting future for China that can be realized through the education of women. Yet it is based on a sweeping condemnation of the ignorance of Chinese women and on the very assumption that, "through thousands of years, women did not acquire fame in learning because they were never guided to that path."[72]

Zeng, by contrast, writes of how a gentry woman like herself took the initiative to address the national crisis rather than waiting to be enlightened. More important, she proudly retraces the tradition of women's learning in her own family and identifies this tradition as the foundation for reforms. In other words, the "path" of learning that Liang imagined was eluding women throughout Chinese history nonetheless revealed itself most clearly in Zeng's delineation of the mother-to-daughter transmission of knowledge in her family. What she learned by this means—and what she subsequently "personally experienced and diligently practiced [shenti lixing]" all her life—suggested to her the truly transforming force for China.

Zeng's crossing of the boundaries between the "old" and the "new" aligned her with a group of late Qing women reformers who quickly changed the campaign for women's education that was originally initiated by men during the reform movement of 1898 into an enterprise aimed at fulfilling women's social and cultural ambitions. Rather than blaming China's backwardness on women's lack of "useful knowledge," these women celebrated the free spirit and intellectual independence found in a tradition of "worthy ladies" (*xianyuan*) and pointed out that what men were now urging women to learn had always been part of women's domestic obligations. Xue Shaohui (1866–1911), for example, systematically responded to Liang and his fellow reformers by arguing for education of women that "aimed not at changing them from useless to useful but at nurturing their long-ignored talents."[73] These included poetic talent—used for the purposes of character development and moral transformation—and a variety of traditional virtues ranging from moral fortitude to practical skills of household management. Xue consequently fit a new-style "women's Way" (*fudao*) into a modern curriculum for women's education.[74]

Zeng promoted a similar "women's Way," which she called *kundao*, or "Womanly Way." In a eulogy that she authored for her own portrait photograph, attached to the front pages of *Treatise on Women's Learning*, she suggests that it is up to no one but herself to revive this "Womanly Way": "The Womanly Way has declined into obscurity, and who can be relied on to revive it? I promote my virtues cultivated from literature, and find pleasure for myself in poetry and the classics. I adhere to my exemplary conduct for the inner quarters, [and put forth measures for] both nurturing and educating [my children]" (see Figs. 4.04a and 4.04b).[75]

Here Zeng offers two remedies for what she perceived as the decline of the Womanly Way: her *wende*, which I have translated as "virtues cultivated from literature," and her *kunfan*, which I have translated as "exemplary conduct for the inner quarters." The former echoes Xue Shaohui's suggestion of using poetry as a means of moral transformation. It also reveals how much Zeng valued her own literary

影小歲五十五卅伯

Figure 4.04a. "Portrait photograph of Zeng Yi." Source: Zeng, *Nüxue pian*, front page. Reprinted by permission from the National Library of China.

cultivation, even though she regarded poetry as not directly relevant to China's crises. The idea of *kunfan* reflects to an even greater extent Zeng's affinity with Xue Shaohui in that, precisely like Xue, she tried to fit traditional values of female exemplarity into a modern curriculum for women's education. Her nine chapters on women's learning laid down in detail how this aim could be achieved. Moreover both the "women's Way" as promoted by Xue and the "Womanly Way" as put forth by Zeng carried tremendous moral authority. By

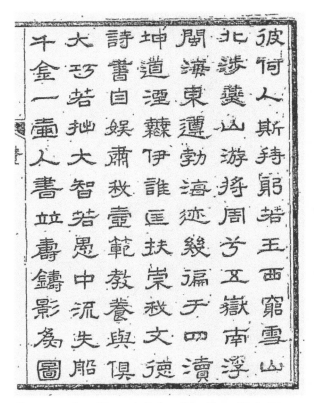

Figure 4.04b. "Portrait Eulogy" by Zeng Yi, in Nüxue pian, front page. Reprinted by permission from the National Library of China.

appropriating such moral authority, the two women and their fellow women reformers were able to claim their centrality to nation-building and reorient women's pivotal roles in the domestic sphere to this national purpose.

A comparison of Zeng Yi and Chen Ershi is illuminating. Both women passed harsh judgments on their contemporaries and expressed their wish to revive a neglected tradition of female virtue. Chen reflected a concern more common to the high Qing period, that is, how to revive appropriate rites from the Confucian classics as a means of precluding the danger of moral decline in the inner quarters.[76] Zeng, on the other hand, demonstrated an awareness of the swiftly changing world following the long and peaceful high Qing period. Unlike Chen, who seemed to be addressing broadly women "in the inner quarters,"[77] Zeng divided women into the three categories of "rich," "poor," and the radical advocates of "new learning." The first two categories conveyed a distinction of classes. While the former's negligence of their domestic duties could be attributed to their indulgence in extravagant lifestyles, the latter's ignorance arose out of their lack of opportunities for education. Zeng tried to expand what used to be the elite women's privileged access to knowledge to the "two hundred million women in China," including a large population of nonelite women. It was thanks to efforts like this, made by Zeng's generation of reformers, that women's education started to be popularized through the newly established women's schools during this time and after.[78]

Zeng's third category of women pointed unmistakably to a late Qing phenomenon, namely, the rise of "new learning" based on the import of a wide variety of Western ideas. Zeng's sarcastic representation of these women is crucial to our understanding of her proclaimed "neutral" position, which differentiated her from both the conservatives who saw no need for change and the radicals who, in her view, missed the real point of change. That is, any efforts at reform, including that of obtaining equal rights for women, had to go beyond empty talk and superficial knowledge of imported terms. Echoing the women reformers who regarded women's education as a precondition for equal rights,[79] Zeng offered her family tradition of women's learning as the basis for a curriculum that would qualify women as equal competitors of men. It was in this sense that she designated her treatise on women's learning as at once "family instructions," "precepts for daughters," and a "textbook." In other words, what fell within the traditional guidebooks for women could also be combined into a "textbook" (a late Qing neologism) catering to new needs.

Among Zeng's major concerns was women's fulfillment of their "heaven-assigned duties" of raising a robust Chinese race and educating future national citizens. As I noted, the curriculum she offers in *Treatise on Women's Learning* indicates her predominant concern with health issues, especially those related to childbirth and child care. Each of the chapters is further divided into several sections for elaboration. The chapter "Nurturing the Infant," for example, includes ten sections that address hygienic issues related to breastfeeding and issues concerning the selection of the wet nurse, a mixed diet other than breastfeeding, and vaccination. Likewise the chapter

"Educating the Young Child" goes beyond general concerns about children's health and education to include the highly contentious issue of footbinding, especially its relation to the weakened female frame. Even in the volume *Zhongkui lu*, which focuses on women's traditional duty of cooking for the family, Zeng identifies the promotion of hygiene as one of her main purposes of compilation.[80] A distinct example can be found in the essay "Hygiene":

> Once a woman is married and starts to run her household, she becomes the key to the household safety and peace. Therefore, strengthening the nation has to start with strengthening the race; and strengthening the race has to start with [the regulation of] family hygiene. The Japanese woman educator Shimoda Utako once said, even if a family is blessed with wealth and leisure, the happiness of the entire family would be ruined when a member of the family groans and sulks, suffering from illness; and a family brimming with peace and harmony would thus turn into a miserable and dreary world. How true these words are![81] Therefore, those who shoulder the responsibility of managing their households must pay attention to sleep, food, living conditions, clothes and bedding, chill, heat, dryness and dampness, and so on. They should in fair weather prepare for foul, and properly plan for daily life or travels. They should also be good at protecting themselves and strengthening their own health so that they can take their workload. . . . *This is why women should not only pay special attention to hygiene, but also study medicine* [my emphasis]. Once the family is strengthened, the nation becomes strengthened; and once the nation is strengthened, the Chinese race also grows stronger.[82]

In this express association of the family with the nation and the race—a variation of the Confucian social scheme that related the individual and the family to the state—Zeng defines women's role as first and foremost that of guarding family health as a step toward strengthening the nation. What was among a gentry wife's daily domestic missions therefore became crucial to the nation, and what women should learn in order to contribute to the nation also came to focus predominantly on medicine and hygienic knowledge (see my emphasis). Here again we can spot the historical shift from Chen's generation of gentry wives to Zeng's generation of women reformers. Recall that Chen's preface to *A Collection of Wifely Duties* does not specifically include among wifely duties women's daily mission of guarding family health. For her this daily chore—like the other practical aspects of running the household—was taken for granted as not worth mentioning. Instead her view of the ideal woman focused on moral qualities, particularly self-control and self-discipline, which had the capacity of bringing order and harmony to the family. By contrast, Zeng show-cased household chores, at once promoting them as ideal female vir-tues (i.e., the Womanly Way) and turning them into a touch point for how "modern" and "useful" a woman could be. Her curriculum for women's education politicized women's role as the guardian of family health and harnessed this role for reformist purposes—in particular for the purpose of strengthening the Chinese race, which constituted the core of national strengthening. In this respect she echoed the pre-vailing concern with the "Chinese race" during her time and antici-pated the spread of eugenic discourse in the Republican period.[83]

"Hygienic Modernity": The Purpose of Medicine under a National Agenda

It is now time to further contextualize Zeng's concern with health issues within the late Qing discourse of hygiene. A recent book-length study on the transforming meanings of health and disease in the treaty port city of Tianjin draws a nuanced picture of how China's effort of seeking "modernity" in the early twentieth century coalesced around the term *hygiene*. During the process the Chinese term *weish-eng* gradually lost its original Daoist associations of "guarding life" and, through the Japanese translation and mediations, became syn-onymous with "public hygiene" developed in Western countries such as France and England. *Weisheng* as a set of techniques aimed at improving individual health and longevity, based on Chinese cosmol-ogy, was consequently replaced by an all-consuming urge to regulate individual health through state intervention. Accompanying this lin-guistic shift were the profound social transformations required by "a foreign-defined modernity," which modernizing elites in China will-ingly embraced for the purpose of coping with China's deficiency, ironically "at the very height of imperialist violence and coercion."[84]

Chronology is crucial to the discussion of how Zeng fit into this narrative of *weisheng*'s transformation into public hygiene. Scholars identify the 1860s, the period of the Second Opium War, as the time of the first medical encounters between China and the West. From the 1880s onward new treatises on hygiene, especially those trans-lated from English by John Fryer (1839–1928), appeared in the treaty port cities and provided an alternative set of meanings for the term. It was not until the 1900s, however, in the aftermath of the Boxer

Uprising and the foreign occupation of Tianjin, that the highly interventionist approach to health regulation started to take firm hold. Before that, although elites in China had internalized a medicalized view of China's deficiency, and although Japan had quickly picked up the interventionist approach to national health regulation and set its example to China, the discourse of hygiene was multivocal. That is, there were competing voices arguing for a variety of means of improving health, including those from the perspective of Chinese medicine and those from a Western medicine that itself was in the process of transformation.[85]

Zeng's publication of her treatises on medicine and women's learning in 1907 therefore occurred in a period when the Western idea of public hygiene, with its interventionist approach, was taking hold in China and starting to triumph over a more individual approach to health. *Treatise on Medicine* shows that she carried on lively conversations with both Chinese and Western medical ideas. Yet in the context of the 1900s she may be understood not simply as illustrating an eclecticism that characterized many physicians of Chinese medicine during this time but more specifically as presenting a twofold approach to "hygienic modernity."[86] That is, on the one hand, she tried to improve individual health by popularizing medical knowledge and techniques of "guarding life" (basically from the Chinese medical system), and, on the other, she embraced the concept of hygiene as key to national strengthening and related the individual body to a national purpose. Thus far in my discussion I have translated the term *weisheng* consistently as "hygiene." Yet we should bear in mind that the term often carried two levels of meanings for Zeng: the individual and the national.

Zeng's emphasis on exercise and fresh air as keys to health illustrates this point. The two concepts appear first in her essay on the etiologies of "cold damage" and "warm disease":

> Although these diseases are triggered by external factors, they most often afflict those who have exhausted their minds/hearts, and those who live in deep, secluded houses where the air does not circulate. . . . In those who exhaust themselves with mental work, their energy of blood [*qixue*] is often obstructed, and wind, chill, summer heat, and dampness congeal in their bodies and do not disperse. Being absorbed into the main organs over a long time, the aforesaid factors will trigger disease whenever the body is stricken by external wind, chill, summer heat, and dampness again . . . .
> Within the human body, the lungs are like a canopy. Above them are two pipes, one is the esophagus that gets food from above, and

the other is the windpipe that lets through the air breathed in and out. Anything that triggers disease gets in through breathing, and, therefore, disease always starts in the channels of the lungs [*feijing*]. If from the start [the doctor knows how to] lighten and disperse the evil in the lungs [*feixie*] through the sweat, the sick person will recover and [the disease] will not be transferred to every channel in the body [*chuanjing*]. *Therefore, although Western medicine is not as effective as Chinese medicine as far as the methods for treating diseases are concerned, it indeed has advantages over Chinese medicine as far as the methods for preventing diseases are concerned* [my emphasis]. As long as a person knows how to save mental labor to protect the brain, often inhales fresh air to protect the energy of the lungs [*feiqi*], and also exercises to let the blood circulate well, he will be immune to hundreds of diseases and attain longevity.[87]

Zeng engages with the important medical doctrine of "warm disease" that emerged during the Qing period. This doctrine rejected the earlier classification of warm disease as a variant of cold damage, regarding it instead as an independent disease that merited specialized studies.[88] Zeng followed this doctrine in a preceding essay to distinguish between cold damage, wind damage, and warm disease.[89] Here she seems to be proposing that, despite their many differences in etiology and treatment, cold damage and warm disease share a common internal factor: a weakened system that is particularly vulnerable to external pathogens. Her theorization further links with an influential argument of the warm disease doctrine, which proposes that pathogens—such as heat, dryness, and dampness—enter the human body through the mouth and nose, reach the lungs, and descend to the stomach and intestines. This path of transmission corresponds with the triple *jiao* (*sanjiao*) schema of the body. Treatments of the disease target different stages of transmission in this schema and provide detoxifying formulas accordingly.[90] It is on the basis of this theory that Zeng offers her "fresh air plus exercise" formula to protect the lungs and facilitate blood circulation as a means of preventing disease.

This formula is a technique of "guarding life," the focus of which is improving individual health. This is especially evident in her intention to prevent "hundreds of diseases" and help people "attain longevity." At the same time, she links this technique of "guarding life" to Western methods for preventing diseases (see my emphasis). She refers to these Western methods in such an offhand way that, clearly, she assumes the reader knows what methods she has in mind: most likely the Western public health measures that were starting to take hold in China during this time. The Qing warm disease theorists had already demonstrated concern with warm diseases' close connection to epidemics and their transmission through contaminated air and water.[91] The physician Wang Shixiong (1808–64), for example, recommended clean drinking water and ventilation as preventative measures for cholera, which arrived in China in the early 1820s and caused pandemics in the following decades.[92] After the 1880s transformations in bacteriology in the West led to discoveries of the causative agents for a range of epidemics, including cholera, and in turn brought about large-scale public health innovations.[93] Zeng's familiarity with the Qing warm disease doctrine explains why she readily embraced the public health measures as better options than Chinese medicine in preventing illness.

These concepts of fresh air and exercise reappear in Zeng's writings on female disorders and eventually link the individual female body to the national body. Let us first turn to how she was bent on treating individual female bodies:

> The methods used to treat women's diseases are exactly the same as those used to treat men's, except that for women it also concerns their reproductive system. In past times, women were confined deep in the inner quarters and could not dispel their unpleasant thoughts in the open air—not only that such unpleasant thoughts were pent up in their hearts but also that the air was not circulating well [in the inner quarters]. [The traditional view that] women are liable to illness can be attributed to the above reason. The main method to treat women's illness—if by careful examination it is found that the female patient has not been affected by external factors or other diseases—is to nourish the blood and let the liver perform its dispersing and discharging functions [*yangxue shugan*]. Fortunately, in recent years, there has been a gradual tendency toward enlightenment [*wenming*], exercise, and hygiene, and women's disease should be reduced accordingly. As far as pre-pregnancy and post-partum [disorders] are concerned, they are indeed matters of life or death and should never be neglected.[94]

In designating women's diseases as the same as men's, Zeng is echoing an important reorientation of the *fuke* doctrine during the late imperial period. A number of *fuke* experts from the elite echelons of scholarly medicine challenged the earlier predominant opinion that women were constitutionally different from men. They proposed instead that women's diseases should be treated in exactly the same ways as men's except when the diseases concerned specifically female conditions, such as irregularity of the menses or postpartum complications. That is, they defined *fuke* more narrowly as a doctrine treating disorders related to the female reproductive system. In developing their arguments, these physicians shifted attention away from bodily disposition to social factors—such as women's seclusion and its contribution to emotional repression—to explain women's presumed emotionality.[95] Zeng's reference to fresh air and exercise reflected precisely this "social" approach to women's diseases. That is, she attributed women's presumed susceptibility to illness to their confinement in the inner quarters, which not only caused their pent-up emotions but prevented them from getting fresh air and exercise. Treatments for women's diseases should then be formulated separately. Fresh air and exercise can serve as preventative measures for diseases triggered by external pathogens. If not caused by external factors or other diseases, women's diseases should be treated by nourishing the blood and adjusting the functions of the liver—the means of treating the *fuke* disorders that can be attributed primarily to emotional factors.[96] It can be argued that, in these cases, fresh air figures again as a preventative measure since it can help women dispel their pent-up "unpleasant thoughts." Finally particular attention should be paid to pre-pregnancy and postpartum complications, the more narrowly defined *fuke* disorders, which the main body of Zeng's *fuke* prescriptions targets.

While Zeng was firmly grounded in the new *fuke* doctrine, her reference to women's confinement deep in the inner quarters as a "past" phenomenon, to be contrasted with the recent trends of "enlightenment, exercise, and hygiene" that can reduce women's diseases, reflected her awareness of a larger national discourse of health and hygiene in which the female body figured as a site of contention. Recent scholarship has brought alive the heated discussions centering on the female body during this time. Many of these discussions targeted women's bound feet, a symbol of their confinement, which was viewed as the cause of their weakened body frames and, in turn, of a weakened Chinese race.[97] Zeng too participated in these discussions. Her essay on footbinding may reveal what she had in mind when she referred to the recent trends that had the potential of changing women's lives:

> Footbinding poses a huge obstacle to women's freedom, and its
> harm is even greater than "floods and fierce brutes [hongshui meng-
> shou]." In recent years, societies promoting natural feet emerged in

metropolises. And yet, only thirty percent of women followed these societies' advice [to unbind their feet], and seventy percent of women did not. Why are [the great majority of women] so hard on themselves? This perplexes me indeed!

I remember that, in my childhood, I saw my brothers coming back home from school in late afternoons: They [ran around to] catch butterflies and look for flowers, enjoying unbounded freedom. I, by contrast, felt that my body was burdened by a tremendously heavy load and that my feet were in fetters. I always touched my feet and wept. Those moments are still vivid in my mind, and I cannot even imagine the torture again.

With the reforms going on in China today, I am truly happy to see that women can be free from this torture from now on. Those who have already bound their feet should unbind their feet immediately. Even for the really tiny bound feet, there are still ways to let them grow bigger if truly desired. Gradually switch to larger sizes of stockings and shoes—every time to one or two *fen* bigger[98]—and make the tips of the shoes in the round, rather than the pointed, shape, then in one year the feet will grow one or two inches, and in two years they will grow back to normal sizes . . . .

What would be the benefits [of freeing the bound feet]? [Women would have] ease in walking and in digesting food, and the hepatic energy disease [*ganqi bing*] common among Chinese women can be prevented. This is called the benefit of protecting the body. Being healthy and energetic, women can bear the burden of hard work and thus perform their household duties. This is called the benefit of managing the household. Bearing sons and daughters who are robust and strong in blood, women can make the race prosper day by day. This is called the benefit of strengthening the nation. With these three benefits, our two hundred million women who are normally seen as toys would all turn into useful citizens. This would not only be good fortune of us women, but also great fortune for China's future.[99]

Zeng contributed to the discussions on footbinding from two perspectives: first, her personal experience, and second, her medical expertise. In the first, she joined the ranks of other women reformers who promoted foot-unbinding for women's own well-being instead of for a national cause, as their male counterparts did.[100] The example of Xue Shaohui again offers a useful point of comparison. Xue argued from women's own bodily experiences that, since footbinding and foot-unbinding were equally painful, men should let women decide what to do with their own bodies.[101] Zeng no doubt highlighted such bodily experiences in writing emotionally about her own childhood memories and the "fetters" that footbinding imposed on her body. Her purpose, however, diverged significantly from Xue's. Precisely because footbinding imposed great pain on women's bodies and consequently posed "a huge obstacle to women's freedom," it had to be abandoned.[102]

In this way Zeng links all her major concerns: freeing the bound feet provides the foundation for personal hygiene (e.g., exercise and good digestion) and for prevention of the diseases caused by the dysfunction of the liver. (Here the "hepatic energy disease" can be read as an alternative name for diseases that were perceived to be caused by women's pent-up emotions.) The reformed female body, then, provides the foundation for reformed female roles: as capable household managers, as mothers of a robust race, and, eventually, as useful citizens of a modern nation.

CONCLUSION

Family letters, essays, and medical texts expand our knowledge about the range of household-based healing that women did and indicate the level of sophistication that this medical knowledge could reach in gentry families. More important, they also delineate a trajectory of change in women's writing consciousness toward the end of the nineteenth century. The case of Zeng Yi in particular reveals how a medically accomplished woman could evoke the female tradition of domestic caregiving and turn it into both an agent of reform and an object of reform. Female medical knowledge would then serve the nation and create strong Chinese citizens instead of being limited to the immediate family.

Zeng's treatises on medicine and women's learning are extremely rich and merit further investigations. Here I have mainly used these writings to make two points. First, Zeng demonstrated how a gentry woman like herself could take the initiative to seek solutions to the national crisis of her time rather than waiting to be enlightened. Unlike her radical male counterparts who condemned "Chinese women" with sweeping generalizations, she proudly retraced the tradition of women's learning in her own family and identified this tradition as the foundation for reforms. Second, Zeng developed a twofold approach to "hygienic modernity," trying to improve individual health by popularizing medical knowledge and techniques of "guarding life" (from the Chinese medical system) and embracing the concept of hygiene as key to national strengthening. Her efforts at improving female health eventually linked individual female bodies to a national purpose. In both aspects she joined her fellow women reformers in pursuing paths of reform unlike those promoted by their male counterparts. In expanding what used to be elite women's privileged access to knowledge to a broader population of women in China, Zeng and her fellow women reformers established the means of reforming women into active agents of nation-building.

Conclusion

Foregrounding their devotion to kinship values allowed the female authors to insert, paradoxically, disruptive voices that questioned the very foundation of the kinship system, namely, the authority of the husband and the father. The writings examined here, however, have implications beyond illustrating rhetorical strategies and representing a few particularly disruptive voices. In articulating the terms of their exemplarity, the authors reveal the production of the discourse of female exemplarity as dynamic *processes* in which they actively intervened as writing subjects. Contrary to the growing tendency during this time to identify female exemplarity with widow chastity, these female authors formulated their exemplary attributes broadly as economic contribution, political critique, managerial skills, practical knowledge, and the social and cultural prestige they brought to their families. Their skillful negotiations with the power discourse simultaneously shed light on the broader social trends underlying the publication and circulation of their writings, particularly the joined forces of writing as a path to fame and the elite family strategy for social metamorphosis. Aside from serving a range of expressive needs, these writings affirmed and expanded the women's social networks, ensured their material means of survival in various ways, fulfilled ritual needs while intervening in family disputes, popularized practical knowledge, and provided avenues of political engagement.

THE SELF IMBRICATED IN WRITING AND RELATIONS

When I began this project, I was drawn by the remarkably authoritative tone in women's writings from this time and found a number of particularly illuminating examples of women's self-empowering strategies in writing. Delving into the personal histories of these female authors enabled me to see a broader picture of their literary and artistic careers, social lives, and interactions with the cultural and sociopolitical trends of their time. Writing empowered these women in more substantial ways than helping them achieve literary immortality: their work attests to the women's rise as agents of social and cultural change and refutes the idea that the birth of the self among Chinese women writers must necessarily begin with the modern era.[1]

Far from reflecting a universal experience of Chinese women during the eighteenth and nineteenth centuries, these selected cases foreground differences in class, marital status, age, region, and a multitude of other factors.[2] The historical contingency of such terms as *funü* and *nüxing* no doubt informs discussions of the construction of Chinese womanhood catering to the shifting trends of Chinese modernity.[3] Nevertheless the writings examined in this book reveal that the construction of ideal womanhood and women's self-construction were ongoing processes imbricated in writing practices and familial and social relations. While there was no uniform selfhood among women, these authors asserted in their own way how their selves evolved in terms different from the modern conception of the self as an autonomous ego—namely, through a dynamic give-and-take with the normative values of the kinship system and out of a complex of roles and relations in the family-society-state continuum. This self-construction addressed national and modernizing purposes when the kinship system and the power discourse built on that system entered a phase of massive transformation.

These writings also lead us to further question such dichotomies as "tradition" versus "modernity" and "normative authority" versus "individual autonomy"—the idea that "tradition" imposes authoritative and irrational constraints on the individual.[4] While studies of Chinese women's history in the past few decades caution against the idea of a monolithic Confucian patriarchy victimizing women and suppressing all their creative energies, a study of women's self-construction in dynamic interplay with the normative values central to their existence sheds light on situations—including even the most disruptive voices incorporated here—that reject being neatly subsumed under such dichotomies. Discussions of the rise of feminism in China around the turn of the twentieth century should therefore be informed by this perception of women's self-construction in relation to normative values instead of being construed as a radical break from these normative values or presuming a teleological process by which women's efforts at self-empowerment became meaningful only when they eventually conformed to standards of feminism proper. In this sense this study also participates in recent discussions of feminism in light of antiessentialist awareness and an emphasis on particularities of women's situations in different cultural and historical contexts.[5]

SUGGESTIONS FOR FURTHER EXPLORATION

Situating these writings into the larger picture of their authors' life courses and social relations opens new directions for further exploration. Take the example of Zuo Xijia: the seventeen years following her return to Chengdu saw her rise to fame as a professional woman painter. Unfortunately little specific information is available regarding the commercial side of her artistic production. Since the price list mentioned by the local gazetteer has not survived, it is unknown how much Zuo's paintings fetched or how her income compared with other artists'. From the Ming period on, it was common practice for a professional painter to put up a price list in his studio. Surviving samples indicate that payment varied greatly depending on the reputation of the painter, as well as practical factors (e.g., size of the paintings, difficulties involved in the commission).[6] Women painters were participants in this lively art market, but studies of their activities have only just begun.[7] In this context, how competitive was Zuo as a woman painter, and what factors aside from artistic merit made her competitive? If the prices of paintings depended heavily on the painter's reputation, what could help a woman painter like her to establish or enhance her reputation? Social networks were important to any painter in this respect, in that they brought in more cash payments, gifts, favors, and a patron's hospitality.[8] How might a woman painter like Zuo have established such social networks?

While much of this broader picture remains obscure due to limited textual evidence, there is little doubt that Zuo became increasingly competitive in the contemporary art market. Aside from what the biographical sources laud as the popularity of her artistic works, she herself proudly stated that "connoisseurs always fought to purchase" her paintings, which caused the price of painting paper to soar. By 1876 her reputation as an artist was so well established that a Japanese diplomat who was visiting Sichuan commissioned thirty-six paintings.

An author who inscribed her autobiographical painting also mentions "rich merchants from Korea [jilin dagu]" who were willing to pay high prices for her work. Another author writes that her works of calligraphy and painting were treated like "rare treasures," her clients "fought to offer her payments," and commissions poured in unceasingly. Such publicity enhanced the marketability of Zuo's poetic works. When her personal collection of poetry was printed in 1891, an author who inscribed the collection predicted that she would make "sufficient profits" out of it. That is, given her renown as a painter in Japan, the Japanese people would also "fight to purchase" her volume of poetry.[9]

These references to Zuo's artistic and literary productions as commercial activities are indicative of the career of such women painters. Her choice of residence in the culturally renowned area of Stream of Washing Flowers instead of the commercial center tells us that a woman painter's livelihood, like her male counterparts', depended no less on her connections to elite culture than on commercial factors. The expansion of her connections during this time hints at a dynamic process by which her reputation generated a form of social currency, which brought her tangible benefits in the form of an increasing number of clients and soaring profits. Further exploration in this direction will shed much light on how women painters like her moved between the lively art market and elite society, as well as how their commercial activities changed their economic roles or status in their families.

The writings of Wang Ying, though not fully examined here, may open a new terrain of research on the rising cultural authority of learned women in mercantile lineages and their roles in the interplay of money, cultural production, and the social ascendancy of their families. Wang's life attests to the social success of the Huizhou mercantile lineages, the wealthiest families of which migrated to the great urban centers in China's cultural and economic heartland. In Yangzhou, Suzhou, and Hangzhou—among other places—these families rapidly translated their fortune into social and cultural capital, so much so that on local and state levels literary and artistic production, intellectual trends, and social and political leadership became permeated with the presence of these "gentry merchants."[10] The salt merchants of Yangzhou emerged especially as a formidable social force and accounted for the "splendid cultural and intellectual developments that characterized the lower Yangtze area during the eighteenth century."[11]

Wang is typical of the women who fit into this extraordinary story of social metamorphosis. They were the cultivated daughters who enhanced the cultural capital of their natal families and multiplied such capital through marriages—for example, by cementing important ties with networks of wealth, power, and cultural influence. They were also the exemplary wives and mothers who advised and aided their husbands on family affairs, business, and social projects and charity works and who supervised the education of their children. When the husbands were less cultivated or incapable of realizing the families' social ambitions, the women educated their husbands and assumed authority in managing the family resources toward success. If fortunes declined—as could happen with the diversion of commercial capital to expensive cultural projects or simply due to the vicissitudes of the trade or of life itself—some women resorted to the social and cultural capital at their disposal to help their families overcome such vicissitudes. A few women, like Zuo Xijia, turned their refined tastes into livelihood skills, such as calligraphy and painting.[12] An inquiry into these women's lives will further illuminate women's changing roles in the Chinese family system and the social transformations and cultural reorientations created by their families' social metamorphoses.

Moreover, these women earned literary and scholarly renown through the publication and circulation of their works and mingled with the eminent female talents of the cultural centers. Just like the male members of their families, in time these women of mercantile background became largely indistinguishable from their peers among the educated gentry. Their pursuit of cultural prestige and their penetration into the networks of cultural elites counted among the forces driving the phenomenal rise of women writers in these areas. An exploration of these forces has the potential of remapping women writers by foregrounding the regional forces underlying the rise of learned womanhood and bringing to light how the regional joined trends with the cultural heartland to produce the now familiar boom in Qing women's writing culture.

CHINESE CHARACTER GLOSSARY

A He 阿荷
Anqing 安慶
A Ying 阿英

Baihua tan 百花潭
baitou xiangshou 白頭相守
"Baitou yin" 白頭吟
baojia 保甲
Bao Shichen 包世臣
beiyin 悲吟
Ben 賁
Bianque 扁鵲
bieji 別集
Biwuhongjiaoguan shiji 碧梧紅
　蕉館詩集
bixue 碧血
Bo Shaojun 薄少君
"Bozhou" 柏舟
buhuo qingjing 不獲請旌
buqi zhi yao 補氣之藥
buwei liangxiang, bianwei liang-
　yi 不為良相，便為良醫
buxiu 不朽

cai 才
cainü 才女
Cao 曹
Cao Rui 曹銳
Cao Zhenxiu 曹貞秀
Chayu 叉魚
Chen Ershi 陳爾士
Cheng Bao 程葆
cheng muxun 承母訓
chengtiao 承祧
Chen Jiwan 陳季婉
Chen Shaoxiang 陳紹翔
Chen Shu 陳書
chenyu 讖語
Chen Yunlian 陳蘊蓮
Chen Zuwang 陳祖望
chifu 尺幅
chuanjing 傳經
chu buzu ruo youyu 處不足若
　有餘
Cishou 慈壽
cisi zongyue 祠祀宗約
Congma daoyu tu 驄馬導輿圖

congrong jiuyi 從容就義

congwu siji qinu zhe 從無私及
妻孥者

dafu 大府

Dao 道

"Daohua xiaohan xiaoying" 道
華消寒小影

daxi ganhuo 大息肝火

de 德

Dingxiang 定襄

Dong Baohong 董寶鴻

Dong Zhongshu 董仲舒

duanchang yin 斷腸吟

Duanfang 端方

Du Fu 杜甫

"Duijing tu" 對鏡圖

dunben xuqin 敦本恤親

Duzhai 篤齋

Fancha tu 泛槎圖

Fan Zhongyan 范仲淹

Feihong ji 飛鴻集

feijing 肺經

feiqi 肺氣

feixie 肺邪

"Fengshui lun" 風水論

Fengxin 奉新

Fengyang 鳳陽

fengzeng 封贈

fudai zizhi 婦代子職

fudao 婦道

fuke 婦科

funü 婦女

Fuzhi jibian 婦職集編

"Ganhuai zayong" 感懷雜詠

Gan Lirou 甘立媃

ganqi bing 肝氣病

gong 公

Guanwan 冠萬

guchu 孤雛

gugen 孤根

Gu Huaisan 顧槐三

gui 閨

Guifan 閨範

Guimen jili 閨門集禮

GuiShu tu 歸蜀圖

guixiu 閨秀

Guizhou anshi tu 歸舟安侍圖

"Guizhou xiehuai shi" 歸舟寫
懷詩

guo you buji zhishi 過猶不及之
失

guren tushu bingxing zhiyi 古人
圖書並行之意

Gu Taiqing 顧太清

Guzhou ruShu tu 孤舟入蜀圖

Han Fei 韓非

Han Taichu 韓太初

heke 合刻

heming 和鳴

hongshui mengshou 洪水猛獸

Hongxue yinyuan tuji 鴻雪因緣
圖記

houfei biao 后妃表

hualu 畫錄

Huan 桓

Huang Shi 黃奭

Huangzhou 黃州

Huanhua ji 浣花集

Huanhua shenchu 浣花深處

Huanhua shishe 浣花詩社

Huanhua xi 浣花溪

Huanxiang xiaocao 浣香小草

huashi 畫史

Huating 華亭

Huayang 華陽

huayuan 畫苑

Huayuan chu 畫院處

huazhao 畫照

huazhuan 畫傳

ji 記

jiachan 家產

Ji'an 吉安

jiancai 剪綵

Jiangyin 江陰

jiannian shangwen 減年上聞

jiapu 家譜

Jiashu 家書

jiating jihui 家庭集會

jiaxue 家學

jiaxun 家訓

Jia Yi 賈誼

jiazhuan 家傳

jie 節

jieshuai 節帥

jieti fahui 借題發揮

jiexiao Fanshi 節孝范氏

jilin dagu 雞林大賈

"Jilu" 記錄

"Jinchandao, Daohua nianhua
   xiaoying" 錦纏道 道華拈花
   小影

Jincheng 錦城

jingbiao 旌表

Jinling 金陵

Jin Luoxian 金洛先

jinshi 進士

jisibu 祭祀簿

jiuyang 就養

jiwen 祭文

Jiyin gangmu 濟陰綱目

Juanshi yin 卷葹吟

"Juguan shize" 居官十則

junmen 軍門

juren 舉人

Kuaiji 會稽

kuang 狂

"Kuhan" 苦寒

kujie 苦節

kundao 坤道

kunfan 壼範

kuxin 苦心

kuzhong 苦衷

langhu zhi ji 狼虎之劑

lei 誄

Lengyin ji 冷吟集

li 禮

lianfeng 廉俸

liangbu 涼補

Liang Hong 梁鴻

Liang Qichao 梁啟超

liaoruo zhizhang 瞭若指掌

Lichen 勵宸

Lidai houfei biao 歷代后妃表

lie 烈

lienü 列女

Lienü zhuan 列女傳 Biographies of Exemplary Women

Lienü zhuan 烈女傳 Biographies of Martyred Women

Liheng 勵衡

Lijie 勵傑

Li Jinyang 李金揚

Lingshu 靈樞

Lingyan ge 凌煙閣

Lin Shangchen 林尚辰

Lisao 離騷

Liu Ao 劉鶚

Liu Jirong 劉季容

Liu Rushi 柳如是

Liu Shu 劉澍

Liu Shuchu 劉樹初

Liu Xiang 劉向

Liu Yin 劉蔭

Lixian 勵賢

liyan 立言

liyan deti 立言得體

Lizhai 禮齋

Lizhen 勵楨

Lizhun 勵準

Lu Desheng 陸得勝

Lü Kun 呂坤

Lu Yitong 魯一同

Meifang shouzu bu 梅房收租簿

Meiliang 梅梁

Meipo 渼坡

meiren hua 美人畫

Meng Guang 孟光

mennei 門內

Miao Quansun 繆荃孫

Miao Zhengjia 繆徵甲

Miao Zhongying 繆仲英

ming 命

Mingluan ji 鳴鸞集

mingshu 冥書

mozhang 魔障

mujiao 母教

Muqing 慕青

muxun 母訓

muzhiming 墓誌銘

Nanling 南陵

nei 內

neizhu 內助

ni 匿

nianpu 年譜

Nü lunyu 女論語

Nü xiaojing 女孝經

nüxing 女性

nüyi 女醫

Pan Gongshou 潘恭壽
Pan Suxin 潘素心
Pan Zhixuan 潘芝軒
Peng Yuwen 彭玉雯
"Pingsheng jiyu fu" 平生際遇賦
Pingyang 平陽
pingyu 評語
Poyang 鄱陽

Qian Baohui 錢保惠
Qian Chenqun 錢陳群
Qiangweilu guanshou tu 薔薇露
　盥手圖
Qianwei 犍為
Qian Yiji 錢儀吉
Qilin ge 麒麟閣
Qinfeng 秦風
qing 情
qingchi 情癡
Qingyang 青陽
Qin Huan 秦煥
qinjia 親家
qiong er yijian 窮而益堅
Qiudeng kezi tu 秋燈課子圖
qixue 氣血
Qixun 頎勳
quan enyi 全恩義
Qu Bingyun 屈秉筠
Qu Yuan 屈原

renxiao 仁孝
Ruan Yuan 阮元
Ruan Yuntai 阮芸臺

ruyi 儒醫
Ruyi guan 如意館

sanjiao 三焦
shangfeng 傷風
Shanghan lun 傷寒論
Shaoxing 紹興
Shen Shanbao 沈善寶
shenti lixing 身體力行
Shen Zhaolin 沈兆霖
Shidai 石埭
"Shi'er" 示兒
shiji 詩集
Shijing 詩經
shimu 世母
Shiqi 仕齊
Shi, shiyu 詩、詩餘
shi yan zhi 詩言志
Shoujing oubi 授經偶筆
"Shu Li xiansheng *Bianyi
　suoyan* 'Qingqiyin' fang
　hou" 書李先生辨疫瓋言清氣
　飲方後
"Shu mingyi Li Zhensheng
　xiansheng *Jingui buzhu* hou"
　書名醫李振聲先生金匱補注
　後
si 私 personal, private
si 絲 silk
si 思 thoughts
Sima Xiangru 司馬相如
sizi lei 思子淚
Song Ruoxin 宋若莘
Suwen 素問

Taiping 太平

Taizhou 泰州

tanci 彈詞

Tang Qiushi 湯秋史

Tao Qian 陶潛

tici 題辭

Tingsonglou nüxun 聽松樓女訓

"Ti Qu Wanxian nianmei tu" 題
屈宛仙撚梅圖

tongju gongcai 同居共財

Tongliang 銅梁

tu 圖

tuce 圖冊

wai 外

waiyang 外洋

Wang Degu 王德固

Wang Qisun 王芑孫

Wang Shixiong 王士雄

Wang Ying 汪嫈

Wang Zhenyi 王貞儀

Wanxian furen xiaoxiang 宛仙夫
人小像

Wanyan Linqing 完顏麟慶

weisheng 衛生

Wei Xiaolan 魏小蘭

wen 文

wenbing 溫病

Wencun 文存

wende 文德

Wen Duanrong 文端容

wenhui 文會

wenji 文集

wenming 文明

Wen Shu 文俶

"Wen Weiru dasao Cao ruren
tanbing ji" 聞蔚如大嫂曹孺人
談疫記

"Wenxi tongzi zhuan" 文熙童
子傳

Wenyuan 文苑

Wu 巫

Wu Bao 吳保

Wu Chunhai 吳春海

Wu Enxi 吳恩熙

Wu Jie 吳傑

Wujin 武進

Wu Qingdi 吳慶坻

Wu Qiu 吳俅

Wu Tang 吳棠

Wu Wenxi 吳文熙

"Wuyi" 無衣

Wu Yonghe 吳永和

Wu Yongqing 吳永清

Wu Yun 吳運

Wu Zhongying 吳鐘瀛

xiang 像

xian'gan 銜感

xiangyue 鄉約

xiangzan 像讚

xianyuan 賢媛

xiao 孝

xiaolian 孝廉

"Xiaorong" 小戎

xiaoxiang 小像

xiaoying 小影

xiaozhao 小照

xiaozi shunsun zhennü yifu 孝子順孫貞女義夫

Xie Qingyang 謝青揚

"Xie Qu Wanxian huiti xiaoying jici yuanyun" 謝屈宛仙惠題小影即次原韻

Xie Xiangtang 謝香塘

xieying 寫影

xiezhao 寫照

xiezhen 寫真

"Xinfangge ziti batu" 信芳閣自題八圖

xinfu 新婦

xingle tu 行樂圖

Xinle 新樂

xinxue 心血

xingzhuang 行狀

Xi Peilan 席佩蘭

"Xiwen jin yapianyan ji" 喜聞禁鴉片煙記

"Xi yi wushi" 習醫五事

xuan'ge yuhua 懸格鬻畫

Xuba zhuanji zan tiba 序跋傳記贊題跋

Xue Shaohui 薛紹徽

xuexing 血性

Xu Xintian 徐心田

Yanghu 陽湖

Yang Juyuan 楊鉅源

yanglian yin 養廉銀

yangsheng 養生

yangxue shugan 養血疏肝

Yangzhou 揚州

Yangzi 揚子

yanliang 炎涼

yantian 硯田

Yao Bo'ang 姚伯昂

Yefang shoujing tu 夜紡授經圖

yi 義

yibo weili 以博微利

yingyang 迎養

"Yin shi wuli fuzi yougan" 因詩無力付梓有感

Yinyun ji 吟雲集

Yishou 頤壽

"Yi shuo" 醫說

"Yixi pian" 憶昔篇

yixue 義學

"Yi yu zheng tong lun" 醫與政通論

Yizheng 儀征

youfen 幽憤

yougan 有感

Yu 育

Yuan Botian 袁柏田

Yuan Houtang 袁厚堂

Yuan Jingrong 袁鏡蓉

Yuan Kejia 袁克家

Yuan Mei 袁枚

Yuan Xuechang 袁學昌

Yue 越

Yuefu 樂府

Yuke 毓科

Yun Bing 惲冰

Yuntai 雲臺

Yun Zhu 惲珠
Yuzhang 豫章

zan 贊/讚
zazheng 雜症
Zeng Guangmin 曾光岷
Zeng Guangwen 曾光文
Zeng Guangxi 曾光禧
Zeng Guangxu 曾光煦
Zeng Guofan 曾國藩
Zeng Jifen 曾紀芬
Zeng Shujun 曾叔俊
Zeng Yan 曾彥
Zeng Yi 曾懿
Zeng Yong 曾詠
Zhang Baixi 張百熙
Zhang Bao 張寶
zhangshi bachi 仗勢把持
Zhang Wenhu 張文虎
Zhang Xie 章燮
Zhang Xigeng 張錫庚
Zhang Xuecheng 章學誠
Zhang Yiniang 張憶娘
Zhang Yuniang 張玉娘
Zhang Zhongjing 張仲景
Zhao Peiyun 趙佩芸
Zhao Wulian 趙悟蓮
Zhending 真定
Zheng Xie 鄭燮
Zheng Yue 鄭越
Zhenzhou 真州
zhi 識

zhile 至樂
Zhixuan 芝軒
Zhonghe 中和
zhong huo nizhi, nanda tiancong 中或尼之，難達天聰
zhongxin 忠信
Zhongzhou 中州
Zhou Li 周笠
zhu 囑
zhuan 傳
Zhuang Biru 莊璧如
Zhuang Xiao 莊斅
Zhuang Yingru 莊瑩如
Zhuang Zhongfang 莊仲方
zhui 贅
Zhuoshi 卓士
Zhuo Wenjun 卓文君
Zhu Shuzhen 朱淑真
Ziguang ge 紫光閣
zihui 自繪
zishu 自述
ziti 自題
"Ziti beihua xiaoying" 自題背花小影
"Ziti Hanmo heming tu xiewai lianju" 自題翰墨和鳴圖偕外聯句
zixie 自寫
ziyin yanggan 滋陰養肝
zizan 自贊
zongji 總集
zongpu 宗譜
Zuo Ang 左昂

Zuo Baiyu 左白玉

Zuo Chen 左晨

Zuo Fu 左輔

Zuo Shengsan 左省三

Zuo Xihui 左錫蕙

Zuo Xijia 左錫嘉

Zuo Xixuan 左錫璇

zupu 族譜

NOTES

INTRODUCTION

1. Etymologically *lienü* referred to "numerous (examples of) women," and only in later times did it acquire the now standard meaning of "exemplary women." See its entry in the dictionary *Ciyuan*, 344.

2. In terms of its power structure and ritual and property inheritance, the Chinese kinship system was headed by the father (patriarch) and determined descent through the male line (patriline). This kinship system was, of course, far more complicated than the terms *patriarchal authority* and *patrilineal succession* indicate. For example, see Lu, "Uxorilocal Marriage among Qing Literati"; Bernhardt, *Women and Property in China*.

3. Judge and Hu, introduction to *Beyond Exemplar Tales*, 8.

4. For a new translation of Liu Xiang's book, see Kinney, *Exemplary Women of Early China*, particularly her detailed introduction to the book's contents and the Han court politics underlying Liu Xiang's compilation of the book, xvi–li.

5. Kinney, *Exemplary Women of Early China*, xvii. There have been controversies regarding Liu Xiang's original intention in compiling the book. See Wu, *The Double Screen*, 86; Zurndorfer, "The *Lienü zhuan* Tradition and Wang Zhaoyuan," 56.

6. For a recent discussion of how the rich corpus of the Tang epitaphs for women offers insights into the Tang gender norms, social lives, and emotional bonds between family members, see Yao, "Women's Epitaphs in Tang China," particularly 139. Yao also points out that these Tang epitaphs differed from the *Lienü zhuan* stories in that they provided a fuller picture of the women's roles at different life stages instead of focusing on the pivotal moments of their lives (140).

7. For a brief introduction to *Classic of Filial Piety for Women* and *Analects for Women*, see Idema and Grant, *The Red Brush*, 54–60. For *Lienü zhuan* as part of the moral literature for women during the late imperial period, see Zurndorfer, "The *Lienü zhuan* Tradition and Wang Zhaoyuan," 59–62.

8. For discussions of the enhanced dramatic appeal of the tales during the late imperial period, which had the effect of sentimentalizing the images

of exemplary women and blurring the boundaries between Confucian fidelity and romantic love, see Carlitz, "The Social Uses of Female Virtue" and "Desire, Danger, and the Body." For a more comprehensive picture of the late imperial printing boom, see Brokaw and Chow, *Printing and Book Culture*.

9. See Raphals's book-length study of the canonical tradition that Liu Xiang's work established and the changing meanings of female virtue across time, *Sharing the Light*. See particularly her discussion of how the portrayal of early exemplary women as "intellectual and moral agents" refutes the idea of Chinese women as eternal victims of a patriarchal system (4–7, 11–59). Also see Kinney, *Exemplary Women of Early China*, xxix–xxxi. Increasing scholarly attention has been paid to female suicide and the cult of female chastity in late imperial China. For quick reference, see Lu, *True to Her Word*; Mann, "Widows in Qing Dynasty China"; Ropp, "Passionate Women"; Sommer, *Sex, Law, and Society*; Theiss, *Disgraceful Matters*; T'ien, *Male Anxiety and Female Chastity*.

10. Bossler, *Courtesans, Concubines, and the Cult of Female Fidelity*, 142.

11. See Elvin's seminal study of the system of court reward, "Female Virtue and the State."

12. For the state-society interactions briefly described here, see particularly Elvin, "Female Virtue and the State," 124–26, 132–33, 135–36; Sommer, *Sex, Law, and Society*, 8–12; Theiss, *Disgraceful Matters*, 7–13.

13. See: Sommer, *Sex, Law, and Society*; Theiss, *Disgraceful Matters*.

14. A group of articles discuss this mourning literature for women in late imperial China, with a focus on how womanhood was constructed through the mediation of male consciousness. See Huang, "Introduction."

15. Two articles in the volume edited by Judge and Hu, *Beyond Exemplar Tales*, propose to use women's letters and poetry as alternative biographical sources: Waltner, "Life and Letters"; Idema, "The Biographical and the Autobiographical." Lu's book-length study of the faithful maiden cult in late imperial China also productively incorporates writings by the women themselves (*True to Her Word*, 101–210). By an old "truth" about China, I refer to the standard narrative about Chinese women's victimization by the Confucian patriarchy, which recent studies have started to problematize. See a brief review of this recent scholarship: Bailey, *Women and Gender in Twentieth-Century China*, 4–23.

16. See the following pathbreaking works: Ko, *Teachers of the Inner Chambers*, particularly 29–67; Mann, *Precious Records*, particularly 76–120.

17. See Idema and Grant, *The Red Brush*, 347–764.

18. Idema and Grant, *The Red Brush*, 347–496.

19. See particularly Idema and Grant, *The Red Brush*, 576.

20. Hu, *Lidai funü zhuzuo kao*; Zhang and Shi, "Appendix," in Hu, *Lidai funü zhuzuo kao*, 1206.

21. Mann uses the term *querelles des femmes* to characterize the debates over women during the High Qing (*Precious Records*, 83).

22. For quick reference to these debates, see Chang, "Ming-Qing Women Poets"; Hamilton, "The Pursuit of Fame," particularly 41; Mann, *Precious*

Records, 83–94; Widmer, "The Trouble with Talent." Also see *Women's Poetry of Late Imperial China*, Li's recent book-length study of the inner quarters or chambers (*gui*) as the normative gender location and women's transformation of the literary conventions and social norms associated with this inner sphere through poetry-writing.

23. Mann, *Precious Records*, 15. Also see 85–92.

24. Mann, *Precious Records*, 94–120. Also see "Gender and Textual Politics," Li's discussion of Yun Zhu's use of her anthology to seek authority for women's literary voices.

25. Elvin, "Female Virtue and the State," 123.

26. Cheng, *Ya'an Shuwu zengyanlu*, "Biography," 4a–b.

27. See the painting and inscriptions in Cheng, *Qiudeng kezi tu tiyongji*. See Ho's discussion of the painting as an example of the elite families' interest in portraying and glorifying the mother's education of the son (*Cai de xianghui*, 172–77).

28. Zhao, *Qingshi gao* 46: 14054.

29. Cheng, *Ya'an Shuwu zengyanlu*, "Biography," 5a. Unofficial biographies were often submitted as material to be included into official history. See Judge and Hu, Appendix A, in *Beyond Exemplar Tales*, 287.

30. These writings survive in four volumes of poetry and two volumes of prose (Wang, *Ya'an Shuwu shiwen ji*). A portion of Wang Ying's writings is discussed in chapter 4. Their richness, however, goes beyond the present study. For the extraordinary social metamorphoses of the Yangzhou merchants, of which Wang Ying's marital family figured as an example, see Ho, "The Salt Merchants of Yang-Chou." For the elite strategies for such social metamorphoses in general, see Ho, *The Ladder of Success*.

31. Elvin, "Female Virtue and the State," 117–18, 134–35.

32. T'ien, *Male Anxiety and Female Chastity*, 6.

33. Elvin, "Female Virtue and the State," 129–35.

34. Fong, *Herself an Author*, 5.

35. In cases where the female authors obtained court rewards, we may presume that it happened during their lifetime because court rewards were usually not bestowed posthumously. However, exceptions were made during the Qing period, and it is unstated in some cases whether the women received the rewards during their lifetime or posthumously. See my summary of the procedures of court rewards in the text and note 32.

36. In the cases examined in this study, the female authors were generally more invested in moral than literary reputation. This, however, does not suggest they were not interested in a literary reputation or that their writings lacked literary merit. Rather they tended to highlight the moral strength of their literary productions or phrase their literary endeavors in terms of moral projects.

37. Zhang and Shi, "Appendix," in Hu, *Lidai funü zhuzuo kao*, 1206.

38. Fong took the initiative in making these women's writings easily accessible by building the digital archive, Ming Qing Women's Writings, which is now frequently used by researchers in the field (http://digital.library.mcgill.ca/mingqing). In China two scholars, Hu Xiaoming and Peng Guozhong, are

leading a reprinting project of Ming-Qing women's *bieji* in cooperation with a number of major Chinese libraries. See the four volumes of Hu and Peng: *Jiangnan nüxing bieji chubian*; *Jiangnan nüxing bieji erbian*; *Jiangnan nüxing bieji sanbian*; *Jiangnan nüxing bieji sibian*.

39. Judge and Hu, Appendix A, in *Beyond Exemplar Tales*, 287–89, particularly 289.

40. Owen, "The Self's Perfect Mirror," particularly 73.

41. The practice of collecting women's works started as early as the Han dynasty (206 BCE –220 CE). For quick references, see Hu Wenkai's listing of the earliest women's collected works during the Han dynasty and the Six Dynasties (*Lidai funü zhuzuo kao*, 1–16). Given that it is unclear whether women themselves were involved in the editing of their own works, and that in most instances it was men who collected, edited, and published women's works, scholars have cautioned that collections of women's works may sometimes reflect "male fantasies" rather than the realities of women's lives. For instance, see Idema, "Male Fantasies and Female Realities." Idema refers specifically to the cases of the Song women poets Zhu Shuzhen (fl.1095–1131) and Zhang Yuniang (1250–76). However, evidence suggests that women were increasingly involved in the publication of their own works during the late imperial period.

42. See Ho, "Encouragement from the Opposite Gender." In *Herself an Author* Fong convincingly establishes a number of women poets of this period as authors of their own lives and examines their active involvement in the editing and publishing of their own works, as well as other women's works. For her general observations on women's use of *bieji* as autobiography during this time, see 9–12.

43. Fong, *Herself an Author*, 10.

44. Fong, "The Life and Afterlife of Ling Zhiyuan," 126–31.

45. Fong, "The Life and Afterlife of Ling Zhiyuan," 130–31. Fong's major case here is the life history of the woman poet Ling Zhiyuan (1831–52) as constructed in her poetry collection, which was posthumously published by her husband and framed by numerous paratexts.

46. Mann, *The Talented Women of the Zhang Family*, 166.

47. For taboo aspects of women's lives, see Judge and Hu, introduction to *Beyond Exemplar Tales*, 6–9.

48. Judge and Hu, *Beyond Exemplar Tales*, 285.

49. Barlow, *The Question of Women in Chinese Feminism*, 37–63.

50. For the relational and role-based self in the Confucian tradition, see Ames, "The Focus-Field Self in Classical Confucianism," 193–98. Also see *The Confucian's Progress*, Wu's pioneering study of the development of the self in the Chinese autobiographical tradition as the "Confucian's progress," centering on self-cultivation and self-transformation.

51. Ames, "The Focus-Field Self in Classical Confucianism," 206–7.

52. See particularly the innovative approaches used by Fong (*Herself an Author*) and Robertson ("Voicing the Feminine" and "Changing the Subject") in their analyses of women's poetic works as a form of self-expression. Also see Li, *Women's Poetry of Late Imperial China*.

53. Scholars have already discussed women's engagement with drama, fiction, and fictional narrative in rhymed verses (*tanci*). See Hu, *Cainü cheye weimian*; Hua, *MingQing funü zhi xiqu chuangzuo yu piping*; Widmer, *The Beauty and the Book*. For discussion of women's poetic criticism, see Fong, *Herself an Author*, 121–58.

54. Barr, "Marriage and Mourning."

55. For pioneering studies of these new artistic trends, see Vinograd, *Boundaries of the Self*; Mao, *Tucheng xingle*.

56. For a discussion of how women crossed the boundaries of the domestic sphere and engaged in literary activities outside their families, see Ko, *Teachers of the Inner Chambers*, 219–94. Also see "The Lady and the State," Mann's discussion of women poets of the late nineteenth century who voiced their political concerns in poems that addressed the social unrest of their time.

1. BREAKING THE SILENCE

1. Owen, "The Self's Perfect Mirror," 79. Owen also refers to Tao Qian as the first "poet-autobiographer" or "poetic autobiographer" in the Chinese literary tradition (78). For the quest for the "genuine" Tao Qian in manuscript culture starting in the Northern Song, see Tian, *Tao Yuanming and Manuscript Culture*. For autobiographical writing as a process of self-construction and self-invention in current Western autobiographical studies, see Eakin, *Fictions in Autobiography* and *How Our Lives Become Stories*.

2. Goodman, "Book Review," 772.

3. Owen, "The Self's Perfect Mirror," 73.

4. Moloughney, "From Biographical History to Historical Biography," 11.

5. Fong, "Writing Self and Writing Lives."

6. Fong, *Herself an Author*, 9–53.

7. Fong, *Herself an Author*, 5.

8. Han Chun, "Liu xiaofu zhuan" (Biography of Filial Woman Liu), in Liu, *Mengchanlou yigao*, reprinted in Hu and Peng, *Jiangnan nüxing bieji chubian* 2: 823.

9. There is a recent reprint of the collection, from which my discussion draws most of its material. See Liu, *Mengchanlou yigao*, reprinted in Hu and Peng, *Jiangnan nüxing bieji chubian* 2: 817-46. The collection was originally printed by the famous Xu family of Piling. Xu Rongjing, a student of Miao, was impressed with Liu's collection and urged Miao to put it in print. See Xu Rongjing, "Epilogue," in Liu, *Mengchanlou yigao*, reprinted in Hu and Peng, *Jiangnan nüxing bieji chubian* 2: 845. Another Xu, Xu Wu, called for donations from his friends to put the collection in print. Xu Wu, "Xiaoyin" (A brief preface), in Liu, *Mengchanlou yigao*, reprinted in Hu and Peng, *Jiangnan nüxing bieji chubian* 2: 846.

10. Liu, *Mengchanlou yigao*, reprinted in Hu and Peng, *Jiangnan nüxing bieji chubian* 2: 819–25, and see 845–46.

11. Dong and Tang, *Guangxu Wujin Yanghu xianzhi*, 25.27b.

12. Liu, "Meinü pian" (Verse on a beautiful woman), in *Mengchanlou yigao*, reprinted in Hu and Peng, *Jiangnan nüxing bieji chubian* 2: 832. The title of the verse was a popular Music Bureau (Yuefu) theme. Liu demonstrates in her collection a tendency to borrow various Music Bureau themes for her self-expression.

13. See Mann's discussion in "Dowry Wealth and Wifely Virtue" of how a woman's "virtuous use" of her dowry could assist her in serving as the exemplary daughter-in-law, wife, and mother.

14. Miao had to leave home so often that, according to him, he was home for hardly ten months during the six years of his marriage ("Wangshi Liu ruren kuangji" [Epitaph for my deceased wife, Lady Liu], in Liu, *Mengchanlou yigao*, reprinted in Hu and Peng, *Jiangnan nüxing bieji chubian* 2: 825). He also reveals that he could barely pay for the debts with his earnings, and it was Liu who pawned her dowry to assist him (824). According to Mann, the declining career opportunities for the growing numbers of degree-holders during the mid-Qing put men increasingly on the road seeking jobs, so that it fell upon the women to manage the households and to support the families during the prolonged absences of their husbands ("Dowry Wealth and Wifely Virtue," 69–70).

15. Gu, "Preface," in Liu, *Mengchanlou yigao*, reprinted in Hu and Peng, *Jiangnan nüxing bieji chubian* 2: 819.

16. Miao, "Kuangji," 825.

17. Gu, "Preface," 819; Miao, "Kuangji," 824. Here Miao clearly prioritizes filial piety over motherly feelings.

18. Gu, "Preface," 820. What Liu said, according to Gu, was "[Your situation can be compared to that of] the roc that takes some time to rest its wings, or the unicorn that will eventually show its horn. You should go through ordeals in order to serve grand purposes in the future, and encourage yourself so that your parents would feel comforted." The auspicious beast *qilin* in Chinese legends has no exact equivalent in English. I translate it as "unicorn."

19. Miao, "Kuangji," 824.

20. See Epstein's discussion in "Writing Emotions" of how ritual and biographical writings in premodern China tended to frame intimate emotions and relationships in terms of rites. More important, Epstein argues that Yan Yuan (1635–1704) and Li Gong (1659–1733), the two prominent ritualists of the Qing dynasty, negotiated ritual codes to express intimate emotions.

21. Zhang Wenhu, "Preface," in Liu, *Mengchanlou yigao*, reprinted in Hu and Peng, *Jiangnan nüxing bieji chubian* 2: 821.

22. For example, see Zhao Fen, "Preface," in Liu, *Mengchanlou yigao*, reprinted in Hu and Peng, *Jiangnan nüxing bieji chubian* 2: 821.

23. According to Miao, Liu left around one hundred poems, around half of which were written before they married ("Kuangji," 825). According to Xu Rongjing, Miao selected seventy pieces of Liu's works and had them printed as her collection ("Epilogue," 845).

24. For instance, see Liu Yin, "Xinglu nan" (Ordeals in traveling), "Kuhan" (Bitter cold), "Bingzhong" (During illness), in *Mengchanlou yigao*,

reprinted in Hu and Peng, *Jiangnan nüxing bieji chubian* 2: 835, 837, 839. The first title is again a Music Bureau theme; the second is a variation of another Music Bureau theme, "Kuhan xing" (Verse on bitter cold).

25. Miao, "Kuangji," 825.

26. In "Childhood Remembered," Wu finds a growing tendency during the late imperial period among parents to write elaborate and sentimental requiems for their deceased children and attributes it to the influence of the discourse of sentiment. Also see Hsiung, "Constructed Emotions." Hsiung approaches this topic from the sons' point of view, namely, how the male scholars and officials reconstructed their relationships with their mothers from memory.

27. Xi Peilan, "Songs of a Broken Heart," in Idema and Grant, *The Red Brush*, 603–7.

28. Liu Yin, "Dao wang'er Danyun" (Mourning over the death of my son Danyun) 1 and 3, in *Mengchanlou yigao*, reprinted in Hu and Peng, *Jiangnan nüxing bieji chubian* 2: 843.

29. For instance, see Liu Yin, "Yinma Changchengku xing" (Verse of feeding my horse at a cave by the Great Wall), "Jiwai" (Sent to my husband), in *Mengchanlou yigao*, reprinted in Hu and Peng, *Jiangnan nüxing bieji chubian* 2: 833, 839. The first title is again a Music Bureau theme.

30. Liu, *Mengchanlou yigao*, reprinted in Hu and Peng, *Jiangnan nüxing bieji chubian* 2: 833.

31. Chen and Miao, *Jiangyinxian xuzhi*, 191.

32. Lu Yitong, "Epilogue," in Liu, *Mengchanlou yigao*, reprinted in Hu and Peng, *Jiangnan nüxing bieji chubian* 2: 845. The poem "Chanted for a Companion Who Would Grow Old with Me" caught the attention of others as well. Among the inscriptions, Zhou Cheng's refers to the poem as "an ominous piece [*chenyu*]." Zhou also relates that his younger sister married Miao after Liu's death. As if to appease Liu, Zhou specifically explains that his sister is now taking good care of Liu's son so Liu can feel consoled in the underworld. Zhou, "Inscription," in Liu, *Mengchanlou yigao*, reprinted in Hu and Peng, *Jiangnan nüxing bieji chubian* 2: 826–27.

33. Wang and Liu, *Pingyang xianzhi*, 427.

34. A copy of Xie Xiangtang's poetry collection as it is attached to her brother Xie Qingyang's is now held by the Shanghai Library. It has recently been reprinted. See Hu and Peng, *Jiangnan nüxing bieji chubian* 2: 1225–41. There is also a recent reprint of Xie Qingyang's collection: *Yuyuzhai shiwen ji*. This reprint does not include Xie Xiangtang's works.

35. Xie Xiangtang, "Preface by Myself," in *Gongyu shici gao*, reprinted in Hu and Peng, *Jiangnan nüxing bieji chubian* 2: 1227.

36. For debates about women's education and literary pursuits in late imperial China, see Chang, "Ming-Qing Women Poets"; Ho, "The Cultivation of Female Talent." Also see Mann, *Precious Records*, 83–93.

37. Xie, "Preface by Myself," 1227.

38. Xie Xiangtang, "Kufu ba jue" (Eight quatrains composed to mourn my husband) 7, in *Gongyu shici gao*, reprinted in Hu and Peng, *Jiangnan nüxing bieji chubian* 2: 1232. For a chaste widow to continue the family

line—in other words, to adopt a son from the lineage of her late husband—
often served as a proper concern that could justify her existence. I pursue this
question later in this chapter.

39. Xie Xiangtang, "Wusu yingshen, qi sangai jie funü suoxiu, yin jingci
yishi yushang" (We have the custom of honoring deities with canopies that
are covered with embroideries by the hands of women. Therefore, with
respect I embroidered a poem on a canopy), in *Gongyu shici gao*, reprinted
in Hu and Peng, *Jiangnan nüxing bieji chubian* 2: 1232.

40. Xie Xiangtang, "Fude feihong xiang yuanyin" (Composed in the
form of the verse "Echoes of the sounds of the swan"), in *Gongyu shici gao*,
reprinted in Hu and Peng, *Jiangnan nüxing bieji chubian* 2: 1232. "Echoes
of the Sounds of the Swan" was a Music Bureau theme.

41. Xie, "Eight Quatrains Composed to Mourn My Husband" 6, 1232.

42. Xie, "Eight Quatrains Composed to Mourn My Husband" 1, 1231.

43. See Lin, "Shilun MingQing daowang shici de yishu tese"; Wang,
"Gudai daowang wenxue de jiannan lichen." Also see Idema's discussion of
mourning poetry's focus on private life and private emotions ("The Biographical and the Autobiographical," 230). Idema finds that, although mourning
poetry as a poetic subgenre can be traced to the third century, women did
not use it to lament their loved ones until the late fifteenth century (230–31).

44. Idema, "The Biographical and the Autobiographical," 232–45. Idema
characterizes the complete set of Bo's mourning poems as "one act of memory" (241).

45. Another of Xie's curious silences concerns her in-laws: quite contrary
to the filial feelings that Liu Yin expresses, nowhere in Xie's collection does
she even mention her in-laws. This may give rise to conjectures about the
tension that could have existed between a chaste widow and her in-laws,
especially regarding the inheritance of family properties or other financial
stresses. See Sommer, "The Uses of Chastity."

46. A poem that follows serves as a note to this line: Xie Xiangtang,
"Xinwu luocheng" (Completion of my new house), in *Gongyu shici gao*,
reprinted in Hu and Peng, *Jiangnan nüxing bieji chubian* 2: 1233. In the
poem Xie expresses her joy at the completion of her new mansion, stating
that what adds to her joy and gives her a sense of security is that, during the
same year, she adopted a son from the fifth branch of the Jin lineage. This
reveals that Xie had succeeded in restoring the family fortune even before her
adoption of a son.

47. Xie Xiangtang, "Shi'er sanshisan yun" (Precepts for my son, composed with thirty-three rhymes), in *Gongyu shici gao*, reprinted in Hu and
Peng, *Jiangnan nüxing bieji chubian* 2: 1233.

48. It is a telling fact that a late Qing anthology of women's poetry leaves
out four of Xie's most explicit lines when incorporating her poem—an editorial choice that testifies to the subversiveness of Xie's anger: "He indulged
in sensual pleasures of all kinds, and squandered our wealth as if it were
worthless. A thousand taels of gold meant nothing to him; he would spend
days and nights in brothels." See Shan, *Guixiu zhengshi zaixuji, juan* 4b,

44b–45a. There are a few other traces of editing, but the four missing lines mark the major difference between the two versions of Xie's poem.

49. Xie Qingyang, *Yuyuzhai shiwen ji*, 13. Xie Qingyang's mourning poems (four in total) are loaded with contempt for Jin Luoxian as well as concerns about how his sister Xie Xiangtang could handle the many burdens left by Jin. Xie Qingyang also reveals that the couple had a son, who unfortunately died when he was only one, and a daughter.

50. See Mann's insight about the pointed vagueness in women's biographies regarding "the precise market transactions that convert dowry assets into savings, investment, and profit for women and their families" ("Dowry Wealth and Wifely Virtue," 70).

51. See Yu, *Wenzhou gudai jingji shiliao huibian*, 444–64.

52. For example, see her later poem to her grandson: Xie Xiangtang, "Shisun" (Precepts for my grandson), in *Gongyu shici gao*, reprinted in Hu and Peng, *Jiangnan nüxing bieji chubian* 2: 1238.

53. Dong, *Yinxiangge shichao*, 958. There is a recent reprint of Dong's collection, from which my discussion draws most of its material. See Hu and Peng, *Jiangnan nüxing bieji chubian* 2: 927–58.

54. For the development of shelters for chaste widows, see Leung, "To Chasten Society"; Rogaski, "Beyond Benevolence," 54–57. For population loss caused by the Taiping Rebellion, see Meyer-Fong, *What Remains*, 1. For the pressure on widows to remarry around this time, see Holmgren, "The Economic Foundations of Virtue"; Waltner, "Widows and Remarriage in Ming and Early Qing China."

55. Liu Shu, "Jilu" (Record), in Dong, *Yinxiangge shichao*, reprinted in Hu and Peng, *Jiangnan nüxing bieji chubian* 2: 930.

56. Ibid.

57. See Hsieh and Spence, "Suicide and the Family." It needs to be emphasized, however, that controversies constantly arose during the Qing period regarding widow suicide and that one aim of the court rewards for chaste widows was to forestall it. See Mann, "Widows in the Kinship, Class and Community Structures," particularly 45.

58. According to Elvin in "Female Virtue and the State," tensions could arise between the conflicting virtues of following one's husband to the grave and of serving one's in-laws or raising the children. One may also observe that suicide or chastity was not the only choice for a woman whose husband died. Government-promoted ideals could be a far cry from reality, and widow remarriages were not uncommon during the late imperial period, often practiced under the pressure of the woman's natal family or her late husband's family. See note 54 on widow shelters.

59. Dong mentions that she had adopted a son, who, however, died soon after: Dong Baohong, "Dielianhua, si'er" (To the melody of "Dielianhua," thinking of my son), "Pingsheng jiyu fu" (An account of my lifetime experiences), in *Yinxiangge shichao*, reprinted in Hu and Peng, *Jiangnan nüxing bieji chubian* 2: 957–58. The death of her adopted son explains why she chose to emphasize her filial concern over that of continuing the family line

in her speech at the shelter, as the family line could not be sustained at this moment.

60. Dong also mentions that her mother-in-law died a short while before her husband ("Pingsheng jiyu fu," 958).

61. See Li's discussion of Dong's poem "Escaping from the Red Turbans," as well as a few of Dong's poems about the boudoir, as examples of how women in this area experienced social upheaval caused by the Taiping Rebellion (*Women's Poetry of Late Imperial China*, 117–20).

62. See Elvin, "Female Virtue and the State."

63. According to Mann, suicide often served as an honorable option for widows resisting remarriage ("Widows in the Kinship, Class and Community Structures," 47).

64. Liu, "Jilu," 930.

65. Ibid. "Martyrdom" here suggests to live as a martyr rather than to die as a martyr.

66. This is the only place in her collection that Dong reveals that Zheng also had a younger sister for her to take care of. If she could barely survive herself, she would not have any means to take care of the sister. But she could not bring this up in her speech at the shelter since it would appear to be a violation of her promise to Zheng.

67. Here Dong reveals that she had had other sources of help before she secured a monthly stipend from the shelter. It was highly probable that, due to the wars, she lost such sources of help so that she had to turn to the shelter.

68. Dong Baohong, "Fu mingshu yize" (Appendix: A letter to the deceased), in *Yinxiangge shichao*, reprinted in Hu and Peng, *Jiangnan nüxing bieji chubian* 2: 947.

69. See the brief entry about sacrificial essays or essays written to mourn or console the deceased (*jiwen*) in Judge and Hu, *Beyond Exemplar Tales*, 288. For such essays as a means of communicating with the underworld, see Xu, *Wentan* 3: 60. For such essays as part of funerary rituals, see Zhang and Xie, "Daojiwen de wenti yuanliu he wenti xingtai." For the notion of continued exchange between living and dead underlying funerary rituals, see Watson, "The Structure of Chinese Funerary Rites," 9–10, 13.

70. For famous examples, see Du, *Lidai diaojiwen*. It needs to be noted that sacrificial essays developed into a literary and biographical subgenre and flourished during the Tang dynasty. Because authors could choose to write such essays to pay tribute to illustrious figures of previous ages—instead of mourning someone newly passed away—not all surviving samples of these essays served funerary purposes.

71. Liu Shu phrases it thus: "The poorer [she was], the more determined [she became] [*qiong er yijian*]" ("Jilu," 930). Also the inscriptions on Dong's collection repeatedly refer to her courage (*xuexing*). For example, see Li Xiangshu, "Inscription"; Kang Yu, "Inscription"; Li Gengtang, "Inscription," in Dong, *Yinxiangge shichao*, reprinted in Hu and Peng, *Jiangnan nüxing bieji chubian* 2: 932–33.

72. This aspect of Dong's words of "blood and tears" was by no means lost on the authors of her eulogies. Chu Yinxi, for instance, comments that

every word of Dong's collection bears a fresh mark of blood ("Inscription," in Dong, *Yinxiangge shichao*, reprinted in Hu and Peng, *Jiangnan nüxing bieji chubian* 2: 935).

73. Dong Baohong, "Zhigan" (Expressing my feelings) 2, in *Yinxiangge shichao*, reprinted in Hu and Peng, *Jiangnan nüxing bieji chubian* 2: 949. This aspect of Dong's self-representation was not lost on the authors of her eulogies either. For instance, see Cheng Pu's reference to Dong's "heart made of steel and stone" and her "bone made of ice" ("Inscription," in Dong, *Yinxiangge shichao*, reprinted in Hu and Peng, *Jiangnan nüxing bieji chubian* 2: 934).

74. Li Xiangshu, "Inscription," 932; Li Xiaoying, "Inscription," in Dong, *Yinxiangge shichao*, reprinted in Hu and Peng, *Jiangnan nüxing bieji chubian* 2: 932.

75. For the development of the system of court reward, see Elvin, "Female Virtue and the State." For data on court rewards for chaste widows during the Daoguang reign, see Wang, "Funü jielie jingbiao zhidu de yanbian," 72. For the relevant official regulations, see Kun et al., *Da Qing huidian shili* 403: 400, 402.

76. T'ien, *Male Anxiety and Female Chastity*, 6. Exceptions were sometimes made for chaste widows who died while their cases were being reviewed by the Board of Rites. See Shen et al., *Da Ming huidian*, 79.10b; Kun et al., *Da Qing huidian shili* 403: 395.

77. Liu Shu, "Preface," in Dong, *Yinxiangge shichao*, reprinted in Hu and Peng, *Jiangnan nüxing bieji chubian* 2: 929.

78. This copy is currently held by the Shanghai Library.

79. Zhixuan, "Preface," front page.

80. Ying and Yan, *Xuzuan Yangzhou fuzhi*, 1064. This gazetteer also records an overwhelming number of local officials and gentries who died in the catastrophes of Yangzhou.

81. The Kangxi emperor ruled in 1688 that widow suicides should not be honored with court rewards, and the Yongzheng emperor implemented the rule vigorously. Although the Qianlong emperor made numerous exceptions, court rewards for widow suicides were not officially restored until the Xianfeng reign. See Kun et al., *Da Qing huidian shili* 403: 395, 399, 404; 404: 414. A consequence of the policy shifts during and after the Xianfeng reign was that chaste widows lost their status as a point of community pride and went on anonymous lists printed in local gazetteers (Mann, "Widows in the Kinship, Class and Community Structures," 51).

2. VISUALIZING EXEMPLARITY

1. For instance, see Vinograd, *Boundaries of the Self*, 1.

2. Seckel, "The Rise of Portraiture in Chinese Art," 12.

3. Wu, *The Double Screen*, 84–86.

4. See Carlitz, "The Social Uses of Female Virtue" and "Desire, Danger, and the Body."

5. See Shen, *Mingyuan shihua*, 377; Weidner, "The Conventional Success of Ch'en Shu"; Ho, *Cai de xianghui*, 159–67; Li, *MingQing guige huihua*

yanjiu, 64–69, 127–28. Also see a book-length study on Chen Shu and her husband's lineage: Li, *Shidai gongqing, guige duxiu*.

6. For example, see Mann, *Precious Records*, 208.

7. Well-known examples include the Western Han portraits in the Qilin Pavilion (Qilin Ge), the Eastern Han portraits in the memorial hall on the Terrace of Clouds (Yun Tai), and the Tang portraits in the Pavilion That Traverses Smoky Clouds (Lingyan Ge). See Yang, "MingQing xiaoxianghua gailun," in *MingQing xiaoxianghua*, 14; Vinograd, *Boundaries of the Self*, 20–21.

8. The best-known examples from the Qing period are the portraits of meritorious generals in the Pavilion of Purple Light (Ziguang Ge). See Nie, "Tan Qingdai 'Ziguang Ge gongchen xiang.'"

9. Mao, *Tucheng xingle*.

10. See Seckel's discussion of the appearance of the first self-portrait in Chinese art history in relation to the individualistic trends of the East Jin period ("The Rise of Portraiture in Chinese Art," 14).

11. Vinograd, *Boundaries of the Self*, 11–13.

12. Vinograd, *Boundaries of the Self*, 2, 29.

13. I am grateful to Professor Grace S. Fong for her suggestion of this term.

14. For example, see Mao, *Tucheng xingle*, 5–6.

15. Vinograd, *Boundaries of the Self*, 97–99. Alternatively Vinograd discusses the use of women's self-portraits and portraits as a prominent plot device in drama authored by men, the most famous example of which is the Ming drama *The Peony Pavilion* (14–18). Also see Zeitlin's discussion in "The Life and Death of the Image" of the rich symbolic and social implications of women's portraits as a literary topos during the sixteenth and seventeenth centuries. The focus of my present discussion is not women's portraits as a literary phenomenon but as a visual means of self-representation. To what extent literary imagination and artistic practices interacted with and impacted each other is a question that, though worthy of serious investigation, goes beyond the scope of my study. Also women's portraits should be clearly differentiated from a popular subgenre of figure painting, "paintings of beautiful women" (*meiren hua*). According to Cahill, *meiren hua* have been too often mistaken for women's portraits, yet the subgenre was firmly rooted in its own painting conventions ("*Meiren hua*," 11, 16).

16. Mao refers to *xingle tu* as "portraits of the male literati" (*Tucheng xingle*, 3).

17. For example, Feng lists a range of pictures or portraits as auto/biographical sources, including Linqing's autobiography. Yet he does not mention women's use of their visual images for autobiographical purposes (*Qingdai renwu zhuanji shiliao yanjiu*, 13–29, 141–43, 439–50). For quick reference to recent studies on print culture, see Clunas, *Pictures and Visuality*; Chow, *Publishing, Culture, and Power*; Brokaw and Chow, *Printing and Book Culture*; Hegel, *Reading Illustrated Fiction*.

18. For quick reference to these recent studies on Chinese women painters, see Weidner et al., *Views from Jade Terrace*; Weidner, *Flowering in the*

Shadows; Li, *MingQing guige huihua yanjiu*. The great majority of women's paintings incorporated by Weidner fall into the categories of flowers, birds, insects, landscape, and, occasionally, figure paintings such as *meiren hua*. See Weidner et al., *Views from Jade Terrace*, 65–173.

19. Mao, *Juanzhong xiaoli yi bainian*.

20. For instance, see De Girolami Cheney et al., *Self-Portraits by Women Painters*, 97–166; Rideal, *Mirror Mirror*, 34–44.

21. For example, see a Qing painting about the lad Shancai paying respect to the Bodhisattva Guanyin, who sits on a rock by a bamboo forest, in Liu et al., *Guanyin pusa tuxiang yu chuanshuo*, 234. I am grateful to one of the anonymous readers for pointing out the similarity between Cao's portrait and the artistic representations of the Bodhisattva Guanyin from this time.

22. Cao, "Ti Shi furen xiaozhao" (Inscriptions for the portrait of Lady Shi), in *Xieyunxuan xiaogao*, 1.4b–5a. Cao's preface to her inscriptions indicates that Lady Shi painted the portrait herself.

23. Cao, "Zhu shiyu qiuti suocang Pan Gongshou lin Wen Duanrong zixie xiaoxiang" (Inscription written at the request of the impeacher Zhu, for a self-portrait by Wen Duanrong that was copied by Pan Gongshou and owned by Zhu), in *Xieyunxuan xiaogao*, 1.17a.Wen Shu's courtesy name was Duanrong.

24. Li, *MingQing guige huihua yanjiu*, 200–201.

25. For the prevalent practice of attaching a self-eulogy or eulogy to an author's portrait during the Ming period, see Mao, *Tucheng xingle*, 99–158.

26. Qu, *Yunyulou ji*, 2.6b, 2.4b, *Cichao* (Drafts of song lyrics), 6a. In addition a title in Qu's collection indicates that Xi painted a portrait for one of her sons who died of illness and asked for Qu's inscription. Qu, "Daohua zhuti lingsi A'an chongsheng tu" (Inscription written at the request of Dao-hua for the picture of her son, A'an, in rebirth), in *Yunyulou ji*, 2.3b.

27. Xi, *Changzhenge ji*, 2.15b, 2.13a, 3.9a.

28. As recent studies of women painters from late imperial China have shown, a cultivated woman was by definition a woman who mastered the "three perfections" that her male counterpart was vested with: poetry, calligraphy, and painting. For instance, see Lo, "Daughters of the Muses of China," 41. Personal collections of these women may therefore yield a wealth of information about their artistic activities, including their engagement with the portraiture genre. By contrast traditional treatises of painting—such as histories of paintings (*huashi*), records of paintings (*hualu*), biographies of paintings (*huazhuan*), and "gardens" of paintings (*huayuan*)—incorporate only sporadic entries of women's portraits. Li, *A History of Poetry by the Qing Painters* (Qing huajia shishi), for example, incorporates a selection of poetic works by over two thousand painters from the Qing period, among which only five entries concern women's portraits (*guishang juan*, 6a, 9b, 36a; *guixia juan*, 9a–b, 18b).

29. The inscriptions and colophons were accorded value as works of calligraphic art or literary composition and could become part of the surface design of the painting. See Vinograd, *Boundaries of the Self*, 85. In more extreme cases, the texts were presumed to have a greater expressive

and mimetic range because words—especially poetic compositions—were endowed with the power of transcending the bounds of the depicted scene or image. See Clunas, *Pictures and Visuality*, 186–87. For lively discussions on the interrelationships among poetry, calligraphy, and painting, see Murck and Fong, *Words and Images*. See particularly two articles in this volume: Fong, "Words and Images"; Cahill, "K'un-ts'an and His Inscriptions."

30. I would like to thank one of the anonymous readers for suggesting this concept of image and text as a "semiotic continuum."

31. Gan, "Tu," in *Yongxuelou gao*. The untranslated part of the painting title, "Anshi," has two layers of meanings: the son finding peace in serving the mother, and the mother finding peace in being served. For a detailed study of Gan Lirou and her personal collection as an autobiography, see Fong, *Herself an Author*, 9–53.

32. Gan, "Guizhou xiehuai shi" (Poem written to express my feelings, on a boat back to my home), in *Yongxuelou gao*, appendix 1a.

33. Xu Xintian, "Inscription," in *Yongxuelou gao*, appendix 1b.

34. See Vinograd's concept of portraiture as "social events" (*Boundaries of the Self*, 10–14). I will refer to this concept again in my interpretations of women's self-portraits.

35. Zeng, "Nianpu zixu" (My own preface for my chronological autobiography), in *Chongde Laoren bashi ziding nianpu*, frontmatter, author preface 1b.

36. Zeng, *Chongde Laoren bashi ziding nianpu*, frontmatter, paintings.

37. Zeng, "Fulu: Lianjian jiuguo shuo" (Appendix: On saving the nation through moral integrity and frugality), in *Chongde Laoren bashi ziding nianpu*, appendix 1a–7a.

38. Li, *Qing huajia shishi, guixia juan*, 32a.

39. See Miao, *Guochao Changzhou cilu*, 912–13; Shan, *Guixiu zhengshi zaixuji*, 2.29b–41b; Shen, *Mingyuan shihua*, 540–41; Xu, *Guixiu cichao*, 13.12a–13a.

40. Shen, *Mingyuan shihua*, 540–41.

41. Xu, *Guixiu cichao*, 13.12a.

42. Pan Suxin, "Preface," in Chen, *Xinfangge shicao*, 1b.

43. Chen, *Xinfangge shicao*, 4.13a.

44. Chen, *Xinfangge shicao*, 4.25a. Although the Qing dynasty did not have an official imperial painting academy similar to that in the Song dynasty, its Painting Academy Office (Huayuan chu) and Hall of Fulfilled Wishes (Ruyi Guan) served basically the same functions. For example, see Yang, "The Development of the Ch'ien-lung Painting Academy."

45. Li, *Women's Poetry of Late Imperial China*, 133–36.

46. Yang, "Ziwo de kunjing."

47. Chen, *Xinfangge shicao*, 1.15a–b.

48. Chen, *Xinfangge shicao*, 1.15b.

49. Chen, *Xinfangge shicao*, 5.33a.

50. Chen, *Xinfangge shicao*, 5.33b.

51. Ibid.

52. Chen, *Xinfangge shicao*, 5.33b–34a.

53. Chen, *Xinfangge shicao*, 5.34a.
54. Chen, *Xinfangge shicao*, 4.5a.
55. Chen, *Xinfangge shicao*, 4.2a.
56. Chen, *Xinfangge shicao*, 4.25a.
57. Chen, *Xinfangge shicao*, 5.25a.
58. Chen, *Xinfangge shicao*, 4.13a.
59. For instances, see: Chen, *Xinfangge shicao*, 4.3b, 5.19b.
60. For instances, see: Chen, *Xinfangge shicao*, 3.5a-7a, 4.14a, 4.16b.
61. For instances, see: Chen, *Xinfangge shicao*, 3.16b; 3.21a-b, 4.4b-5a.
62. Chen, *Xinfangge shicao*, 5.34a–b.
63. Chen, *Xinfangge shicao*, 5.34b–35a.
64. Liu, *Lienü zhuan*, reprinted from the Zhibuzuzhai cangban, 15.2 a–b, 15.26 a–b, 15.36 a–b.
65. Liu, *Lienü zhuan*, reprinted from the Zhibuzuzhai cangban, 15. 27b.
66. Liu, *Lienü zhuan*, reprinted from the Zhibuzuzhai cangban, 15.3a.
67. Mann, *Precious Records*, 208. For more information on the popularity of the Zhibuzuzhai cangban, see "Conclusion" in *Precious Records*, note 23.
68. Chen, *Xinfangge shicao*, 5.35a.
69. Ibid.
70. Yang, "Ziwo de kunjing."
71. Shan, *Guixiu zhengshi zaixuji*, 2.29b. A biographical entry on Chen Yunlian's daughter Zuo Baiyu further reveals that Chen's husband, Zuo Chen, was a brother of Zuo Xijia's father, Zuo Ang. See Huang, *Guochao guixiu shi liuxu ji* 4: 1845. This fact may tell much about the two women's artistic achievements, moral stances, and economic contributions to their families as part of the local elite culture of Changzhou, especially in eminent lineages like the Zuos. As Mann argues about the Zhang family of Changzhou, local culture nurtured and promoted female talents, thus giving women in straitened circumstances the means to support themselves as men did. Women's economic contributions to their families, including a variety of productive activities and managerial skills, were both integral to what was represented as their virtue and central to the survival and prosperity of the elite families. See Mann, *The Talented Women of the Zhang Family*, 174–77, 181–82, 196–99. In the cases of Chen Yunlian and Zuo Xijia, we may observe in addition that their subscription to female virtue sometimes took dramatic forms, such as self-mutilation for the purpose of curing an ill family member. (I introduce Zuo's life in more detail below.) In this respect it is useful to recall that Chen's daughter, Zuo Baiyu, was glorified as a moral exemplar specifically for this reason. This fact suggests family influences and, perhaps more broadly, women's more zealous practices of female virtue in eminent lineages in this area. Despite her affinal ties to Chen Yunlian, Zuo Xijia remained utterly silent over Chen's autobiographical paintings. This fact may attest to the subversive nature of these paintings.
72. See Chen, *Xiaodaixuan lunshi shi*, 2.8b; Lei and Lei, *Guixiu cihua*, 4.7a–b; Li , *Qing huajia shishi, guixia juan*, 34a–35a; Shan, *Guixiu zhengshi zaixuji, juan* 1a, 45a–51b; Xu, *Xiaotanluan shi huike guixiu ci*, 1.1a–19b.

73. See Chen et al., *Minguo Huayang xianzhi*, 19.4b–5b; Lin Shangchen, "Gaofeng furen waigu Zengmu Zuo tairuren shouyan jielue" (A biographical sketch in honor of the birthday of Grand Lady Zuo, who earned this official title from the court, and who is my mother-in-law and the mother of Zeng; hereafter "Shouyan jielue"), in Zuo, *Lengyinxianguan shigao*, appendix 32a–36a. Unless otherwise noted, my introduction of Zuo's life is based on these two main sources, which are more detailed than the other available sources. For a recent study of the female talents in the Zuo family, uncovered from a web of their familial relations, see Lin, "Shilun Yanghu Zuoshi."

74. The local gazetteer records it as the age of nine.

75. I will return to this part of Zeng's life experience later in this chapter. My exploration of a number of Zuo's biographical accounts of Zeng will reveal it to be much more complicated than the present sources suggest.

76. Lin, "Shouyan jielue," in Zuo, *Lengyinxianguan shigao*, appendix 34a. For brief introductions to a few extant paintings by Zuo Xijia, which were sold in auctions in 2002, 2003, and 2004, see Dayunhe, *Zhongguo shuhua paimai qingbao* 2: 111.

77. For the system of granting an official title or post to the son due to the father's contribution to the state (*yinzi*) during the Qing period, see Wang, "Qingdai baqi guanyuan de yinzi zhidu" and "Qingdai de yinzi zhidu." I will return to Guangxu's assignment as county magistrate in relation to the complexities involved in Zeng Yong's career.

78. Chen et al., *Minguo Huayang xianzhi*, 19.5b–6b.

79. Zeng Yi is crucial to my discussion in chapter 4 as an example of how this family tradition of female exemplarity generated strategies for the redefinition of women's roles in a new national context.

80. According to the local gazetteer of Huayang, Zuo had started to collect her writings and had at least a portion of these writings printed before she left Sichuan (Chen et al., *Minguo Huayang xianzhi*, 19.5b). The complete version of her personal collection eventually came out in print in 1891 in Dingxiang.

81. Zeng Yong's collection is titled *Poetry Drafts from the House of Immortals Chanting about the Cloud* (Yinyunxianguan shigao). See Zuo's preface for information regarding her compilation of the collection (*Yinyunxianguan shigao*, preface 2a–b).

82. These volumes are currently held by the Shanghai Library. The copy of Zuo's *Poetry Drafts from the House of Immortals Chanting in the Chilly Season* in Shanghai Library also includes a biography of Zuo authored by Guangmin and inscribed by Guangxu. This piece does not appear in other versions of Zuo's personal collection. See Zeng Guangmin, "Gaofeng furen jingbiao jiexiao Zengmu Zuotaifuren shilue" (A brief account of the life of Grand Lady Zuo, the mother of Zeng, who earned the court title of "Lady" and court reward for her chastity and filial piety; hereafter "Shilue"), in Zuo, *Lengyinxianguan shigao*, "Shilue" 1a-5b.

83. The local gazetteer of Huayang does not specify when the court reward was granted to Zuo (Chen et al., *Minguo Huayang xianzhi*, 19.5b). The biographical material included in *Lengyinxianguan shigao* indicates that, by

the time of Zuo's sixtieth birthday, the reward had not been granted yet. Since court rewards were not normally granted posthumously, Zuo probably obtained the reward between 1891 and 1894. The piece "Shilue" by Guangmin was added to Zuo's personal collection in 1896, when Zuo's coffin was moved back to Chengdu and buried with Zeng Yong. By this time Zuo had no doubt been granted the reward.

84. *Juanshi* was a plant with a pith that was said to have a bitter taste. The phrase was a standard metaphor for people going through tough situations. Zuo's personal collection includes four volumes of poetry: *Drafts Written While Washing Perfumed [Clothes]* (Huanxiang xiaocao), *Collection [of Poetry] Chanted about the Clouds* (Yinyun ji), *[Poetry] Chanted for Juanshi*, and *Collection [of Poetry] Chanted in Chilly Seasons* (Lengyin ji). For the English translations of a selection of poems included in *Juanshi yin*, see Fong, "A Widow's Journey." Also see Fong's introduction to this part of Zuo's life, particularly her demonstration of courage when exposed to disorder and violence (49–50).

85. Zuo, *Lengyinxianguan shigao*, 4.1a.

86. Zuo, *Lengyinxianguan shigao*, 4.1a–b.

87. Zuo, *Lengyinxianguan shigao*, 4.1b–2a.

88. Zuo, *Lengyinxianguan shigao*, 4.2a. The record for the portrait that Zuo painted for her husband can be found in the poem "Fujiu zhi Ji'an zhuihua xianfu yixiang" (I painted a posthumous portrait for my late husband after I took his coffin to Ji'an). In the body of the poem Zuo indicates her intention to use the portrait for funerary and commemorative purposes.

89. Zuo, *Lengyinxianguan shigao*, 4.2a–b. The record for Zuo's self-portrait can be found in the poem "Bingzhong huixiang ziti" (My own inscription for a portrait that I painted [for myself] when I was ill).

90. Zuo, *Lengyinxianguan shigao*, 4.2b–3b.

91. Zuo, *Lengyinxianguan shigao*, 4.3b–4a.

92. Zuo, *Lengyinxianguan shigao*, 4.4a–b.

93. Zuo, *Lengyinxianguan shigao*, 4.4b–6b.

94. Zuo, *Lengyinxianguan shigao*, 4.6b–7a.

95. This painting also fits into a larger picture of Zuo's engagement with the portraiture genre while she was coping with an intensely traumatic period of her life. We are aware of two other portraits she painted following her husband's death: a posthumous portrait of her husband used for commemorative and ritual purposes, and a self-portrait used as an emotional outlet for herself.

96. Zuo referred to Zeng Guofan as *jieshuai*, which I translate as "commander-in-chief." In November 1861 he was authorized to command the armies of the four provinces of Jiangsu, Anhui, Jiangxi, and Zhejiang and also to direct officials of these four provinces, including the governors, the provincial military commanders, and all those ranked blow. See Qian, *Qingdai zhiguan nianbiao* 4: 3005–6. By "Provincial Military Commander Bao," Zuo is referring to Bao Chao (1828–86), who was then a renowned general under the command of Zeng Guofan. Bao was promoted to provincial military commander of Zhejiang in 1862 and served at the post until 1867. The

title *junmen* refers to this later title. See Zhao, *Qingshi gao* 39: 11981–86. Also see Qian, *Qingdai zhiguan nianbiao* 3: 2567–71.

97. The phrase "martyr's blood" (*bixue*) alludes to a story in the *Zhuangzi* about a loyal official, Chang Hong (ca. 5 BCE), who was executed on wrongful charges and whose blood turned into green jade three years after his death. See Guo, *Zhuangzi jishi*, 920. The phrase was often used to refer to the blood of loyal officials and martyrs, especially those who were wrongly charged. Zuo's allusion to this story is crucial to my discussion about the complexities surrounding her husband's death and her intention to vindicate him.

98. It was a commonly used literary trope to state that one's anguish could even affect the surroundings.

99. Zuo, *Lengyinxianguan shigao*, 4.5b–6a.

100. Zuo, *Lengyinxianguan shigao*, 4.6a-b. Zuo refers elsewhere to Zeng Yong's deathbed wish, namely, that she should serve his parents in his place. See Zuo, "Muzhi" (Inscription for the tomb [of Zeng Yong]), in *Lengyinxianguan shigao*, *Wencun* (Preserved prose) 4a-8a. See particularly page 7a. I will return to this important text later in this chapter.

101. For these earliest inscriptions, see Zuo, *Lengyinxianguan shigao*, appendix 2b–4a.

102. For the physical form in which the painting circulated, see Wang Jiabi, "Inscription," in Zuo, *Lengyinxianguan shigao*, appendix 5b; Zhao Zhixie, "Inscription," in Zuo, *Lengyinxianguan shigao*, appendix 27b; Hu Yuyun, "Inscription," in Zuo, *Lengyinxianguan shigao*, appendix 19a. For the time when Guangxu left for the Capital, see Zuo, *Lengyinxianguan shigao*, 6.17b–18b. For the fact that Guangxu went to the National University as a reward for his father's contribution to the state, see Miao Quansun, "Zeng taifuren Zuoshi jiazhuan" (A family biography for Grand Lady Zeng, natal name Zuo), quoted in Lin, "Shilun Yanghu Zuoshi erdai cainü zhi jiazu guanxi," 197.

103. For inscriptions from this later time, see Zuo, *Lengyinxianguan shigao*, appendix 15b–30b.

104. Vinograd, *Boundaries of the Self*, 10–14.

105. In addition there is an inscription authored by Zuo Xijia's uncle, Zuo Shengsan (*Lengyinxianguan shigao*, appendix 2b). For the posts that Wu Tang and Wang Degu held, see Qian, *Qingdai zhiguan nianbiao* 2: 1479–83, 3: 1934–37.

106. Wang Jiabi, "Inscription," in Zuo, *Lengyinxianguan shigao*, appendix 5a.

107. Zeng, "Shilue," in Zuo, *Lengyinxianguan shigao*, "Shilue" 2b; Lin, "Shouyan jielue," in Zuo, *Lengyinxianguan shigao*, appendix 33b–34a.

108. Lin, "Shouyan jielue," in Zuo, *Lengyinxianguan shigao*, appendix 33b–34a.

109. Zeng, "Shilue," in Zuo, *Lengyinxianguan shigao*, "Shilue" 2b.

110. We may also need to take into account the considerable regional and cultural differences between Sichuan and the Jiangnan area—where Zuo was born—in order to understand the difficult transition she was making.

111. Lin, "Shouyan jielue," in Zuo, *Lengyinxianguan shigao*, appendix 33b.

112. For a study on the practice of household division during this time, see Wakefield, *Fenjia*.

113. An alternative translation of the phrase *quan enyi* in the first line is "to keep affections and loyalty intact." This translation suggests an even higher degree of tension in the household. The words *gong* and *si* in the second line have very rich meanings in the Chinese language. In the context of the poem they refer to the common properties of the household and the personal properties of individual members, respectively.

114. Zuo alludes in the fourth line to the story of Ouyang Xiu's (1007–72) mother, who personally taught him by using a straw to draw characters on the ground. The story highlights the motherly virtue of personally instructing the son and raising him to be an upright person despite poverty. See Tuotuo et al., "Ouyang Xiu liezhuan," particularly 10375.

115. The phrase *yanliang* in the fifth line refers to the radically changing attitudes with which a person is treated by other people; such changing attitudes are usually caused by the person's declining fortunes or status. Zuo here personifies the lamp to refer to her own situation. The word *si* (silk threads) in the sixth line is a homophone of the word *si* (thoughts), and is therefore used as a standard metaphor for thoughts or feelings. Zuo, *Lengyinxianguan shigao*, 5.2b.

116. She stated in at least two places that she pawned her jewelry to purchase food. However, the rice she was able to get by this means was barely 1 *dou* (around 750 grams). See Zuo, *Lengyinxianguan shigao*, 5.7a.

117. For instance, see Zuo, *Lengyinxianguan shigao*, 5.7b, 5.8a–b, 6.6a–b; 6.11a, 6.16b–17a, 6.23b, 6.26b; *Song Lyrics*, 12a–14a, 17a, 17b–18a.

118. For instance, see Zuo, *Lengyinxianguan shigao*, 6.18b; *Song Lyrics*, 17a.

119. See Bray, *Technology and Gender*, 183–84.

120. Zuo, *Lengyinxianguan shigao*, 6.11a, 6.23b, 6.26b. The "poor woman" refers to none other than Zuo herself.

121. Zuo, *Lengyinxianguan shigao*, 5.8a–b.

122. See Zuo's abundant poetic exchanges with these women (*Lengyinxianguan shigao*, 5.9a–b, 5.11a, 5.11b, 5.12a–b, 5.13b, 6.1b, 6.3a–b, 6.4a–b, 6.7a, 6.15a–b, 6.19a, 6.22a–23b; *Song Lyrics*, 15a). Also see Lin's summary of the backgrounds of these women and their connections with Zuo ("Shilun Yanghu Zuoshi erdai cainü zhi jiazu guanxi," 198).

123. See Zuo's poetic exchanges with the Miao family (*Lengyinxianguan shigao*, 6.5a–6a, 6.7a, 6.11a–b). Also see Lin, "Shilun Yanghu Zuoshi erdai cainü zhi jiazu guanxi," 198.

124. Zuo, *Lengyinxianguan shigao*, 6.17a–b.

125. See Zuo's reference to this fact (*Lengyinxianguan shigao*, 6.5b, 6.12a–13b). Also see Zeng, "Shilue," in Zuo, *Lengyinxianguan shigao*, "Shilue" 3a. Zeng Guangmin mentions another official named Wen Ge who was among Zeng Yong's connections and who admired Zuo's paintings.

126. See Zuo, *Lengyinxianguan shigao*, 5.18b; Lin, "Shouyan jielue," in Zuo, *Lengyinxianguan shigao*, appendix 35b. Also see the family tree drawn

by Lin Meiyi ("Shilun Yanghu Zuoshi erdai cainü zhi jiazu guanxi," 193). There are a number of other poems that indicate Zuo's connection with Wu Chunhai. See Zuo, *Lengyinxianguan shigao*, 6.1b–2a, 6.2a–3a, 6.15b–16a.

127. Zuo married her second daughter, Zeng Yi, to Yuan Xuechang, the son of her sister Zuo Xixuan. Xixuan had married well, and Yuan already had a budding career at this time. The younger sisters all married into gentry families of Sichuan. See Lin, "Shouyan jielue," in Zuo, *Lengyinxianguan shigao*, appendix 35b–36a.

128. See Zuo, *Lengyinxianguan shigao*, 6.1a. Jincheng was sometimes used as an alternative name of Chengdu. For its history and the commercial activities around this area (roughly, south to the urban center of Chengdu), see Chen et al., *Minguo Huayang xianzhi*, 27.4b–6a, 28.3a–8b.

129. See Zuo, *Lengyinxianguan shigao*, 6.3a–4b. For the location and history of the stream, see Chen et al., *Minguo Huayang xianzhi*, 28.41a–43a.

130. See Zuo, *Lengyinxianguan shigao*, 6.13b–15a, 17a–b. For the construction of Du Fu's memorial hall, see Chen et al., *Minguo Huayang xianzhi*, 28.12a–b. During a visit to the site I took a photo of the hall's original layout inscribed on a piece of stone, dated 1793.

131. For instance, see Chen et al., *Minguo Huayang xianzhi*, 28.21b–23b, 26b–28b, 30a–b, 41b–43a.

132. Zeng, "Shilue," in Zuo, *Lengyinxianguan shigao*, "Shilue" 3b.

133. For the painter's livelihood, see Cahill, *The Painter's Practice*, 32–70. For his mention of gentry women painters, see particularly 70.

134. Wu Tang, "Inscription," in Zuo, *Lengyinxianguan shigao*, appendix 3a; Wang Degu, "Inscription," in Zuo, *Lengyinxianguan shigao*, appendix 3b; Zhao Wulian, "Inscription," in Zuo, *Lengyinxianguan shigao*, appendix 3b–4a.

135. Zuo, *Lengyinxianguan shigao*, 6.13b.

136. Zuo, *Lengyinxianguan shigao*, 5.9b–10a.

137. In her inscription for Wu Chunhai's painting, Zuo refers to him as "father-in-law of my daughter" (*qinjia*). There are also a line and a brief note toward the end of her inscription stating that she had arranged a good marriage for her fourth daughter (*Lengyinxianguan shigao*, 5.16a, 5.18b).

138. Zuo, *Lengyinxianguan shigao*, 5.15b–19a.

139. Zuo, *Lengyinxianguan shigao*, 5.19a.

140. Zuo, *Lengyinxianguan shigao*, appendix 31a, 31b.

141. Zuo, *Lengyinxianguan shigao*, 5.17b.

142. Zuo, *Lengyinxianguan shigao*, 5.18a.

143. See chapter 2, note 97 about the phrase's allusion to the story in the *Zhuangzi*.

144. Both Zuo and the local gazetteer referred to Zeng Yong's superior as *dafu*. The phrase meant "government administration" in general terms. However, it was also an alternative way of addressing the governor of a province. The contexts suggest that Zuo and the local gazetteer are referring to Yuke, who was governor of Jiangxi during 1860–61. For Yuke's tenure, see Qian, *Qingdai zhiguan nianbiao* 2: 1703–4. Yuke was demoted in late 1861. On the recommendation of Zeng Guofan, Shen Baozhen (1820–79) replaced

Yuke as governor of Jiangxi, serving from 1861 to 1865. See Zhao, *Qingshi gao* 39: 12043–46. Also see Qian, *Qingdai zhiguan nianbiao* 2: 1704. For background information concerning a protracted period of battles in Ji'an, see Zhao, *Qingshi gao* 39: 12037–38.

145. Soon after Zeng Yong assumed office in Ji'an, he declined the governor's request for heavier taxation on the people there. He also prevented Li Jinyang and Lu Desheng, the two directors sent by the governor as reinforcements, from extorting money from the people and gave them a sum out of his own pocket. It was Zeng's integrity that led to the two directors' discontent and hence their intrigues against him. The governor did not look into the matter until the entire prefecture was stirred by Zeng's dismissal and made an appeal on his part. See Chen et al., *Minguo Huayang xianzhi*, 15.1b–2a.

146. Chen et al., *Minguo Huayang xianzhi*, 15.2a.

147. Chen et al., *Minguo Huayang xianzhi*, 15.2b. For the system of granting posthumous titles to officials who had made contributions to the state, see Pan, "Lun Qingdai shifa"; Shu and Qiao, "Qingdai wenguan zhidu gailun," particularly 71–74.

148. Chen et al., *Minguo Huayang xianzhi*, 15.3a–4b. The epitaph dated the Eighth Day of the Third Lunar Month of 1880. It is also incorporated into Zuo's volume of prose, *Lengyinxianguan shigao*, *Wencun*, 4a–8a.

149. Zuo, *Lengyinxianguan shigao*, *Wencun*, 1a–2b. Zuo incorporated three texts into this volume. Aside from the epitaph and the portrait eulogy for Zeng Yong, there is a preface to the Zeng lineage genealogy (*Wencun*, 3a). Taken together these three texts indicate her efforts to honor Zeng's death and to place him properly in the Zeng lineage tree. Her preface is a rare example of a woman's involvement in the compilation of her husband's lineage genealogy. I briefly cite this example in chapter 3, which focuses on the genre of genealogy writing.

150. The traumatic effects of Zeng Yong's death were still fresh for Zuo. She prompted a series of questions of how she was supposed to shoulder all the familial responsibilities confronting her in the wake of his death. A few lines indicate in particular that she had not yet embarked on her long journey to Sichuan: "To hold a wake for you, I temporarily stayed in this land (in Jiangxi). How will your parents react when they hear of your death in the countryside (of Chengdu)?" See Zuo, *Lengyinxianguan shigao*, *Wencun*, 2a. In other words, the posthumous title was added to the caption at a later time, after Zeng's achievements successfully reached the emperor and won him the title. It was most probably added when Zuo's collection was published in 1891. I am grateful to Professor Allan Barr for suggesting this point to me.

151. Zuo, *Lengyinxianguan shigao*, *Wencun*, 2a.

152. Zuo, *Lengyinxianguan shigao*, appendix 2b–3b.

153. Zuo, *Lengyinxianguan shigao*, 5.18b. Other evidence found in Zuo's inscription for Wu Chunhai's painting suggests that, by 1872, her earlier efforts to vindicate Zeng Yong had been to no avail because she had been unable to reach her most powerful connections (*Lengyinxianguan shigao*, 5.18a). Her inscription for Wu's painting partly served this purpose of reaching the powerful.

154. See Zuo, *Lengyinxianguan shigao*, appendix 4a–14b.

155. Some of the authors referred to these details of Guangxu's visits. For instance, see Zuo, *Lengyinxianguan shigao*, appendix 5b, 11b–12a.

156. Zuo, *Lengyinxianguan shigao*, 5.18a–b. It was also during this year that she moved twice so that her sons would have better educational opportunities (6.1a–b, 6.4a).

157. These poems bear the title "Chanted by a Son Traveling away from Home" (Youzi yin) (Zuo, *Lengyinxianguan shigao*, 6.17b–18b). For the following selections from the poems, see 6.18a.

158. The city of Yan refers to Beijing, former capital of the Yan State during the Warring States period.

159. These two lines allude to the story of the Han founding general, Han Xin (ca. 231–196 BCE) as recorded in *Records of the Historian* (Shiji). Before Han Xin had the chance to establish his glorious career, he was driven by poverty to beg for food. "Mother Piao" was an old woman who was cleaning silk by a river. She brought food for Han Xin and said encouraging words to him. See Sima, *Shiji*, 251. Zuo uses this episode to express her worries about the uncertainty lying ahead of Guangxu, especially his lack of support and help in the capital.

160. See Wang, "Qingdai baqi guanyuan de yinzi zhidu," 29–30; Wang, "Qingdai de yinzi zhidu," 92–93. These studies also refer to the corruptions of this system.

161. Wang Jiabi, the first author who inscribed the painting in the capital, stated that Guangxu took the album to pay him a visit during the time when Guangxu was waiting for the assignment from the Board of Personnel (Zuo, *Lengyinxianguan shigao*, appendix 5a–b).

162. At various places *Lengyinxianguan shigao* bears the following line: "Proofread by the son-in-law Lin Shangchen, and printed with respect by the son Guangxu." There is also ample evidence of Zuo's involvement in the publications of her own collection and that of her husband. See my introduction of her life earlier in this chapter.

163. See note 83 about the probable time when Zuo was granted the reward (between 1891 and 1894).

3. STAGING FAMILY DRAMA

1. For a list of what genealogy usually includes, see Wang, *Zhongguo jiapu tonglun*, 279–348. For the development of genealogies in relation to lineages and their ancestral rites, see Feng, *Zhongguo zongzu zhidu*, 13–44, 252–332; Feng, *Zhongguo gudai de zongzu yu citang*, 57–78. Also see Ebrey, *Confucianism and Family Rituals*.

2. Feng, *Zhongguo gudai de zongzu yu citang*, 45.

3. Rowe, "Ancestral Rites and Political Authority," 389–90.

4. Feng, *Zhongguo zongzu zhidu*, 271.

5. See Bray, *Technology and Gender*, 102; Ebrey, *The Inner Quarters*, 124; Feng, *Zhongguo gudai de zongzu yu citing*, 73–74.

6. Bray, *Technology and Gender*, 107.

7. Maclaren and Chen, "The Oral and Ritual Culture," 206.

8. Zuo Xijia, *Lengyinxianguan shigao*, *Wencun*, 3a.

9. According to Feng's exhaustive study of the biographical sources from the Qing period, *jiazhuan* has two definitions: first, biography, epitaph, or elegy for a family or lineage member; second, family or lineage genealogy (*Qingdai renwu zhuanji shiliao yanjiu*, 5). A few records of *jiazhuan* by female authors fall into the former category. The woman poet Zhang Wanying (1800–ca. 1868), for example, published a collection of biographical writings titled *Canfengguan wenji*. This collection includes two *jiazhuan* for gentry women: "Zhangmu Suntairuren jiazhuan" and "Wangtaigongren jiazhuan," in *Jiangnan nüxing bieji sanbian* 2: 1388–90. Zhang indicates that she authored the biographies at the invitation of the two ladies' families. Women's engagement with biographical writings, including *jiazhuan*, is a topic worthy of further investigation. For the purpose of my discussion, I focus on writings directly related to genealogies.

10. Mann, "Dowry Wealth and Wifely Virtue," 70.

11. Chen, *Xiaodaixuan lunshi shi*, 2.38a; Shan, *Guixiu zhengshi zaixuji*, juan 4b, 5b. Also see Hu, *Lidai funü zhuzuo kao*, 494.

12. Copies of Yuan's collections are currently held by the National Library of China. There are also recent reprints, from which this chapter draws most of its materials: Yuan, *Yuequxuan shicao*, reprinted in *Jiangnan nüxing bieji erbian* 2: 901–48. Yuan, *Yuequxuan zhuanshulue*, reprinted in *Jiangnan nüxing bieji erbian* 2: 949–80.

13. These include, in the original order: Shen Zhaolin, "Preface"; Yuan Kejia, "Preface"; Zhuang Zhongfang, "Preface"; Luo Benzhou, "Preface"; Zhuang Xiao, "Epilogue"; Cai Zhenwu, "Epilogue"; Yu Chengde, "Epilogue," in Yuan, *Yuequxuan shicao*, reprinted in *Jiangnan nüxing bieji erbian* 2: 903–7, 928–30. Zhuang Zhongfang, "Preface"; Yang Juyuan, "Epilogue," in Yuan, *Yuequxuan zhuanshulue*, reprinted in *Jiangnan nüxing bieji erbian* 2: 951, 980.

14. See Yuan, "Xianfuzi Meiliang gong zhuan" (Biography of my late husband, Mr. Meiliang), in *Yuequxuan zhuanshulue*, reprinted in *Jiangnan nüxing bieji erbian* 2: 960. Also see the entry about Wu Jie in the local gazetteer of Kuaiji: Wang and Shen, *Daoguang Kuaiji xianzhi gao*, 93.

15. Luo Benzhou, "Preface," in Yuan, *Yuequxuan shicao*, reprinted in *Jiangnan nüxing bieji erbian* 2: 906.

16. Ibid.

17. Wang and Shen, *Daoguang Kuaiji xianzhi gao*, 93.

18. Luo Benzhou, "Preface," 906.

19. Yuan, "Xianfuzi Meiliang gong zhuan," 965.

20. Shen Zhaolin, "Preface," in Yuan, *Yuequxuan shicao*, reprinted in *Jiangnan nüxing bieji erbian* 2: 903.

21. Luo Benzhou, "Preface," 906.

22. Shen Zhaolin, "Preface," 903.

23. Zhuang Zhongfang, "Preface," in Yuan, *Yuequxuan zhuanshulue*, reprinted in *Jiangnan nüxing bieji erbian* 2: 951.

24. Zhuang Xiao, "Epilogue," in Yuan, *Yuequxuan shicao*, reprinted in *Jiangnan nüxing bieji erbian* 2: 928.

25. Yuan, "Chongxiu citang ji" (Account of the restoration of the Lineage Ancestral Hall), in *Yuequxuan zhuanshulue*, reprinted in *Jiangnan nüxing bieji erbian* 2: 953–54.

26. Yuan, "Laodangnian jisibu xu" (Preface to the book for the ancestral rites that are held for those from the seventh generation to the tenth); "Xiaodangnian jisibu xu" (Preface to the book for the ancestral rites that are held for those from the eleventh to the twelfth generations), in *Yuequxuan zhuanshulue*, reprinted in *Jiangnan nüxing bieji erbian* 2: 954–56. To judge from Yuan's prefaces to these two books, their contents would have included a chronological list of the ancestors and brief biographies of them, a list of offerings to the ancestors, an account of the funds and land allocated for the rituals, and an alternating schedule according to which different descendants would take charge of various categories of ancestral rites.

27. For the preface to the *jisibu*, see Yuan, *Yuequxuan zhuanshulue*, reprinted in *Jiangnan nüxing bieji erbian* 2: 957–58. For the preface to the account book, see 974–75. For the fifteen biographies, see 958–74.

28. In addition to the pieces related to ancestral rites, *Yuequxuan zhuanshulue* also includes an autobiographical account and an additional account on burial matters (975–79).

29. Yuan, "Zishu" (An account about myself), in *Yuequxuan zhuanshulue*, reprinted in *Jiangnan nüxing bieji erbian* 2: 975.

30. Yuan, "Xianfuzi Meiliang gong zhuan," 961.

31. Wu Jie's mother passed away when he was only seven. See Yuan, "Xiangu Qian taifuren zhuan" (Biography of my late mother-in-law, the Grand Lady Qian), in *Yuequxuan zhuanshulue*, reprinted in *Jiangnan nüxing bieji erbian* 2: 959.

32. Yuan, "Xianfuzi Meiliang gong zhuan," 961.

33. Ibid.

34. I elaborate on this point in my later discussion.

35. Yuan, "Xianfuzi Meiliang gong zhuan," 961.

36. Lu, "Uxorilocal Marriage among Qing Literati."

37. Wang and Shen, *Daoguang Kuaiji xianzhi gao*, 93.

38. Yuan, "Xianfuzi Meiliang gong zhuan," 960.

39. Yuan Kejia, "Preface," in Yuan, *Yuequxuan shicao*, reprinted in *Jiangnan nüxing bieji erbian* 2: 904.

40. Lu, "Uxorilocal Marriage among Qing Literati," 102. Also see 89–91.

41. The Yuan government mandated that agreements should be drawn up to specify terms of uxorilocal marriages. See Ebrey, "Property Law and Uxorilocal Marriage," 65–66. For samples of the contract for uxorilocal marriages, see Cohen, "Writs of Passage in Late Imperial China," 61–62.

42. Lu, "Uxorilocal Marriage among Qing Literati," 91.

43. Yuan, "Zishu," 975.

44. For reasons of space, I provide only a brief summary here.

45. Yuan, *Yuequxuan zhuanshulue*, reprinted in *Jiangnan nüxing bieji erbian* 2: 958, 961–66, 975–76.

46. Yuan, "Zishu," 976.

47. For the practice of household division during this time, see Wakefield, *Fenjia*, 64–67.

48. See Shen, *DaQinglü jizhu*, 216–17. Also see A, *MingQing shidai funü de diwei yu quanli*, 233.

49. For the power of the patriarch over either household properties or household members, see Zhang, *Qingdai minfa zonglun*, 213–16.

50. Shen, *DaQinglü jizhu*, 216–17.

51. Birge, *Women, Property, and Confucian Reaction*, 228–29. Birge sees in this legal case a new rule for uxorilocal marriages during the Yuan because, during the Song, an uxorilocally married man should renounce his rights to his natal father's patrimony.

52. For instance, see Yuan, "Xianjiu Meipo gong zhuan" (Biography of my late father-in-law, Mr. Meipo [style name of Wu Yonghe]), in *Yuequxuan zhuanshulue*, reprinted in *Jiangnan nüxing bieji erbian* 2: 958. Yuan qualifies the situation as *jiuyang* (invited to stay with one's son as a means of being supported). For instance, she mentions that both Wu Yonghe and his concubine Wang were invited by Wu Jie to stay in his home. See Yuan, "Wang ruren zhuan" (Biography of Lady Wang), in *Yuequxuan zhuanshulue*, reprinted in *Jiangnan nüxing bieji erbian* 2: 960.

53. Wakefield, *Fenjia*, 78–79.

54. See Li, "Qingdai guanfeng zhidu"; Qi, "Qingdai Xinjiang guanyuan de yanglian yin." Also see the entry about the subsidy in Hucker, *A Dictionary of Official Titles*, 96.

55. Yuan, "Xianfuzi Meiliang gong zhuan," 964.

56. Yuan, "Xianjiu Meipo gong zhuan," 958.

57. Yuan, "Xianbojiu Lizhai gong zhuan" (Biography of my late uncle-in-law, Mr. Lizhai), in *Yuequxuan zhuanshulue*, reprinted in *Jiangnan nüxing bieji erbian* 2: 972.

58. Yuan, "Xianfuzi Meiliang gong zhuan," 962.

59. Yuan, "Xianbojiu Lizhai gong zhuan," 972.

60. Yuan, "Xianfuzi Meiliang gong zhuan," 962.

61. Yuan, "Fengshui lun" (On selecting a propitious tomb site), in *Yuequxuan zhuanshulue*, reprinted in *Jiangnan nüxing bieji erbian* 2: 979.

62. "Fengshui lun" is much more than an implied criticism of Wu Yongqing's descendants. Yuan refutes the idea that she should spend extravagantly on the tomb of Wu Jie because it would be a waste of what should be spent on the education of Wu Jie's son. She denounces the concept of *fengshui* as unreliable and openly criticizes Wu Yonghe for being deluded by the concept in choosing the tomb sites for himself and for his concubine Wang. She proposes instead that the example of Wu Yongqing (i.e., the fact that his descendants failed to take care of his burial) proves that nothing can be predetermined (Yuan, "Fengshui lun," in *Yuequxuan zhuanshulue*, 977–79).

63. For widows' property rights during the Ming and Qing periods, see Bernhardt, *Women and Property*, 62–72.

64. Yuan, "Xianfuzi Meiliang gong zhuan," 965–66.

65. Yuan, "Xianfuzi Meiliang gong zhuan," 967.

66. Yuan mentions Cao as the mother of Wu Jie's twin sons ("Xianfuzi Meiliang gong zhuan," 965).

67. Yuan, "Zishu," 976.

68. This account is, of course, written entirely from Yuan's point of view. From Wu Yonghe's perspective—if he regarded himself as the head of a large household that had not been divided between Wu Jie and Wu Jie's younger brother—his supreme power over the household properties would not be affected by Wu Jie's death. From this perspective we can also understand why Yuan was careful to emphasize that the funds at her disposal were entirely derived from the donations, not from the Wu family wealth. That is, neither Wu Yonghe nor the Wu kin could lay claim to the funds or the properties that she held in Beijing.

69. Yuan, "Xianfuzi Meiliang gong zhuan," 966.

70. Yuan, *Yuequxuan shicao*, reprinted in *Jiangnan nüxing bieji erbian* 2: 920–21. Swallows were believed to find shelter only in illustrious families, such as the Wangs and the Xies of the Eastern Jin period (317–420). See, for example, the famous line of the Tang poet Liu Yuxi (772–842), which refers to the swallows (flying) before the halls of the Wangs and the Xies.

71. See Yuan's poetic exchanges with her female friends during this time (*Yuequxuan shicao*, reprinted in *Jiangnan nüxing bieji erbian* 2: 918–19, 921–24). These poetic works served socializing purposes and indicated that Yuan was well connected with a number of elite women in Beijing.

72. Yuan, "Wenxi tongzi zhuan" (A biography for my child Wenxi), in *Yuequxuan zhuanshulue*, reprinted in *Jiangnan nüxing bieji erbian* 2: 962–63.

73. Yuan, "Wenxi tongzi zhuan," 969.

74. Qian Yiji, "Wu tongzi kuangming" (Funerary epitaph for the child, Wu [Enxi]), and "Dao hui ci" (Poems mourning the death of Hui[sheng]/The talented child), in Yuan, *Yuequxuan zhuanshulue*, reprinted in *Jiangnan nüxing bieji erbian* 2: 969–71.

75. Yuan, "Xianjiu Meipo gong zhuan," 958.

76. Yuan, "Zishu," 976–77.

77. One *mu* equals around 666.67 square meters. One *fen* equals around 66.67 square meters. One *li* equals around 6.67 square meters. One *hao* equals around 0.67 square meters. Here Yuan is counting the fields to their smallest proportions.

78. Yuan, "Meifang shouzubu xu" (Account book for the rent incomes of Wu Jie's household), in *Yuequxuan zhuanshulue*, reprinted in *Jiangnan nüxing bieji erbian* 2: 974–75.

79. Yuan's correspondence with a female friend at a later time indicated that she had taken the trip to bury her father-in-law and to rebuild her husband's tomb (*Yuequxuan shicao*, reprinted in *Jiangnan nüxing bieji erbian* 2: 923).

80. Bernhardt, *Women and Property*, 161–62.

81. Bernhardt, *Women and Property*, 161–78.

82. Bernhardt, *Women and Property*, 163.

83. Legal cases from this time show that the avaricious kin of the deceased husband was a familiar presence in disputes over inheritance. See Sommer,

"The Uses of Chastity," 117. The Wu kin tried to prevent Yuan from taking over the household accounts probably because they expected to have a share of Wu Jie's patrimony.

84. For the principles of inheritance during the Qing period, see Zhang, *Qingdai minfa zonglun*, 222–37. Also see Guo, *Zhongguo caichanfa shigao*, 171–78.

85. Feng, *Zhongguo zongzu zhidu*, 27–28, 33–35.

86. Ebrey, *Confucianism and Family Rituals*, 23, 222.

87. Ancestral sacrifice was the defining element of the lineage, and participation in these sacrifices was directly equated with lineage membership. See Rowe, "Ancestral Rites and Political Authority," 381.

88. Yuan, "Chongxiu citang ji," 953.

89. Yuan, "Laodangnian jisibu xu," 955; Yuan, "Xiaodangnian jisibu xu," 956.

90. Yuan, "Xiaodangnian jisibu xu," 955–56.

91. See Wu, "Guangzong yaozu"; Zhao and Liu, "Mingchao wenguan fuzu fengzeng zhidu shulun."

92. See Wolf and Huang, *Marriage and Adoption*, 105.

93. Yuan, "Chongxiu citang ji," 953. For unknown reasons the name of Wu Jie's son is erased at all places where he is mentioned. However, it is clear from the context that the "fifteenth-generation descendant" refers to him.

94. Yuan, "Meifang jisibu xu" (Book of ancestral rites for Meiliang's household), in *Yuequxuan zhuanshulue*, reprinted in *Jiangnan nüxing bieji erbian* 2: 957–58.

95. Yuan, "Zishu," 977.

96. These included Yin Debu, the county magistrate of Shanyin (a neighboring county of Kuaiji), and Tang Tinglun, an instructor at the local academy. See Yuan, "Xianjiu Meipo gong zhuan," 959.

97. For example, see Sommer, *Sex, Law, and Society*, 15.

98. Yuan Jingrong, *Yuequxuan shicao*, reprinted in *Jiangnan nüxing bieji erbian* 2: 924.

99. Yuan Jingrong, *Yuequxuan shicao*, reprinted in *Jiangnan nüxing bieji erbian* 2: 924–25.

100. Yuan Jingrong, *Yuequxuan shicao*, reprinted in *Jiangnan nüxing bieji erbian* 2: 926.

101. Yuan Jingrong, *Yuequxuan shicao*, reprinted in *Jiangnan nüxing bieji erbian* 2: 925. The theme of this poem is the changing fate of a pot of peonies, which Yuan uses as a metaphor for the unpredictability of her own fate. Some of her lines refer to her loss of the sole surviving root (*gugen*) of the peony, which implies her loss of the sole surviving root of the family (i.e., heir). In any case Yuan's son was only eleven when she took him to Kuaiji in 1844. By the time she adopted her grandson in 1848, her son would be only fifteen. It is unlikely that she would adopt an heir for her son without arranging a marriage for him first. The only explanation is that she lost her son between 1844 and 1848.

102. Zhuang Xiao, "Epilogue," 928.

103. Yang Juyuan, "Epilogue," in Yuan, *Yuequxuan zhuanshulue*, reprinted in *Jiangnan nüxing bieji erbian* 2: 980.

104. Zhuang Zhongfang, "Preface," 905.

105. For instance, see Shen Zhaolin, "Preface," 903.

4. ENACTING GUARDIANS OF FAMILY HEALTH

1. Wu, *Reproducing Women*, 57–59. Also see Brook, *The Confusions of Pleasure*, 167–71; Chia, *Printing for Profit*, 256–57.

2. Furth, *A Flourishing Yin*, 156–63.

3. Furth, *A Flourishing Yin*, 266.

4. Wu, *Reproducing Women*, 19, 77.

5. Hu, "Naming the First New Woman," 201–2.

6. The collection is composed of the following four volumes: *Noted in Random While I Taught the Classics to My Children* (Shoujing oubi); *Prefaces, Epilogues, Biographies, Eulogies, and Inscriptions* (Xuba zhuanji zan tiba, thirteen pieces); *Family Letters* (Jiashu, twenty-nine pieces); *Poetry and Song Lyrics* (Shi, shiyu). The collection is appended with three essays. There is a recent reprint of the collection, from which my discussion draws most of its material. See Chen, *Tingsonglou yigao*, reprinted in Hu and Peng, *Jiangnan nüxing bieji chubian* 1: 569–636.

7. Chen, *Xiaodaixuan lunshi shi*, 1.26a–b; Xu, *Guixiu cichao*, 14.5a–7b; Yun, *Guochao guixiu zhengshi ji*, 19.8a–10b.

8. Chen et al., *Minguo Hangzhou fuzhi*, 892.

9. See my brief discussion of Chen Shu in chapter 2.

10. Chen, *Tingsonglou yigao*, reprinted in Hu and Peng, *Jiangnan nüxing bieji chubian* 1: 590–92, 597–98.

11. Chen, *Tingsonglou yigao*, reprinted in Hu and Peng, *Jiangnan nüxing bieji chubian* 1: 586.

12. Han, "Zhongguo gudai zhuanji wenxue luelun."

13. Waltner, "Life and Letters."

14. Here Chen reveals the financial straits of her family. Her management of the household accounts also reminds us of what Mann refers to as women's role as the family bursar in "Dowry Wealth and Wifely Virtue."

15. Mann, *The Talented Women of the Zhang Family*, 183–85.

16. For instance, see Furth, *A Flourishing Yin*, 129, 235–37; Wu, *Reproducing Women*, 18; Hinrichs and Barnes, *Chinese Medicine and Healing*, 13–4, 153–54, 166–67.

17. As it is unclear which of the children Chen refers to as "San xiaoxiao" and "Si xiaoxiao," I list them separately. Here she also reveals her own fragile health situation. Her "Fire disorders" and "hepatic disorders" involve a variety of symptoms that are both mentally and physically related. I do not discuss her health in detail but focus on how she dealt with the health issues of her household.

18. Chen, *Tingsonglou yigao*, reprinted in Hu and Peng, *Jiangnan nüxing bieji chubian* 1: 611.

19. One *liang* equals around 31.3 grams. One *qian* equals around 3.13 grams. One *fen* equals around 0.313 grams.

20. Chen, *Tingsonglou yigao*, reprinted in Hu and Peng, *Jiangnan nüxing bieji chubian* 1: 610.

21. Ibid.

22. Chen, *Tingsonglou yigao*, reprinted in Hu and Peng, *Jiangnan nüxing bieji chubian* 1: 604.

23. Ibid.

24. Furth, *A Flourishing Yin*, 156–63.

25. For this fact, see Chen, *Tingsonglou yigao*, reprinted in Hu and Peng, *Jiangnan nüxing bieji chubian* 1: 597.

26. Chen's letters indicate that Qian Yiji wrote to her on similar matters, such as how he treated the illness of a boatman's son on his trip. He also advised her on her health situation and sent her medicine and diet supplements for her "hepatic disorders." See Chen, *Tingsonglou yigao*, reprinted in Hu and Peng, *Jiangnan nüxing bieji chubian* 1: 601, 606, 608.

27. For instance, see Li, "Qingdai cangshujia jiqi shumu"; Jiao, *Zhongguo cangshu shihua*; Tan et al., *Qingdai cangshulou fazhanshi*, 37–53.

28. Furth, *A Flourishing Yin*, 156–61, 157, 163.

29. Liao and Lin, "Qingdai yixue jiaoyu xingshi juyao."

30. Furth, *A Flourishing Yin*, 284–85.

31. Wu, *Reproducing Women*, 20.

32. Wang Zhenyi draws recent scholarly attention mainly because of her voluminous works on mathematics and astronomy, areas of study that were rarely explored by gentry women of the time. See Xu, "Qingdai nüxuezhe Wang Zhenyi."

33. Wang, *Defengting chuji*, 8.3b–4a. Wang grew up in a family of scholars and bibliophiles. Her grandfather was a government official who owned seventy-five trunks of books (8.1a). Her father was among the medical and cultural elite discussed by Furth, publishing a collection of prescriptions that proved to be effective in his practice as a literati physician.

34. Wang, *Defengting chuji*, 4.6b–7b.

35. Leung, "Women Practicing Medicine in Pre-modern China," 126.

36. Leung, "Women Practicing Medicine in Pre-modern China," 126–27.

37. Zhao, *Qingshi gao*, 46: 14054. Also see my brief discussion of Wang Ying in the introduction.

38. Wang, *Ya'an Shuwu wenji*, 1.5a–b.

39. Wang, *Ya'an Shuwu wenji*, 1.33a–b.

40. Wang, *Ya'an Shuwu wenji*, 1.36a–b.

41. Wang, *Ya'an Shuwu wenji*, 2.22a–b. *The Bronze Cabinet* was a medical classic from the Han period.

42. Wang, *Ya'an Shuwu wenji*, 2.23a–b.

43. Wang, *Ya'an Shuwu wenji*, 1.33a.

44. Wang, *Ya'an Shuwu wenji*, 1.24b.

45. Zhang, *Han Feizi jiaozhu*, 222.

46. According to Furth, the aphorism reflected the rise of the ideal of the literati physicians (*ruyi*), the learned amateurs who increasingly joined the ranks of medical authors (*A Flourishing Yin*, 63).

47. Wang, *Ya'an Shuwu wenji*, 1.36a–43a.

48. This opening sentence is a direct quotation from the Han scholar-official Huan Kuan's political essay. See Huan, *Yantie lun*, 580.

49. Wang Ying is here quoting from Han Fei. See Zhang, *Han Feizi jiaozhu*, 301. The artisan Shi was said to have superior skills, and the warriors Ben and Yu were known for their physical strength.

50. Wang, *Ya'an Shuwu wenji*, 1.5a–b.

51. The essay bears no date of its composition. Given that Wang's essays are organized by genre rather than chronological order, it is not possible to determine the date by judging from the essay's location in the collection.

52. For an explanation of the *baojia* system, see Hucker, *A Dictionary of Official Titles*, 90.

53. Wang, *Ya'an Shuwu wenji*, 2.12a–13b.

54. Wang, *Ya'an Shuwu wenji*, 2.9a–b.

55. Zeng Guangxu, "Preface," in Zeng Yi, *Guhuanshi shiciji*, Preface 1a.

56. Ibid.

57. Yan Qianrun, "Preface," in Zeng, *Guhuanshi shiciji*, Preface 11a. A few of Zeng's poetic works entered the Qing anthologies of women's poetry. See Lei and Lei, *Guixiu cihua*, 4.7b–8a; Shan, *Guixiu zhengshi zaixuji, juan* 1a, 52a–57a.

58. Zeng, *Guhuanshi shiciji*, 3.11b–13b.

59. Zeng Guangxu, "Preface," in Zeng Yi, *Guhuanshi shiciji*, Preface 1b–2a.

60. Lin, "Shilun Yanghu Zuoshi erdai cainü zhi jiazu guanxi," 204–5, 193.

61. Zeng Guangxu, "Preface," in Zeng Yi, *Guhuanshi shiciji*, Preface 2a–b.

62. For the timeline I provide here, see Zeng's prefaces to her volumes of writings: "Preface," in *Yixue pian*, 2a–3a; "Preface," in *Nüxue pian*, 4a–6a. Also see Duanfang, "Preface," in Zeng, *Yixue pian*, 1a; Duanfang, "Preface," in Zeng, *Nüxue pian*, 1.1a–b; Zhang Baixi, "Preface," in Zeng, *Nüxue pian*, 1.2a–3a; Wu Qingdi, "Preface," in Zeng, *Nüxue pian*, 2.1a–2a.

63. Yang, "You Zeng Yi (1852–1927) de ge'an kan wanQing."

64. Zeng, "Zixu," in *Nüxue pian*, 4a. China had a long tradition of *muxun* or *mujiao*, both of which refer to the education that the mother gave to the children. Gentry women during the Qing period produced a tremendous amount of writings on educating their children. See Ho, "Qingdai nüxing kezishu juyao."

65. Zeng, "Zixu," in *Nüxue pian*, 5b.

66. Zeng, "Zixu," in *Yixue pian*, 2b, 3a.

67. Both poems are from the *Odes of Qin* (Qinfeng) in the *Book of Odes*. In general Zeng is referring to an ancient tradition of female virtue, which she believes to be central to the rise of the Qin state. "Xiaorong" is written in the voice of a woman who expresses her admiration for her husband, who is at war. "Wuyi" is generally believed to be written in the voice of a soldier who expresses his wish to devote himself to his state despite shortages of resources (such as clothes). It is not entirely clear why Zeng cites the latter poem. See Cheng, *Shijing yizhu*, 221–24, 231–33.

68. The concept of patriotism was introduced to late Qing modern schools through Japan. See Zinda, "Propagating New 'Virtues.'"

69. Zeng, "Zixu," in *Nüxue pian*, 4a–6a.

70. Hu, "Naming the First New Woman."

71. Zurndorfer, "Wang Zhaoyuan and the Erasure of 'Talented Women.'"

72. Liang, "Lun nüxue." Also see Ko's recent translation of this text in Liu et al., *The Birth of Chinese Feminism*, 189–203. See 199 for my quotation of the text.

73. Qian, "Revitalizing the *Xianyuan* Tradition," 424.

74. Qian, "Revitalizing the *Xianyuan* Tradition," 426–27. Also see Qian's recent book-length study on Xue Shaohui and her social and intellectual networks, *Politics, Poetics, and Gender in Late Qing China*. She argues that women reformers like Xue prioritized women's self-improvement over the "patriarchal nationalism" of the leading male reformers who subordinated women's issues to national strengthening (see particularly 9). In Zeng Yi we find the same emphasis on women's self-empowerment, and to the benefit of the nation at the same time.

75. Zeng, "Eulogy," in *Nüxue pian*, front page.

76. See, for example, Mann's discussion of Yun Zhu's moral stance in *The Precious Records*, 116–17.

77. It can be argued that Chen assumed her audiences to be women of the gentry class, who could afford to be educated and could therefore read her moral guides.

78. For the transformation of women's education during the late Qing period, see Cong, "From '*Cainü*' to '*Nü Jiaoxi.*'"

79. Zeng was probably echoing a newspaper essay by a late Qing female student Zhang Jianren, titled "Yu chang pingdeng xian xing nüxue lun" (To have equal rights we must first promote women's learning). See Xia, *Wan-Qing nüxing yu jindai Zhongguo*, 93. At the same time, Zeng's attack of the radical women reformers reminds us that there were not only male and female reformers' sides of the story, but a complex continuum of positions that were not determined by the factor of gender alone.

80. Zeng, "General Remarks," in *Zhongkui lu*, 1a.

81. For the introduction of the Japanese woman educator Shimoda Utako to China, see Huang, "Cong 'jianghu zhiyuan' dao 'miaotang zhigao.'"

82. Zeng, *Nüxue pian*, 29a–b.

83. For a discussion of eugenics in Republican China, see Dikötter, *Imperfect Conceptions*, 61–118.

84. Rogaski, *Hygienic Modernity*, 13.

85. Rogaski, *Hygienic Modernity*, 73, 104–25, 165, 92, 125–35; 161–64.

86. He, *Xiyi dongjian yu wenhua tiaoshi*, 299–305.

87. Zeng, *Yixue pian*, 1.1.4b–5a.

88. See Hanson, "The 'Warm Diseases' Current of Learning." Also see Hanson's book-length study of the history of the disease from antiquity to modern times, *Speaking of Epidemics*.

89. Zeng, *Yixue pian*, 1.1.3a–4b.

90. Hanson, *Speaking of Epidemics*, 110–17. In a few other essays Zeng provides different treatments for warm disease based precisely on the Triple *jiao* schema. See Zeng, *Yixue pian*, 1.1.21a–1.3.4b.

91. Hanson, *Speaking of Epidemics*, 111, 141–42.
92. Hanson, *Speaking of Epidemics*, 138, 142. For cholera's arrival in China, see 134.
93. Hanson, *Speaking of Epidemics*, 151.
94. Zeng, *Yixue pian*, 2.2.1a.
95. Wu, *Reproducing Women*, 42–51, 47–49.
96. The blood and the liver system were viewed in close relation to women's presumed emotionally generated disorders. For example, see Furth's discussion of nourishing the *yin* blood and making the Ministerial Fire lodged in the liver system descend as strategies of treating female disorders caused by unsatisfied passion (*A Flourishing Yin*, 171).
97. For example, see Xia, *WanQing nüxing yu jindai Zhongguo*, 95–101, 128–42.
98. One *fen* equals 0.33 cm.
99. Zeng, *Nüxue pian*, 1.21b–22a.
100. The 1898 anti-footbinding movement was largely a "male discourse" that lacked substantial participation by women. See Yang, "Lun Wuxu weixin," 210.
101. Xue Shaohui, *Daiyunlou yiji*, *Wenji, juan* b, 22a. Xue expressed this point in her "Letter to Ms. Shen" (Fu Shen nüshi shu), *juan* b, 21a–22b.
102. By contrast, Xue argued primarily that "footbinding is a trivial, private matter; bound or unbound, a woman's foot is simply irrelevant to her mission in life and her contributions to the nation" (Ko, *Cinderella's Sisters*, 39).

CONCLUSION

1. For example, see Wang, *When "I" Was Born*.
2. We should bear in mind, for example, that the vast majority of highly educated women writers originated from gentry-class families of the Yangtze delta. The distinction of class and marital status among women was a crucial factor, as I have argued in Yuan Jingrong's case.
3. Barlow, *The Question of Women in Chinese Feminism*, 37–63.
4. For example, see a study of ritual (including that in early China) that questions these dichotomies: Seligman et al., *Ritual and Its Consequences*.
5. For quick reference to this antiessentialist trend, see Scott, *Gender and the Politics of History*, 29–50; Scott, "Experience." For the decentering of feminism into "feminisms," see Kemp and Squires, *Feminisms*. For an emphasis on particularities of women's situations in different cultural and historical contexts, see, for example, Green, *Making Space for Indigenous Feminism*.
6. Cahill, *The Painter's Practice*, 54–65. For example, a renowned painter like Zheng Xie (1693–1765) could earn an annual income of as high as 1,000 taels of silver; by comparison a second-rank official of this time received a basic annual salary of 256 taels (57–58).
7. Cahill, *The Painter's Practice*, 69–70.
8. Cahill, *The Painter's Practice*, 59–67.

9. Zuo, *Lengyinxianguan shigao*, 6.6a, 6.16b–17a, appendix 20b, appendix 21b, 8.19a.

10. See Ho, "The Salt Merchants of Yang-Chou" and *The Ladder of Success in Imperial China*; Zurndorfer, *Change and Continuity in Chinese Local History*.

11. Ho, "The Salt Merchants of Yang-Chou," 168.

12. There are several important sources on women writers from the Huizhou area and its adjoining counties, including those who migrated to the urban centers of the lower Yangtze delta: Fu Ying, *MingQing Anhui funü wenxue zhushu jikao*; Guang Dazhong, *Anhui caiyuan jilue chugao*; Guang Tiefu, *Anhui mingyuan shici zhenglue*. The instances that I summarize here result from my preliminary research following these sources.

PRIMARY SOURCES

Cao Zhenxiu 曹貞秀. *Xieyunxuan xiaogao* 寫韻軒小藁 (Drafts from the Pavilion for Composing Rhymed Verses). 1815.

Chen Ershi 陳爾士. *Tingsonglou yigao* 聽松樓遺稿 (Remaining drafts from the Tower for Listening to the [Sounds of] Pine Trees). Ca. 1821.

Chen Fajia 陳法駕, et al., comps. *Minguo Huayang xianzhi* 民國華陽縣誌 (Republican period gazetteer of Huayang county). 1934; repr., Chengdu: Bashu Shushe, 1992.

Chen Qiong 陳璚, et al., comps. *Minguo Hangzhou fuzhi* 民國杭州府志 (Republican period gazetteer of Hangzhou prefecture). 1926; repr., Shanghai: Shanghai Shudian, 1993.

Chen Si 陳思 and Miao Quansun 繆荃孫, comps. *Jiangyinxian xuzhi* 江陰縣續志 (A sequel to the gazetteer of Jiangyin county). 1921; repr., Nanjing: Jiangsu Guji Chubanshe, 1991.

Chen Yun 陳芸. *Xiaodaixuan lunshi shi* 小黛軒論詩詩 (Poetry as commentary on poetry, written in the Small Black Pavilion). 1911.

Chen Yunlian 陳蘊蓮. *Xinfangge shicao* 信芳閣詩草 (Poetry drafts from the Pavilion of True Fragrance). 1851, 1859.

Cheng Bao 程葆, ed. *Qiudeng kezi tu tiyongji* 秋燈課子圖題詠集 (Collection of inscriptions for Picture [of Wang Ying] teaching her son under an autumnal lamp). 1844.

———, ed. *Ya'an Shuwu zengyanlu* 雅安書屋贈言錄 (Records of writings in honor of Ya'an's [courtesy name of Wang Ying] Study Room). 1844.

Cheng Junying 程俊英, trans. and annot. *Shijing yizhu* 詩經譯注 (The book of odes, annotated and translated into modern Chinese). Shanghai: Shanghai Guji Chubanshe, 1995.

Ciyuan 辭源 (Origins of words). 1915; repr., Beijing: Shangwu Yinshuguan, 1979.

Dong Baohong 董寶鴻. *Yinxiangge shichao* 飲香閣詩鈔 (Poetry collection from the Drinking-Fragrance Pavilion). 1857.

Dong Sigu 董似穀 and Tang Chenglie 湯成烈, comps. *Guangxu Wujin Yanghu xianzhi* 光緒武進陽湖縣誌 (Guangxu reign gazetteer of Wujin and Yanghu counties). 1879; repr., Taibei: Taiwan Xuesheng Shuju, 1968.

Du Min 杜敏. *Lidai diaojiwen* 歷代弔祭文 (Essays written to mourn the deceased from all dynasties). Xi'an: Sanhua Chubanshe, 1998.

Fu Ying 傅瑛. *MingQing Anhui funü wenxue zhushu jikao* 明清安徽婦女文學著述輯考 (Compiled sources of literary works by women of Anhui during the Ming and Qing periods). Hefei, Anhui: Huangshan Shushe, 2010.

Gan Lirou 甘立媃. *Yongxuelou gao* 詠雪樓稿 (Drafts from the Tower for Chanting about Snow). 1840.

Guang Dazhong 光大中. *Anhui caiyuan jilue chugao* 安徽才媛紀略初稿 (A preliminary draft of brief accounts about the talented women of Anhui). 1934–35.

Guang Tiefu 光鐵夫. *Anhui mingyuan shici zhenglue* 安徽名媛詩詞徵略 (Selected poetry and song lyrics by gentry women of Anhui). 1936.

Guo Qingfan 郭慶藩, annot. *Zhuangzi jishi* 莊子集釋 (An annotated edition of the *Zhuangzi*). Beijing: Zhonghua Shuju, 1982.

Huang Zhimo 黃秩模, comp. *Guochao guixiu shi liuxu ji* 國朝閨秀詩柳絮集 (A collection of willow catkins: Poetry by gentry women of our dynasty). 1853; repr., Beijing: Renmin Wenxue Chubanshe, 2011.

Huan Kuan 桓寬. *Yantie lun* 鹽鐵論 (On salt and iron). Ca. 81 BCE; repr., Yili: Yili Renmin Chubanshe, 2002.

Hu Wenkai 胡文楷. *Lidai funü zhuzuo kao* 歷代婦女著作考 (Research on works by women from all dynasties). Amended edition; Shanghai: Shanghai Guji Chubanshe, 2008.

Hu Xiaoming 胡曉明 and Peng Guozhong 彭國忠, eds. *Jiangnan nüxing bieji chubian* 江南女性別集初編 (The first anthology for personal collections of women from the Jiangnan area). Hefei, Anhui: Huangshan Shushe, 2008.

———, eds. *Jiangnan nüxing bieji erbian* 江南女性別集二編 (The second anthology for personal collections of women from the Jiangnan area). Hefei, Anhui: Huangshan Shushe, 2010.

———, eds. *Jiangnan nüxing bieji sanbian* 江南女性別集三編 (The third anthology for personal collections of women from the Jiangnan area). Hefei, Anhui: Huangshan Shushe, 2012.

———, eds. *Jiangnan nüxing bieji sibian* 江南女性別集四編 (The fourth anthology for personal collections of women from the Jiangnan area). Hefei, Anhui: Huangshan Shushe, 2014.

Kun Gang 昆岡, et al., comps. *Da Qing huidian shili* 大清會典事例 (Examples

for the Qing statutes). Ca. 19 cent.; repr., Shanghai: Shanghai Guji Chubanshe, 1995.

Lei Jin 雷瑨 and Lei Jian 雷瑊. *Guixiu cihua* 閨秀詞話 (Remarks on song lyrics by gentry women). 1916.

Li Junzhi 李濬之. *Qing huajia shishi* 清畫家詩史 (A history of poetry by the
Qing painters). 1930.

Liang Qichao 梁啟超. "Lun nüxue" 論女學 (On women's education). In
Shen Peng 沈鵬, et al., eds. *Liang Qichao quanji* 梁啟超全集 (A complete collection of Liang Qichao's works) (Beijing: Beijing Chubanshe,
1999), 30–33.

———. "Lun nüxue." Trans., Dorothy Ko. In Lydia H. Liu, Rebecca E. Carl,
and Dorothy Ko, eds. *The Birth of Chinese Feminism: Essential Texts
in Transnational Theory* (New York: Columbia University Press, 2013),
189–203.

Liu Xiang 劉向. *Lienü zhuan* 列女傳 (Biographies of exemplary women). 1st
cent. BCE; repr., Beijing: Zhonghua Shuju, 1985.

———. *Lienü zhuan*. Illustrated by Qiu Ying 仇英. Amended by Wang Geng
汪庚. Reprinted from the Zhibuzuzhai Cangban 知不足齋藏版, Tokyo:
Zuhon Sokankai, 1923–1926.

Liu Yin 劉蔭. *Mengchanlou yigao* 夢蟾樓遺稿 (Remaining drafts from the
Dreaming-of-the-Moon Tower). 1846.

Miao Quansun 繆荃孫, comp. *Guochao Changzhou cilu* 國朝常州詞錄 (The
dynasty's records of song lyrics from Changzhou). 1896; repr., Nanjing:
Nanjing Daxue Chubanshe, 2011.

Qian Shifu 錢實甫, comp. *Qingdai zhiguan nianbiao* 清代職官年表 (Chronological tables for the official posts of the Qing period). Beijing: Zhonghua
Shuju, 1980.

Qu Bingyun 屈秉筠. *Yunyulou ji* 韞玉樓集 (Collection from the Tower of
Hidden Jade). 1811.

Shan Shili 單士釐, comp. *Guixiu zhengshi zaixuji* 閨秀正始再續集 (Another
sequel to the Correct beginnings for gentry women).1911.

Shen Shanbao 沈善寶. *Mingyuan shihua* 名媛詩話 (Remarks on poetry of
notable women). 1845; repr., Nanjing: Fenghuang Chubanshe, 2010.

Shen Shixing 申時行, et al., comps. *Da Ming huidian* 大明會典 (The Ming
statutes). Ca. 16 cent.; repr., Shanghai: Shanghai Guji Chubanshe, 1995.

Shen Zhiqi 沈之奇, comp. *DaQinglü jizhu* 大清律輯注 (Annotations to the
Qing legal code). 17–18c.; repr., Beijing: Beijing Daxue Chubanshe, 1993.

Sima Qian 司馬遷. *Shiji* 史記 (Records of the historian). Ca. 104 BCE—91
BCE; repr., Shanghai: Shangwu Yinshuguan, 1933.

Tuotuo 脫脫, et al. "Ouyang Xiu liezhuan" 歐陽修列傳 (Biography of Ouyang Xiu). In Tuotuo et al., comp. *Songshi* 宋史 (The history of the

Song Dynasty) (1345; repr., Beijing: Zhonghua Shuju, 1977), vol. 30, pp. 10375–83.

Wang Lifu 王理孚 and Liu Shaokuan 劉紹寬, comps. *Pingyang xianzhi* 平陽縣誌 (Gazetteer of Pingyang county). 1926; repr., Shanghai: Shanghai Shudian, 1993.

Wang Rongpo 王蓉坡 and Shen Mozhuang 沈墨莊, comps. *Daoguang Kuaiji xianzhi gao* 道光會稽縣誌稿 (Gazetteer of Kuaiji county, drafted during the Daoguang reign). 1936; repr., Shanghai: Shanghai Shudian, 1993.

Wang Ying 汪嫈. *Ya'an Shuwu shiwen ji* 雅安書屋詩文集 (Collection of poetry and essays from Ya'an's Study Room). 1844.

Wang Zhenyi 王貞儀. *Defengting chuji* 德風亭初集 (The first collection from the Pavilion of Moral Influence). 1916.

Wanyan Linqing 完顏麟慶. *Hongxue yinyuan tuji* 鴻雪因緣圖記 (Drawings of fleeting traces and karma). 1849.

Xi Peilan 席佩蘭. *Changzhenge ji* 長真閣集 (Collection from the Pavilion of Perpetual Truth). 1891.

Xie Qingyang 謝青揚. *Yuyuzhai shiwen ji* 愈愚齋詩文集 (Collection of poetry and essays from the Studio of Dullness Cured [by Learning]). 1884; repr., Shanghai: Shanghai Guji Chubanshe, 2004.

Xie Xiangtang 謝香塘. *Gongyu shici gao* 紅餘詩詞稿 (Drafts of poetry and song lyrics written after womanly work). 1884.

Xu Naichang 徐乃昌, comp. *Xiaotanluan shi huike guixiu ci* 小檀欒室匯刻閨秀詞 (Joint prints of song lyrics by gentry women, from the Small Studio Made of Bamboos). 1896.

———, comp. *Guixiu cichao* 閨秀詞鈔 (Selections of song lyrics by gentry women). 1909.

Xue Shaohui 薛紹徽. *Daiyunlou yiji* 黛韻樓遺集 (Posthumously collected writings from Black-Jade Rhymes Tower). 1914.

Ying Jiexiu 英傑修 and Yan Duanshu 晏端書, comps. *Xuzuan Yangzhou fuzhi* 續纂揚州府志 (A sequel to the gazetteer of Yangzhou prefecture). 1874; repr., Taibei: Chengwen Chubanshe, 1970.

Yuan Jingrong 袁鏡蓉. *Yuequxuan shicao* 月蕖軒詩草 (Poetry drafts from the Studio of Yuequ [courtesy name of Yuan Jingrong]). 1848.

———. *Yuequxuan zhuanshulue* 月蕖軒傳述略 (Brief biographies and records from the Studio of Yuequ). 1848.

Yun Zhu 惲珠. *Guochao guixiu zhengshi ji* 國朝閨秀正始集 (Correct beginnings: Women's poetry of our august dynasty). 1831.

Zeng Jifen 曾紀芬. *Chongde Laoren bashi ziding nianpu* 崇德老人八十自訂年譜 (Chronological autobiography composed by the Elderly Lady Who Admires Virtue at the age of eighty). Shanghai: Nieshi jiayan xunkanshe, 1933.

Zeng Yi 曾懿. *Guhuanshi shiciji* 古歡室詩詞集 (Collection of poetry and song lyrics from the Studio of Ancient Joy). 1907.

———. *Nüxue pian*女學篇 (Treatise on women's learning). 1907.

———. *Yixue pian* 醫學篇 (Treatise on medicine). 1907.

———. *Zhongkui lu* 中饋錄 (Records of doing the cooking). 1907.

Zhang Bao 張寶. *Fancha tu* 泛槎圖 (Drawings of myself floating in a raft). 1831.

Zhang Jue 張覺, ed. *Han Feizi jiaozhu* 韓非子校注 (Annotations to the *Han Feizi*). Changsha: Yuelu Shushe, 2006.

Zhang Wanying 張紈英. *Canfengguan wenji* 餐楓館文集 (Collection of prose from the House of Eating Maple [Leaves]). Preface 1849.

Zhao Erxun 趙爾巽, comp. *Qingshi gao* 清史稿 (Draft of the Qing history). 1927; repr., Beijing: Zhonghua Shuju, 1977.

Zuo Xijia 左錫嘉. *Lengyinxianguan shigao* 冷吟仙館詩稿 (Poetry drafts from the House of Immortals Chanting in the Chilly Season). 1891.

SECONDARY SOURCES

A Feng 阿風. *MingQing shidai funü de diwei yu quanli—yi MingQing qiyue wenshu, susong dang'an wei zhongxin* 明清時代婦女的地位與權利——以明清契約文書、訴訟檔案為中心 (Women's status and rights during the Ming and Qing periods: with a focus on contracts and legal documents from the Ming and Qing periods). Beijing: Shehui Kexue Wenxian Chubanshe, 2009.

A Ying 阿英. *Zhongguo lianhuan tuhua shihua* 中國連環圖畫史話 (A history of Chinese chain pictures). Beijing: Renmin Meishu Chubanshe, 1980.

Ames, Roger T. "The Focus-Field Self in Classical Confucianism." In Roger T. Ames, Wimal Dissanayake, and Thomas P. Kasulis, eds. *Self as Person in Asian Theory and Practice*. New York: State University of New York Press, 1994, 187–212.

Bailey, Paul J. *Women and Gender in Twentieth-Century China*. Basingstoke: Palgrave and Macmillan, 2012.

Barlow, Tani E. *The Question of Women in Chinese Feminism*. Durham, NC: Duke University Press, 2004.

Barr, Allan. "Marriage and Mourning in Early Qing Tributes to Wives." *NanNü: Men, Women, and Gender in China* 15.1 (2013): 137–78.

Bernhardt, Kathryn. *Women and Property in China, 960–1949*. Stanford: Stanford University Press, 1999.

Birge, Bettine. *Women, Property, and Confucian Reaction in Sung and Yuan China (960–1368)*. Cambridge: Cambridge University Press, 2002.

Borzello, Frances. "Behind the Image." In Liz Rideal, ed. *Mirror Mirror:*

Self-Portraits by Women Artists. London: National Portrait Gallery, 2001, 22–31.

Bossler, Beverly. *Courtesans, Concubines, and the Cult of Female Fidelity: Gender and Social Change in China, 1000–1400.* Cambridge, Massachusetts: Harvard University Asia Center, 2013.

Bray, Francesca. *Technology and Gender: Fabrics of Power in Late Imperial China.* Berkeley: University of California Press, 1997.

Brokaw, Cynthia J., and Kai-wing Chow, eds. *Printing and Book Culture in Late Imperial China.* Berkeley: University of California Press, 2005.

Brook, Timothy. *The Confusions of Pleasure: Commerce and Culture in Ming China.* Berkeley: University of California Press, 1998.

Cahill, James. "K'un-ts'an and His Inscriptions." In Alfreda Murck and Wen C. Fong, eds. *Words and Images: Chinese Poetry, Calligraphy, and Painting.* New York: Metropolitan Museum of Art, Princeton University Press, 1991, 513–34.

———. *The Painter's Practice: How Artists Lived and Worked in Traditional China.* New York: Columbia University Press, 1994.

———. "*Meiren hua*: Paintings of Beautiful Women in China." In Cahill et al., eds. *Beauty Revealed: Images of Women in Qing Dynasty Chinese Painting.* University of California, Berkeley Art Museum and Pacific Film Archive, 2013, 9–21.

Carlitz, Katherine. "The Social Uses of Female Virtue in Late Ming Editions of *Lienü Zhuan.*" *Late Imperial China* 12.1 (1991): 117–48.

———. "Desire, Danger, and the Body: Stories of Women's Virtue in Late Ming China." In *Engendering China: Women, Culture, and the State.* Christina K. Gilmartin et al., eds., 101–24. Cambridge, Massachusetts: Harvard University Press, 1994.

Chang, Kang-I Sun. "Ming-Qing Women Poets and the Notions of 'Talent' and 'Morality.'" In Theodore Huters, R. Bin Wong, and Pauline Yu, eds. *Culture and State in Chinese History: Conventions, Accommodations and Critiques.* Stanford: Stanford University Press, 1997, 236–58.

Chia, Lucille. *Printing for Profit: The Commercial Publishers of Jianyang, Fujian (11th—17th Centuries).* Cambridge, Massachusetts: Harvard University Press, 2002.

Chow, Kai-wing. *Publishing, Culture, and Power in Early Modern China.* Stanford: Stanford University Press, 2004.

Clunas, Craig. *Pictures and Visuality in Early Modern China.* Princeton, NJ: Princeton University Press, 1997.

Cohen, Myron L. "Writs of Passage in Late Imperial China: The Documentation of Practical Understandings in Minong, Taiwan." In Madeleine

Zelin, et al., eds. *Contract and Property in Early Modern China*. Stanford: Stanford University Press, 2004, 37–93.

Cong, Xiaoping. "From '*Cainü*' to '*Nü Jiaoxi*': Female Normal Schools and the Transformation of Women's Education in the Late Qing Period, 1895–1911." In Nanxiu Qian, Grace S. Fong, and Richard J. Smith, eds. *Different Worlds of Discourse: Transformations of Gender and Genre in Late Qing and Early Republican China*. Leiden: Brill, 2008, 115–44.

Dayunhe 大運河, comp. *Zhongguo shuhua paimai qingbao* 中國書畫拍賣情報 (Information on the auctions of Chinese calligraphies and paintings), vol. 2. Xiamen: Lujiang Chubanshe, 2005.

De Girolami Cheney, Liana, et al., eds. *Self-Portraits by Women Painters*. Aldershot, UK: Ashgate, 2000.

Dikötter, Frank. *Imperfect Conceptions: Medical Knowledge, Birth Defects, and Eugenics in China*. London: Hurst, 1998.

Eakin, Paul John. *Fictions in Autobiography: Studies in the Art of Self-Invention*. Princeton, NJ: Princeton University Press, 1985.

———. *How Our Lives Become Stories: Making Selves*. Ithaca, NY: Cornell University Press, 1999.

Ebrey, Patricia B. *Confucianism and Family Rituals in Imperial China: A Social History of Writing about Rites*. Princeton: Princeton University Press, 1991.

———. "Property Law and Uxorilocal Marriage in the Sung Period." In *Jinshi jiazu yu zhengzhi bijiao lishi lunwenji* 近世家族與政治比較歷史論文集 (Proceedings for comparative histories of lineages and politics in early modern China). Taibei: Zhongyang Yanjiuyuan Jindaishi Yanjiusuo, 1992.

———. *The Inner Quarters: Marriage and the Lives of Chinese Women in the Sung Period*. Berkeley: University of California Press, 1993.

Elvin, Mark. "Female Virtue and the State in China." *Past and Present* 104 (1984): 111–52.

Epstein, Maram. "Writing Emotions: Ritual Innovation as Emotional Expression." *Nan Nü: Men, Women and Gender in China* 11.1 (2009): 155–96.

Feng Erkang 馮爾康. *Zhongguo gudai de zongzu yu citang* 中國古代的宗族與祠堂 (Lineages and ancestral halls in ancient China). Beijing: Shangwu Yinshuguan, 1996.

———. *Qingdai renwu zhuanji shiliao yanjiu* 清代人物傳記史料研究 (A study of biographical sources for noted persons from the Qing period). Tianjin: Tianjin Jiaoyu Chubanshe, 2005.

———. *Zhongguo zongzu zhidu yu pudie bianzuan* 中國宗族制度與譜牒編纂 (The system of Chinese lineages and the compilation of genealogies). Tianjin: Tianjin Guji Chubanshe, 2011.

Fong, Grace S. "Writing Self and Writing Lives: Shen Shanbao's (1808–1862) Gendered Auto/Biographical Practices." *Nan Nü: Men, Women and Gender in China* 2.2 (2000): 259–303.

———. "A Widow's Journey during the Taiping Rebellion: Zuo Xijia's Poetic Record." *Renditions: A Chinese-English Translation Magazine* 70 (2008): 49–58.

———. *Herself an Author: Gender, Agency, and Writing in Late Imperial China.* Honolulu: University of Hawai'i Press, 2008.

———, and Ellen Widmer, eds. *The Inner Quarters and Beyond: Women Writers from Ming through Qing.* Leiden: Brill, 2010.

———. "The Life and Afterlife of Ling Zhiyuan (1831–1852) and Her Poetry Collection." *Journal of Chinese Literature and Culture* 1.1–2 (2014): 125–54.

Fong, Wen C. "Words and Images in Late Ming and Early Ch'ing Painting." In Alfreda Murck and Wen C. Fong, eds. *Words and Images: Chinese Poetry, Calligraphy, and Painting.* New York: Metropolitan Museum of Art, Princeton University Press, 1991, 501–12.

Furth, Charlotte. *A Flourishing Yin: Gender in China's Medical History, 960–1665.* Berkeley: University of California Press, 1999.

Goodman, Catherine R. "Book Review: *Autobiography and Questions of Gender* by Shirley Neuman, *Essays on Life Writing: From Genre to Critical Practice* by Marlene Kadar, *Colette and the Fantom Subject of Autobiography* by Jerry Aline Flieger, and *Fictions of Authority: Women Writers and Narrative Voice* by Susan Sniader Lanser." *Signs* 20.3 (1995): 771–75.

Green, Joyce, ed. *Making Space for Indigenous Feminism.* Black Point, Nova Scotia: Fernwood, 2007.

Guo Jian 郭建. *Zhongguo caichanfa shigao* 中國財產法史稿 (A draft history of property laws in China). Beijing: Zhongguo Zhengfa Daxue Chubanshe, 2005.

Hamilton, Robyn. "The Pursuit of Fame: Luo Qilan (1755–1813?) and the Debates about Women and Talent in Eighteenth-century Jiangnan." *Late Imperial China* 18.1 (1997): 39–71.

Han Zhaoqi 韓兆琦. "Zhongguo gudai zhuanji wenxue luelun" 中國古代傳記文學略論 (A brief study of biographical writings in pre-modern China). *Beijing shifan daxue xuebao* 北京師範大學學報 (Journal of Beijing Normal University) 4 (1997): 13–20.

Hanson, Marta E. *Speaking of Epidemics in Chinese Medicine: Disease and the Geographic Imagination in Late Imperial China.* London: Routledge, 2011.

———. "The 'Warm Diseases' Current of Learning." In T. J. Hinrichs and Linda L. Barnes, eds. *Chinese Medicine and Healing: An Illustrated*

History. Cambridge, Massachusetts: Belknap Press of Harvard University Press, 2013, 204–5.

He Xiaolian 何小蓮. *Xiyi dongjian yu wenhua tiaoshi* 西醫東漸與文化調適 (The transmission of Western medicine into China and its cultural adaptations). Shanghai: Shanghai Guji Chubanshe, 2006.

Hegel, Robert E. *Reading Illustrated Fiction in Late Imperial China*. Stanford: Stanford University Press, 1998.

Hinrichs, T J, and Linda L. Barnes, eds. *Chinese medicine and Healing: An Illustrated History*. Cambridge, Massachusetts: Belknap Press of Harvard University Press, 2013.

Ho, Clara W. "The Cultivation of Female Talent: Views on Women's Education in China during the Early and High Qing Periods." *Journal of the Economic and Social History of the Orient* 38.2 (1995): 191–223.

———. "Encouragement from the Opposite Gender: Male Scholars' Interests in Women's Publications in Ch'ing China—A Bibliographical Study." In Harriet T. Zurndorfer, ed. *Chinese Women in the Imperial Past: New Perspectives*. Leiden: Brill, 1999, 308–53.

———. "Qingdai nüxing kezishu juyao." 清代女性課子書舉要 (Major examples of women's instructions for their sons during the Qing period). *Donghai zhongwen xuebao* 東海中文學報 (Journal of the Chinese Department, Donghai University) 20 (2008):187–216.

———. *Cai de xianghui: Zhongguo nüxing de zhixue yu kezi* 才德相輝：中國女性的治學與課子 (Talent shines with virtue: Chinese women's efforts in pursuing scholarship and educating their children). Hong Kong: Sanlian shuju, 2015.

Ho, Ping-ti. "The Salt Merchants of Yang-Chou: A Study of Commercial Capitalism in Eighteenth-Century China." *Harvard Journal of Asiatic Studies* 17.1 (1954): 130–68.

———. *The Ladder of Success in Imperial China: Aspects of Social Mobility, 1368–1911*. New York: Columbia University Press, 1962.

Holmgren, Jennifer. "The Economic Foundations of Virtue: Widow-Remarriage in Early and Modern China." *Australian Journal of Chinese Affairs* 13 (Jan. 1985): 1–27.

Hsich, Andrew C. K., and Jonathan D. Spence. "Suicide and the Family in Pre-Modern Chinese Society." In Arthur Kleinman and Tsung-yi Lin, eds., *Normal and Abnormal Behavior in Chinese Culture*. Dordrecht: D. Reidel, 1981, 29–47.

Hsiung, Ping-chen. "Constructed Emotions: The Bond between Mothers and Sons in Late Imperial China." *Late Imperial China* 15.1 (1994): 87–117.

Hu Siao-chen 胡曉真. *Cainü cheye weimian: Jindai Zhongguo nüxing xushi wenxue de xingqi* 才女徹夜未眠：近代中國女性敘事文學的興起 (Burning the midnight oil: The rise of female narrative in early modern China). Tai-bei: Maitian Chuban, 2003.

Hu, Ying. "Naming the First New Woman." *Nan Nü: Men, Women and Gender in China* 3.2 (2001): 196–231.

Hua Wei 華瑋. *MingQing funü zhi xiqu chuangzuo yu piping* 明清婦女之戲曲創作與批評 (Criticism on works of drama by women from the Ming and Qing periods). Taibei: Zhongyang Yanjiuyuan Zhongguo Wenzhe Yanjiusuo, 2003.

Huang, Martin W. "Introduction: Remembering Female Relatives: Mourning and Gender in Late Imperial China." *NanNü: Men, Women, and Gender in China* 15.1 (2013): 4–29.

Huang Xiangjin 黃湘金. "Cong 'jianghu zhiyuan' dao 'miaotang zhigao'—Xiatian Gezi Jiazheng xue zai Zhongguo." 從"江湖之遠"到"廟堂之高"——下田歌子家政學在中國 (From the "margins" to the "ritual center": The introduction of *Domestic Science* by Shimoda Utako into China). *Shanxi shida xuebao* 山西師大學報 (Journal of Shanxi Normal University) 34.5 (2007): 88–92.

Hucker, Charles O. *A Dictionary of Official Titles in Imperial China.* Stanford: Stanford University Press, 1985.

Idema, Wilt. "Male Fantasies and Female Realities: Chu Shu-chen and Chang Yü-niang and Their Biographers." In Zurndorfer, ed. *Chinese Women in the Imperial Past*, 19–52.

———. "The Biographical and the Autobiographical in Bo Shaojun's One Hundred Poems Lamenting My Husband." In Judge and Hu, eds. *Beyond Exemplar Tales*, 230–45.

Idema, Wilt, and Beata Grant. *The Red Brush: Writing Women of Imperial China.* Cambridge, Massachusetts: Harvard University Asia Center, 2004.

Jiao Shu'an 焦樹安. *Zhongguo cangshu shihua* 中國藏書樓史話 (A history of book collecting in China). Beijing: Shangwu Yinshuguan,1997.

Judge, Joan, and Hu Ying, eds. *Beyond Exemplar Tales: Women's Biography in Chinese History.* Berkeley: University of California Press, 2011.

Kemp, Sandra, and Judith Squires, eds. *Feminisms.* Oxford: Oxford University Press, 1998.

Kinney, Anne Behnke, trans. and ed. *Exemplary Women of Early China: The Lienü zhuan of Liu Xiang.* New York: Columbia University Press, 2014.

Ko, Dorothy. *Teachers of the Inner Chambers: Women and Culture in Seventeenth-Century China.* Stanford: Stanford University Press, 1994.

———. *Cinderella's Sisters: A Revisionist History of Footbinding.* Berkeley: University of California Press, 2005.

Leung, Angela K. C. "Women Practicing Medicine in Pre-modern China." In Zurndorfer, ed. *Chinese Women in the Imperial Past*, 101–34.

———. "To Chasten Society: The Development of Widow Homes in the Qing, 1773–1911." *Late Imperial China* 14.2 (1993): 1–32.

Li Shi 李湜. *MingQing guige huihua yanjiu* 明清閨閣繪畫研究 (A study of paintings from the inner quarters during the Ming and Qing periods). Beijing: Zijincheng Chubanshe, 2008.

———. *Shidai gongqing, guige duxiu: Nühuajia Chen Shu yu Qianshi jiazu* 世代公卿，閨閣獨秀：女畫家陳書與錢氏家族 (A distinguished woman painter from a lineage of dukes and ministers: The woman painter Chen Shu and the Qian lineage).

Li Wanjian 李萬健. "Qingdai cangshujia jiqi shumu" 清代藏書家及其書目 (Bibliophiles from the Qing period and their bibliographies). *Tushuguan gongzuo yu yanjiu* 圖書館工作與研究 (Library work and research) 167 (2010):10–14.

Li, Xiaorong. "Gender and Textual Politics during the Qing Dynasty: The Case of the *Zhengshi ji*." *Harvard Journal of Asiatic Studies* 69.1 (2009): 75–107.

———. *Women's Poetry of Late Imperial China: Transforming the Inner Chambers*. Seattle: University of Washington Press, 2012.

Li Zhiming 李志茗. "Qingdai guanfeng zhidu jiqi tedian" 清代官俸制度及其特點 (The salary system for the Qing officials and its characteristics). *Huazhong shifan daxue xuebao* 華中師範大學學報 (Journal of Central China Normal University) 36.2 (1997): 94–98.

Liao Xiaoyu 廖曉渝 and Lin Huiguang 林暉光. "Qingdai yixue jiaoyu xing-shi juyao" 清代醫學教育形式舉要 (A brief introduction to the forms of medical training during the Qing period). *Zhongyiyao wenhua* 中醫藥文化 (The culture of Chinese medicine) 3 (2011): 34–35.

Lin Binhui 林彬暉. "Shilun MingQing daowang shici de yishu tese" 試論明清悼亡詩詞的藝術特色 (A tentative study on the artistic features of mourning poetry from the Ming and Qing periods). *Zhongguo wenxue yanjiu* 中國文學研究 (Studies of Chinese literature) 36.1 (1995): 56–62.

Lin Meiyi 林玫儀. "Shilun Yanghu Zuoshi erdai cainü zhi jiazu guanxi" 試論陽湖左氏二代才女之家族關係 (A tentative study of the familial relation-ships among the two generations of female talents from the Zuo lineage of Yanghu). *Zhongguo wenzhe yanjiu jikan* 中國文哲研究集刊 (Bulletin of the Institute of Chinese Literature and Philosophy Academia Sinica) 30 (March 2007): 179–222.

Liu, Lydia H., Rebecca E. Carl, and Dorothy Ko, eds. *The Birth of Chinese Feminism: Essential Texts in Transnational Theory*. New York: Columbia University Press, 2013.

Liu Qiulin 劉秋霖, Liu Jian 劉健, and Wang Yaxin 王亞新, comps. *Guanyin pusa tuxiang yu chuanshuo* 觀音菩薩圖像與傳說 (The visual images and legends of the Bodhisattva Guanyin). Beijing: Zhongguo Wenlian Chubanshe, 2005.

Lo, Irving Yucheng. "Daughters of the Muses of China." In Marsha Weidner, et al., eds. *Views from Jade Terrace: Chinese Women Artists 1300–1912*. Indianapolis: Indianapolis Museum of Art, 1988, 41–51.

Lu, Weijing. "Uxorilocal Marriage among Qing Literati." *Late Imperial China* 19.2 (1998): 64–110.

———. *True to Her Word: The Faithful Maiden Cult in Late Imperial China*. Stanford: Stanford University Press, 2008.

Maclaren, Anne, and Chen Qinjian. "The Oral and Ritual Culture of Chinese Women: Bridal Lamentations of Nanhui." *Asian Folklore Studies* 59 (2000): 205–38.

Mann, Susan. "Widows in the Kinship, Class, and Community Structures of Qing Dynasty China." *Journal of Asian Studies* 46.1 (1987): 37–56.

———. *Precious Records: Women in China's Long Eighteenth Century*. Stanford: Stanford University Press, 1997.

———. *The Talented Women of the Zhang Family*. Berkeley: University of California Press, 2007.

———. "Dowry Wealth and Wifely Virtue in Mid-Qing Gentry Households." *Late Imperial China* 29.1 S (2008): 64–76.

———. "The Lady and the State: Women's Writings in Times of Trouble during the Nineteenth Century." In Grace S. Fong and Ellen Widmer, eds. *The Inner Quarters and Beyond: Women Writers from Ming through Qing*. Leiden: Brill, 2010, 283–313.

———. "Biographical Sources and Silences." In Judge and Hu, eds. *Beyond Exemplar Tales*, 17–35.

Mao Wenfang 毛文芳. *Tucheng xingle: MingQing wenren huaxiang tiyong xilun* 圖成行樂：明清文人畫像題詠析論 (Pictures completed to record leisurely enjoyment: An analysis of the inscriptions for literati's portraits from the Ming and Qing periods). Taibei: Xusheng Shuju, 2008.

———. *Juanzhong xiaoli yi bainian: MingQing nüxing huaxiang wenben tanlun* 卷中小立亦百年：明清女性畫像文本探論 (Preserved in the scrolls for a hundred years: An exploration of women's portraits and relevant texts during the Ming and Qing periods). Taibei: Xuesheng Shuju, 2013.

Meyer-Fong, Tobie S. *What Remains: Coming to Terms with Civil War in 19th Century China*. Stanford: Stanford University Press, 2013.

Moloughney, Brian. "From Biographical History to Historical Biography: A Transformation in Chinese Historical Writing." *East Asian History* 4 (1992): 1–30.

Murck, Alfreda, and Wen C. Fong, eds. *Words and Images: Chinese Poetry, Calligraphy, and Painting*. New York: Metropolitan Museum of Art, Princeton University Press, 1991.

Nie Chongzheng 聶崇正. "Tan Qingdai 'Ziguang Ge gongchen xiang'" 談清代紫光閣功臣像 (Qing-Dynasty portraits of meritorious generals in the Pavilion of Purple Light). *Wenwu* 文物 (Cultural relics) 1 (1990): 65–69.

Owen, Stephen. "The Self's Perfect Mirror: Poetry as Autobiography." In Shuen-fu Lin and Stephen Owen, eds. *The Vitality of the Lyric Voice: Shi Poetry from the Late Han to the T'ang*. Princeton: Princeton University Press, 1982, 71–102.

Pan Honggang 潘洪鋼. "Lun Qingdai shifa" 論清代諡法 (The Qing laws on the granting of posthumous titles). *Wen shi zhe* 文史哲 (Literature, history, philosophy) 299 (2007): 69–77.

Platt, Stephen R. "Introduction: War and Reconstruction in 1860s Jiangnan." *Late Imperial China* 30 (December 2009): 1–8.

Qi Qingshun 齊清順. "Qingdai Xinjiang guanyuan de yanglian yin" 清代新疆官員的養廉銀 (The subsidy system for the Qing officials in Xinjiang). *Xinjiang daxue xuebao* 新疆大學學報 (Journal of Xinjiang University) 58 (1990): 35–42.

Qian, Nanxiu. "Revitalizing the *Xianyuan* (Worthy Ladies) Tradition: Women in the 1898 Reforms." *Modern China* 29.4 (2003): 399–454.

———. "The Mother *Nü Xuebao* versus the Daughter *Nü Xuebao*: Generational Differences between 1898 and 1902 Women Reformers." In Nanxiu Qian, Fong, and Smith, eds. *Different Worlds of Discourse*, 257–91.

———. "*Lienü* versus *Xianyuan*: The Two Biographical Traditions in Chinese Women's History." In Judge and Hu, eds. *Beyond Exemplar Tales*, 70–87.

———. *Politics, Poetics, and Gender in Late Qing China: Xue Shaohui and the Era of Reform*. Stanford: Stanford University Press, 2015.

Raphals, Lisa. *Sharing the Light: Representations of Women and Virtue in Early China*. New York: State University of New York Press, 1998.

Rideal, Liz, ed. *Mirror Mirror: Self-Portraits by Women Artists*. London: National Portrait Gallery, 2001.

Robertson, Maureen. "Voicing the Feminine: Constructions of the Gendered Subject in Lyric Poetry by Women of Medieval and Late Imperial China." *Late Imperial China* 13.1 (1992): 63–110.

———. "Changing the Subject: Gender and Self-inscription in Authors' Prefaces and 'Shi' Poetry." In Pauline Yu, ed. *Voices of the Song Lyric in China*. Berkeley: University of California Press, 1994, 171–217.

Rogaski, Ruth. "Beyond Benevolence: A Confucian Women's Shelter in Treaty-Port China." *Journal of Women's History* 8.4 (1997): 54–90.

———. *Hygienic Modernity: Meanings of Health and Disease in Treaty-Port China*. Berkeley: University of California Press, 2004.

Ropp, Paul S. "Passionate Women: Female Suicide in Late Imperial China—Introduction." *Nan Nü: Men, Women, and Gender in China* 3.1 (2001): 3–21.

Rowe, William T. "Ancestral Rites and Political Authority in Late Imperial China: Chen Hongmou in Jiangxi." *Modern China* 24.4 (1998): 378–407.

Scott, Joan W. *Gender and the Politics of History*. New York: Columbia University Press, 1988.

———. "Experience." In Judith Butler and Scott, eds. *Feminists Theorize the Political*. New York: Routledge, 1992, 22–40.

Seckel, Dietrich. "The Rise of Portraiture in Chinese Art." *Artibus Asiae* 53.1 (1993): 7–26.

Seligman, Adam B., et al. *Ritual and Its Consequences: An Essay on the Limits of Sincerity*. Oxford: Oxford University Press, 2008.

Shu Sunlin 舒順林 and Qiao Runling 喬潤令. "Qingdai wenguan zhidu gailun" 清代文官制度概論 (A general study on the system of civil officials during the Qing period). *Neimenggu shehui kexue* 內蒙古社會科學 (Social sciences in Inner Mongolia), no. 3 (1989): 71–77.

Sommer, Matthew H. "The Uses of Chastity: Sex, Law, and the Property of Widows in Qing China." *Late Imperial China* 17.2 (1996): 77–130.

———. *Sex, Law, and Society in Late Imperial China*. Stanford: Stanford University Press, 2000.

Tan Zhuoyuan 譚卓垣, et al. *Qingdai cangshulou fazhanshi* 清代藏書樓發展史 (A history of the development of libraries during the Qing period). Shenyang: Liaoning Renmin Chubanshe, 1988.

Theiss, Janet M. *Disgraceful Matters: The Politics of Chastity in Eighteenth-Century China*. Berkeley: University of California Press, 2004.

Tian, Xiaofei. *Tao Yuanming and Manuscript Culture: The Record of a Dusty Table*. Seattle: University of Washington Press, 2005.

T'ien, Ju-k'ang. *Male Anxiety and Female Chastity: A Comparative Study of Chinese Ethical Values in Ming-Ch'ing Times*. Leiden: E. J. Brill, 1988.

Vinograd, Richard. *Boundaries of the Self: Chinese Portraits, 1600–1900*. Cambridge: Cambridge University Press, 1992.

Wakefield, David. *Fenjia: Household Division and Inheritance in Qing and Republican China*. Honolulu: University of Hawai'i Press, 1998.

Waltner, Ann. "Widows and Remarriage in Ming and Early Qing China." *Historical Reflections* 8.3 (1981): 129–46.

———. "Life and Letters: Reflections on Tanyangzi." In Judge and Hu, eds. *Beyond Exemplar Tales*, 212–29.

Wang Chuanman 王傳滿. "Funü jielie jingbiao zhidu de yanbian" 婦女節烈旌表制度的衍變 (Transformations of the system of court reward for chaste widows and female martyrs). *Xihua daxue xuebao* 西華大學學報 (Journal of Xihua University) 27.5 (2008): 70–73.

Wang Guiwen 王貴文. "Qingdai baqi guanyuan de yinzi zhidu" 清代八旗官員的蔭子制度 (The system of granting an official title/post to the son [due to the father's contribution to the state] among the Eight Banners officials during the Qing period). *Manzu yanjiu* 滿族研究 (Manchu studies) 3 (1988): 25–30.

———. "Qingdai de yinzi zhidu" 清代的蔭子制度 (The system of granting an official title/post to the son [due to the father's contribution to the state] during the Qing period). *Liaoning daxue xuebao* 遼寧大學學報 (Journal of Liaoning University) 95 (1989): 90–93.

Wang Heming 王鶴鳴. *Zhongguo jiapu tonglun* 中國家譜通論 (A general study of genealogies in China). Shanghai: Shanghai Guji Chubanshe, 2010.

Wang, Jing M. *When "I" Was Born: Women's Autobiography in Modern China*. Madison: University of Wisconsin Press, 2008.

Wang Li 王立. "Gudai daowang wenxue de jiannan licheng—jiantan gudai de daofu shici" 古代悼亡文學的艱難歷程——兼談古代的悼夫詩詞 (The tough journeys of pre-modern mourning literature; and a concurrent discussion of pre-modern women's mourning poetry for their deceased husbands). *Shehui kexue yanjiu* 社會科學研究 (Studies of social sciences) 102.2 (1997): 128–33.

Watson, James L. "The Structure of Chinese Funerary Rites: Elementary Forms, Ritual Sequence, and the Primacy of Performance." In James L. Watson and Evelyn S. Rawski, eds., *Death Ritual in Late Imperial and Modern China*. Berkeley: University of California Press, 1988, 3–19.

Weidner, Marsha, et al., eds. *Views from Jade Terrace: Chinese Women Artists 1300–1912*. Indianapolis: Indianapolis Museum of Art, 1988.

———, ed. *Flowering in the Shadows: Women in the History of Chinese and Japanese Painting*. Honolulu: University of Hawaii Press, 1990.

———. "The Conventional Success of Ch'en Shu." In Weidner, ed. *Flowering in the Shadows*, 123–56.

Widmer, Ellen. "The Trouble with Talent: Hou Zhi (1764–1829) and Her *Tanci Zai zaotian* of 1828." *Chinese Literature: Essays, Articles, Reviews* 21 (Dec. 1999): 131–50.

———. *The Beauty and the Book: Women and Fiction in Nineteenth-Century China*. Cambridge, Massachusetts: Harvard University Asia Center, 2006.

Wolf, Arthur P., and Chieh-shan Huang. *Marriage and Adoption in China, 1845–1945*. Stanford: Stanford University Press, 1980.

Wu, Hung. *The Double Screen: Medium and Representation in Chinese Painting.* Chicago: University of Chicago Press, 1996.

Wu Liyu 吳麗娛. "Guangzong yaozu: shilun Tangdai guanyuan de fuzu fengzeng 光宗耀祖:試論唐代官員的父祖封贈" (To glorify the ancestors: A tentative study on the title-granting system for the Tang officials). *Wenshi* 文史 (Literature and history) 86 (2009): 141–80.

Wu, Pei-yi. *The Confucian's Progress: Autobiographical Writings in Traditional China.* Princeton: Princeton University Press, 1990.

———. "Childhood Remembered: Parents and Children in China, 800–1700." In Anne B. Kinney, ed. *Chinese Views of Childhood.* Honolulu: University of Hawai'i Press, 1995, 129–56.

Wu, Yi-Li. *Reproducing Women: Medicine, Metaphor, and Childbirth in Late Imperial China.* Berkeley: University of California Press, 2010.

Xia Xiaohong 夏曉虹. *WanQing nüxing yu jindai Zhongguo* 晚清女性與近代中國 (Women in the late Qing and modern China). Beijing: Beijing Daxue Chubanshe, 2004.

Xu Ang 徐昂. *Wentan* 文談 (A discussion of essays). Nantong: Hanmolin Shuju, 1929.

Xu Wenxu 徐文緒. "Qingdai nüxuezhe Wang Zhenyi he tade Defengting chuji" 清代女學者王貞儀和她的德風亭初集 (The Qing woman scholar Wang Zhenyi and her First volume from the Defeng Pavilion). *Wenxian* 文獻 (Literary documents) 1 (1980): 211–14.

Yang Binbin 楊彬彬. "You Zeng Yi (1852–1927) de ge'an kan wanQing 'jibing de yinyu' yu cainü shenfen" 由曾懿（1852-1927）的個案看晚清"疾病的隱喻"與才女身份 ("Illness as metaphor" and the "talented woman" identity during the late Qing—seen through the case of Zeng Yi (1852–1927)). *Jindai Zhongguo funüshi yanjiu* 近代中國婦女史研究 (Research on women in modern China)16 (2008): 1–28.

———. "Ziwo de guijing—yibu Qingdai guixiu shiji zhong de jibing chengxian yu zizhuan yuwang" "自我"的困境——一部清代閨秀詩集中的疾病呈現與自傳欲望 (The "self's' dilemma: illness and autobiographical desire in the poetry collection of a Qing-Dynasty woman poet). *Zhongyang yanjiuyuan Zhongguo wenzhe yanjiu jikan* 中央研究院中國文哲研究集刊 (Bulletin of the Institute of Chinese literature and philosophy Academia Sinica) 37 (2010): 95–130.

Yang, Boda. "The Development of the Ch'ien-lung Painting Academy." In Alfreda Murck and Wen C. Fong, eds. *Words and Images: Chinese Poetry, Calligraphy, and Painting.* New York: Metropolitan Museum of Art, Princeton University Press, 1991, 333–56.

Yang Nianqun 楊念群. "Lun Wuxu weixin shidai guanyu 'xixing' gaizao de gouxiang jiqi yiyi" 論戊戌維新時代關於 "習性" 改造的構想及其意義 (On the significance of the 1898 idea of reforming social customs). In Wang Xiaoqiu 王曉秋, ed. *Wuxu weixin yu jindai Zhongguo de gaige* 戊戌維新 與近代中國的改革 (The 1898 movement and reforms in modern China). Beijing: Shehui Kexue Wenxian Chubanshe, 2000, 209–22.

Yang Xin 楊新, ed. *MingQing xiaoxianghua* 明清肖像畫 (Portraiture from the Ming and Qing periods). Shanghai: Shanghai Kexue Jishu Chubanshe; Hong Kong: Shangwu Yinshuguan, 2008.

Yao, Ping. "Women's Epitaphs in Tang China (618–907)." In Judge and Hu, eds. *Beyond Exemplar Tales*, 139–57.

Yu Guang 俞光, ed. *Wenzhou gudai jingji shiliao huibian* 溫州古代經濟史料 彙編 (A compendium for the sources of the pre-modern economic history of Wenzhou). Shanghai: Shanghai Shehui Kexueyuan Chubanshe, 2005.

Zeitlin, Judith. "The Life and Death of the Image: Ghosts and Female Portraits in Sixteenth-and-Seventeenth-Century Literature." In Wu Hung and Katherine R. Tsiang, eds. *Body and Face in Chinese Visual Culture.* Cambridge, Massachusetts: Harvard University Press Asia Center, 2005, 229–56.

Zhang Hai'ou 張海鷗 and Xie Minyu 謝敏玉. "Daojiwen de wenti yuanliu he wenti xingtai" 悼祭文的文體源流和文體形態 (Origins and stylistic features of essays written to mourn the deceased). *Shenzhen daxue xuebao* 深圳大學學報 (Journal of Shenzhen University) 27.2 (2010): 83–88.

Zhang Hongsheng 張宏生 and Shi Min 石旻. "Fulu: Zhongguo funü wenxue yanjiu de xiandai qidian jiqi tuozhan—Hu Wenkai *Lidai funü zhuzuo kao* de jiazhi he yiyi" 附錄：中國婦女文學研究的現代起點及其拓展——胡 文楷歷代婦女著作考的價值和意義 (Appendix: the modern starting point and developments of studies on Chinese women's literature: the significance of Research on works by women from all dynasties by Hu Wenkai). In Hu Wenkai, *Lidai funü zhuzuo kao*, 1199–224.

Zhang Jinfan 張晉藩. *Qingdai minfa zonglun* 清代民法綜論 (A comprehensive study of the Qing civil law). Beijing: Zhongguo Zhengfa Daxue Chubanshe, 1998.

Zhao Kesheng 趙克生 and Liu Qunying 劉群英. "Mingchao wenguan fuzu fengzeng zhidu shulun 明朝文官父祖封贈制度述論" (A study on the title-granting system for the Ming civil officials). *Shehui kexue jikan* 社會科學 輯刊 (Journal of social sciences) 188 (2010):184–89.

Zinda, Yvonnes. "Propagating New 'Virtues'—'Patriotism in Late Qing Textbooks for the Moral Education of Primary Students." In Michael Lackner and Natascha Vittinghoff, eds. *Mapping Meanings: The Field of New Learning in Late Qing China.* Leiden: Brill, 2004, 685–710.

Zurndorfer, Harriet T. *Change and Continuity in Chinese Local History: The Development of Hui-chou Prefecture, 800 to 1800.* Leiden: Brill, 1989.

————. "Wang Zhaoyuan (1763–1851) and the Erasure of 'Talented Women' by Liang Qichao." In Nanxiu Qian, Fong, and Smith, eds. *Different Worlds of Discourse*, 29–56.

————. "The *Lienü zhuan* Tradition and Wang Zhaoyuan's (1763–1851) Production of the *Lienü zhuan buzhu* (1812)." In Judge and Hu, eds. *Beyond Exemplar Tales*, 55–69.

Figures and tables are indicated by "f" and "t" following page numbers.

9 780295 744261